Religion and the Human Prospect

Religion and the Human Prospect

Alexander Saxton

Monthly Review Press
New York

Library of Congress Cataloging-in-Publication Data

Saxton, Alexander.
    Religion and the human prospect / Alexander Saxton.
    p. cm.
    ISBN 1-58367-133-1 (pbk.) — ISBN 1-58367-134-X (cloth)

1. Religion. 2. Religion and culture. 3. Faith development.
    4. Developmental psychology. I. Title.
    BL48.S28 2006
    200'.1—dc22
            2005036814

Designed by Terry J. Allen

Monthly Review Press
122 West 27th Street
New York, NY 10001

www.monthlyreview.org

10 9 8 7 6 5 4 3 2 1

Contents

Acknowledgments

For their generosity of time and effort in reading and commenting on all, or parts, of this book during its slow years of gestation, I wish to express my gratitude to Tom Ace, J. D. Bear, Dwight Furrow, Marvin Gettleman, Jeanne Giovannoni, Gene Gordon, Eva Herzer, Michael Kuttnauer, June Levine, Jonathan McLeod, Gary Nash, John Raines, Marcus Rediker, Robert Rydell, Martha Saxton, Charles Sellers, and Jack Weston.

Chapter 8, in an earlier version titled "Milton and the Problem of Evil," was presented at a colloquium of faculty and graduate students organized by Professor Robert Rydell at Montana State University, Bozeman. Chapter 11, "Marxism and the Failed Critique of Religion," began as the topic of a faculty-graduate Seminar in Labor History conducted by Professor Marcus Rediker at the University of Pittsburgh. I want to thank participants in both those gatherings for their perceptive criticisms and helpful suggestions. "Marxism and the Failed Critique of Religion" will appear as an article in a forthcoming issue of *Science and Society*. I am grateful to the editor, David Laibman, and to the anonymous peer readers, for their assistance in pinpointing conceptual problems and helping me resolve them.

My work on this book began in 1990 when I retired from teaching at UCLA. Most of my reading and research was done in University of California libraries at Los Angeles, Berkeley, and Irvine, and in the libraries of Sonoma State University (Rohnert Park) and Montana State University in Bozeman. I am enormously indebted to the skilled and enthusiastic librarians who came to my assistance in all those locations. To my wife, Trudy, I remain grateful for patient readings and intense discussions. She carried a major share in creating the book, although she did not live to see it in print.

I have not hesitated to discuss themes and problems of this book with friends, even casual acquaintances. Such conversations sometimes became stressful or painful for participants. Yet (in most cases) their responses were serious, civil, concerned, and *responsible*. I remain deeply appreciative of these exchanges, which I take to be tokens of hope for our collective future.

1

The Human Condition

The historical sequence that defines the human condition at the start of the twenty-first century began sometime before the origin of our species. It centered on the struggle for survival in seldom friendly environments of an animal that sought to elude death by making tools, speaking in tongues, imagining life after death. Even with tools, language, and religion, human existence remained marginal. Nature and death wore the same face. Most of our ancestors went hungry most of the time. When their social systems became complex enough to sustain division of labor, they also produced gender and class divisions because food, housing, and clothing never stretched all the way around. Separations of class mainly developed between tiny minorities with the leisure (as well as obligation) to pursue religion, politics, art, literature, technology, science, thus powering the onset of civilization, and vast majorities that labored to support their privileged superiors.

Such would remain the essence of the human condition until about the time of the American and French revolutions, when a breakthrough to capitalist industrialization revolutionized productive technology. Weaned on two centuries of global warfare, the Industrial Revolution escalated from scarcity to abundance. More people died in wars, but more people ate more food. Killer diseases came under public health control. Populations multiplied. The Second World War, with its gigantic upsurges of production, especially demonstrated that industrial technology had achieved sufficient power at last to abolish hunger from the world. Victors of the war proclaimed "One World," confederated into the United Nations. But though hunger remained widespread even during the bonanza decades after the war, it could no longer be ascribed simply to natural scarcity.

The fault must lie in obstacles of human origin such as ethnic and racial prejudice, nationalism, and class. Hunger, after the Second World War, had to be seen
as socially constructed. And if so, then those deferred expectations, those discontents internalized or imposed on others—long deemed indispensable to the
building and maintenance of civilization—could no longer rationally be justified.
Since to feed everyone was technically possible, reason demanded it be done; for
in "one world" freed of hunger and deprivation, discontents could be brushed
aside, class conflicts would heal over, international tensions relax. Even war might
become obsolete. Thus reason pleaded the cause of consumer society, already so
vividly incarnated in film and television. Why should love's body not be available
to all? It was this sense of immediate gratification that fueled the so-called youth
counterculture of the 1960s. Prometheus, unbound at last by the Industrial Revolution, came knocking (again?) at the gates of paradise.

I.

Paradise, alas, was not so easily reclaimed. Institutions of class control, habits of
domination and acquisitive individualism had sunk deep roots in human culture, perhaps human biology as well. How much historical time would suffice to
revise them? Time was running out. Hiroshima-Nagasaki, followed by nuclear
testing, made clear that the same science that could liberate humankind from
hunger and disease might just as readily obliterate it. Behind this lay a deeper
and more menacing realization. The industrial expansion needed to generate
such powers entailed costs no one either in the progeny of Adam Smith or Karl
Marx had adequately projected: ecological limits. That accelerating industrial
growth must sooner or later run short of space and materials should hardly have
occasioned surprise. Nonetheless the intrusion of ecological limits at the precise
historical moment when abundance came within reach seemed bitterly ironic.
New fears invaded public consciousness. Nuclear holocaust, air pollution, water
pollution, pesticide pollution, destruction of rain forest, poisoning the continental shelves, escalating costs of energy, perforation of the ozone layer—these
would bedevil the children of Adam in their post-industrial order more ruthless-
ly even than had scarcity during the pre-industrial. The conjunction of opposites
induced contrasting moods in adjacent generations: in one, self-indulgence and
utopian expectation; in the next a sense of being (unjustly?) deprived of its
birthright.[1]

The great leap forward of industrial technology and the bleak prospect that leap brought into view together define the human condition as we enter the twenty-first century. How long can our species survive on earth? Perhaps, human beings once believed forever. Modern astronomy and physics reduced forever to a long time; yet relative to individual life the time seemed so inconceivably long that it could continue to approximate eternity. At the start of the twenty-first century, however, we can easily imagine termination of our species within a single generation: ours? our grandchildren's? I am old enough to recall the first impact of that realization on adult consciousness. I remember also the speed with which the impact became routinized. It gummed over in the same way that intolerable knowledge, like awareness of one's own death, gums over. Human beings (like most other organisms) come equipped, in case of immediate threat to life, with biological responses that break through this routinization. Then the adrenalin flows; teeth clench, hair bristles, legs begin to run, hands grasp for weapons. Even a mouse or scorpion will bite and slash in the face of death. Perhaps amoebas and viruses do likewise in their own style. Accustomed to comparing biological organisms to social institutions, we expected some comparable reaction within our species to the threat of extinction. None occurred. There were speeches, books, talk, exhortations; not much slashing and biting.

If evolution has prepared individual organisms to go for broke in life-threatening emergencies, it neglected comparable arrangements on behalf of those social institutions within which many of its creatures normally abide. Yet it did make a beginning in that direction. The simplest organization of all, the family, is certainly a social institution; and rats, tigers, human mothers—all certainly family members— fight ferociously for their young. Ferocity in defense of social organization varies inversely as one moves from simple to complex, or from oldest in evolutionary time to more recent. A mother's defense of the young would be adrenalin-triggered, whereas defense of the tribe by its members appears less spontaneous, more socially conditioned. By the time we reach the social organization of the nation, citizens' obligations are rationalized, abstracted, politicized; they may even require the draft lottery as adrenalin substitute. Yet we should not make light of draft lotteries. Tribes, city-states, nations—over a time span long in history if short in evolution—have developed social, moral, political, even intellectual, defenses that work powerfully.

Let me sum up this line of speculation. An individual organism fights instinctively to preserve life. So, also, it seems, does the simplest of social organizations, the family. Larger social organizations such as tribes and nations possess powerful defense mechanisms developed historically and residing in culture. But if the species goes down, nations, tribes, families, individuals go with it. What sort of mechanism defends the human species? The answer appears to be that neither evolution nor history has had time to devise any such mechanism. Moreover, it seems unlikely, on a single planet, that the biological principle of natural selection could ever do so. Defensive mechanisms selected by natural selection would, like the defense of Singapore in 1941, all be pointing in the wrong direction.

What we need, then, is an ad hoc worldwide program of collective action, powered not much by instinct, mainly by reason, that can act at least with the compulsive power of a family or nation. We need to respond to the nuclear/ecological crises (intensified now by biological weaponry) at a level of commitment comparable to that shown by many nations, including the United States, during the Second World War. History (cultural evolution) moves more rapidly than natural evolution. Human history doubtless has been moving sideways toward defense of the species—otherwise we could hardly even pose the question for discussion. Yet judging from world responses to the danger of nuclear war and the certainty of ecological burnout, history still has a long way to go. The heart of our problem is that industrial proliferation came too fast; history (running its own course, so to speak) has lagged behind industrialization in generating cultural structures appropriate to protection of the species. Is it possible to intervene in this process? Can human intelligence transcend both biological evolution and historical development?

Upon what cultural foundations might such an intervention be based? For the best possibility of success it would need to be based on institutions worldwide in scope, controlling essential knowledge and skills, capable of organizing public information and public behavior, and possessing authority to speak in collective moral judgment. This sounds like an enormous requisition, but institutions making precisely these claims are by no means in short supply. They can be bracketed for convenient reference under four general headings: the scientific/technological establishment, the nation-state with its incumbent apparatus, corporate industry, and institutionalized religion. All have contributed to the present crises of the human condition, religion perhaps less than the other three. Since it is to leading institutions of these categories that the mass of humankind will look for guidance under increasingly difficult circumstances, it seems reasonable to inquire how well equipped they are for the task. In the remainder of this introduction I will comment on institutions of each category with respect to their potential for helping to resolve, or escape from, the oncoming crises of ecological burnout and nuclear/biological self-destruction. The two middle terms—corporate industry and the nation-state—because of their closely intermeshed origins, I will treat jointly, under a single heading.

II.

Little need be said about the scientific/technological category because a great deal has been said already, much of which is obviously true. Science and technology made possible the industrial expansion that brought on the crisis and we have no choice but to rely on scientists and technologists for guiding us out. Whether they will be able to do so is another question. By themselves, they cannot take us out of the crisis any more than, by themselves, they brought us into it. At most, they provided knowledge to which nation-states, including governments, their electorates if any, military establishments, and industrial and educational systems all responded. No one doubts that science can blueprint what needs to be done to halt perforation of the ozone layer, prevent further destruction of rain forests, restore fertility to the continental shelves and bypass both petroleum- and nuclear-based power sources; nor is there much doubt that technology can offer means to accomplish these ends. But long-range directions in scientific research and applied technology are not selected through the wisdom of individual scientists. They are socially and politically determined.

The real difficulties, then, are not scientific and technological but social and political; that is, they are moral decisions. If, for example, science taught us how to budget world resources so as, on the one hand, to extend present levels of production (plus "realistic" annual growth rates) over the next three generations; or, on the other hand, to achieve a balance of use and replacement that could be sustained for an unlimited future—which would we choose? More realistically, which would our political, industrial, and military leaders select? We know the answer already: they would opt for the latter alternative in public discourse, the first in actual practice. And might we be inclined to go along with this platonic evasion? Have we not earned—we would be telling ourselves—by enterprise and hard work in our competitive world, whatever modest comforts we and our children now enjoy? Are we under moral obligation to make outrageously difficult sacrifices for great-great-grandchildren whom none of us will ever see? How do we know such sacrifices would do any good? Maybe things will get better by that time. Science may unwrap new discoveries. Hasn't it worked that way in the past? Has there not always been forward movement and progress? Better let things go as they are and trust in the creative powers of the future—trust, that is, in the omnipotent hand of the free market.

III.

The dominant political institution of modern times is the nation-state. Its apparatus permeates human society. Nation- states come in three varieties: industrialized, industrializing, and those in what used to be called the third world, which remains largely pre-industrial. Industrial and industrializing nations (now that the Cold War hegemony exerted by the United States until a few decades ago has yielded, presumably, to a global market place) understand their best strategy as one of ferocious competition for export markets. Populations of pre-industrial countries, glimpsing by way of the media what life can be like for (some) people in industrial nations, envy the industrialized sector and angrily press their own rulers to find ways of breaking into it. The gap between wealth and poverty in our twenty-first century is probably wider than in any previous human society.

Nation-states have been structured historically on economic growth. Of all nation-states presently existing, only four—England, Spain, France, and the United States—came into existence before the Industrial Revolution. Spain, mesmerized by the glories of its colonial empire, permitted industrialization to pass it by; the other three embraced the Industrial Revolution, merged into and rose with it. They became the classic modernizers, the western (or Atlantic) models that all subsequent nation-states have striven to emulate and outdo. The era of nation-states coincides with the industrial era. When, during the late eighteenth and early nineteenth centuries, national identities coalesced from the post-feudal vortex of regional cultures, vernacular languages, ethnic art, and folkish religion, industrialism stepped forward as the adjunct to nationalism. Urban bourgeoisies, presiding over this transition, wooed the rural hinterland as well as their own sometimes reluctant labor forces with jobs, markets, intimations of abundance and variety. New nations generally defined their identities in opposition to other ethnic or national formations. Industrial growth validated the superiority of *our* identity over *theirs*. Moreover, new nations competed with others, old or new, for markets and raw materials. Growth paved the way to success. Successful competition resulted in economic empires that led to military conflict; victories in war flowed obviously from industrial capacity; and the vanquished healed their gaping wounds by means of industrial growth. The human condition, with nationalism in full flux at the end of the nineteenth century, approximated Hobbes's war of all against all. History, all too brief with respect to oncoming nuclear and ecological disasters, allowed ample time for cultural adaptations of nation-states in their Hobbesian environment. Thus we might see the First World War as the decisive induction of our species to the culture of industrial nationalism.

I turn now to another aspect of that historic adaptation. Doubtless there was class before nationality and class conflict before industrialization. In tandem, however, industrialism and nationalism worked to accentuate class and class conflict. Stripping away customary mediations of artisanry and craft, dehumanizing human exploitation by economizing it and then generalizing it across the terrain of each political state, industrialism exposed class domination to open view. Yet industrial growth required some level of willing input from national labor forces. Coercion might be necessary but never sufficient; and this held true especially for nations at war. If nationalism had not already been coming into existence, political leaders of industrializing states would have been obliged to invent it. Defining national identity against outsiders, nationalism offered a special status—citizenship—to those who were inside. Throughout Western Europe and North America, eighteenth-century subjects became nineteenth-century citizens. Citizenship implied shared decisions, mutuality of obligations and benefits. Consequently it pointed toward democracy, eventually to welfare-statism.

Welfare states extended to working-class citizens (as recompense for their acquiescence in upper-class control of the industrial apparatus) a protective margin against being reduced to the absolute level of the world market. Nationalism thus domesticated class conflict by containing class within citizenship and legitimating class politics. Labor parties became emblems of the industrializing nation-state. If labor politics are successful, they must improve, or at least maintain, living standards for working people. This might be attempted by targeting entrepreneurial profits and professional salaries, but such an attack would plunge the nation into disruptive controversies that might impede industrial expansion. A comparable result could be arrived at, however, simply by means of growth. Slices of expanding pies get bigger even though their shapes remain unaltered. That is, standards can continue to rise for all sectors of a society without modification of existing class structure—so long as industrial growth flourishes. Potential class antagonists thus become collaborators in support of growth; industrial expansion functions as the universal solvent to class conflict.[2]

Despite spectacular successes, capitalist industrialization did not go unchallenged. Evangelical Christians sometimes condemned it for exalting Mammon over Christ. Christian Socialists contrasted its spirit unfavorably to the egalitarian ethos of early Christian communities. Middle-class nationalists (in the North American experience known as "progressives") sought to transform the nation-state into an omsbudsman for the public interest. The classic and most enduring criticism, however, was the work of philosophical materialists—Karl Marx and Friedrich Engels—who applauded industrialization for at last bringing an end to humanity's age of scarcity. Although Marx and Engels were better informed than most of their contemporaries on the complex relationships between industrial production and natural environment, little of this found its way into socialist politics. No one in those days was registering much anxiety with respect to ecological limits. The age-old trauma of scarcity, the identification of nature with gigantic and relentless death, had rendered almost inconceivable any thought that human enterprise might ever make a dent in nature. Thus Marxian polemics against capitalism breathed the same euphoria for unbounded productivity that infused capitalist celebrationism.[3]

The Marxist critique of capitalism rested on different grounds. Capitalist productivity, it argued, was linked structurally to human exploitation. Compulsions to produce, and to exploit, inhered in the system itself rather than being arrived at through collectively willed decision; and since, in this analysis, the system contained no effective checks to its structural compulsions, it must continue to escalate inequality and universalize human exploitation. But exploitive inequality destroys the only possible basis for a moral society. That was (and remains) the bottom line of the Marxist indictment. Its practical conclusion was that working-class collaboration in politics of growth would ultimately prove self-defeating. For this reason, Marxian labor politics could never fully converge with nationalizing labor politics. As counterpart to its negative prognosis for capitalist industrialization, Marxism projected the positive image of an industrial order without human exploitation—socialism. Millions of people around the world have seen in that image a road to the future. The road itself, however, was premised on growth. Marxian parties generally assumed that socialism, unfettered by class conflict, would outdo capitalism in the dynamics of industrial expansion. During the twentieth century, the Soviet Union, Communist China, and the Soviet-bloc nations (leaving aside the question of how close any of these actually came to being socialist societies) retained the Marxist enthusiasm for industrial production. They attempted to overturn capitalism by outproducing it, and failed.

Capitalism's rebuttal of Marxian criticism—and its counterstatement to the utopian image of a social order beyond human exploitation—was to marshal the industrializing nations in all their immense power for a series of bloody repressions (the so-called Cold War formed only one phase) that stretch from the Paris Commune of the 1870s to military and CIA-style interventions in Iran, Korea, Cuba, Vietnam, Chile, Central America, Indonesia—and beyond. Capitalism organized to outproduce its enemies, and succeeded. If working people in capitalist nations were sometimes moved by class consciousness to resist this crusade against socialism, they also were moved to concur with it by national loyalties, as well as by their prior commitment to the politics of growth.

From this retrospect into the genealogy of nation-states, what may we infer as to their potential for resolving the nuclear/biological and ecological crises? The obvious inference is that they are likely to remain part of the problem rather than promote a solution. Nation-states have made themselves synonymous with industrial growth. Industrial growth dissolves inner tensions. It enhances commercial competitiveness and military striking power, two attributes closely linked throughout the history of nation-states. The political economies of nation-states have been so consistently geared to growth that it is difficult to imagine any other type of response to any conceivable demand. Yet industrial growth cannot offer an appropriate response to demands that are likely to emerge from the nuclear/biological and ecological crises. It might seem desirable, for example, to deconstruct certain industries: we can think of lumbering, or whale fisheries, or nuclear power. Whatever long-range benefits their phasing out might bring for the human species, the immediate results will include job loss as well as social costs of developing substitute products and retraining or absorbing the unemployed. For industrialized nation-states such costs might not be unbearable; although obviously this would be only the beginning, since other industries and traditional occupations would certainly also require downsizing.

Thus far, we have glimpsed only the tip of the iceberg. Deconstruction costs would fall most heavily on marginally industrial and pre-industrial societies, which include most of the world's population. Ecological motivations decrease as one moves down the scale of industrial development. Where life expectancy is thirty years and infant mortality over 50 percent, the condition of the ozone layer will rouse less anxiety than among suburbanites of Kent or California. It may seem better to work in a Malaysian plywood factory (atmospheric pollution notwithstanding), or tolerate nuclear reactors along the banks of the Ganges, than watch one's children die of malnutrition. These are priorities that will inform both the domestic politics and international relations of marginally industrial and pre-industrial nations. They will prefer environmentally destructive methods whenever such methods (immediately at least) yield rapid growth for minimal investment.[4]

Industrial growth, regardless of method, exacerbates class conflict. In earlier industrializations, class conflict was mediated through labor politics and welfare statism. Especially during the Cold War, welfare states formed the home base for capitalism's war against socialism, since they instilled in workers of capitalist nations the impression—often the reality—of faring better than their counterparts in countries that were trying to construct socialism. When, with the collapse of the Soviet Union and China's entry into the world market, the Cold War came to an end, capitalist governments proceeded with amazing speed to deconstruct their welfare state apparatus. In any case, no such mediations would be available to newly industrializing nations of the twenty-first century. Their desperate need precludes the old-fashioned, slow process of capital accumulation through individual savings. Consequently they depend on foreign capital, which can come to them only from already industrialized nation-states. Industrial nations, however, since the end of the Cold War, govern their investments in accord with free market principles that aim at maximizing short-run profits. The effect is to compel governments of underdeveloped nations to rely on coercion rather than class collaboration. Coercive technologies and military hardware for carrying them out are available—on credit.

Global mobility has accelerated since the Second World War. For shipment of commodities, export of machinery and technology—especially for the export of capital—mobility increased more rapidly than for transfers of labor. Consequently the traditional exchange by which mines and plantations in the periphery extracted raw materials while industrial nations at the core manufactured finished products has been partially reversed. Sweatshops, factories, steel mills, and shipyards are as common as mining or agriculture nowadays in new third world nations; whereas the older industrial nations at the core, divesting themselves of less profitable investment, move into high-tech (high profit) specializations of information/management systems together with proconsular CEOs to install and supervise them. Third world nations, meanwhile, dependent on borrowed capital, are driven to maximize exports and cut labor costs. They face rising levels of exploitation and intensified class conflict totally unmitigated by the sorts of welfare politics that characterized earlier industrializations.

Not all third world leaders will be willing to make themselves instruments in exploiting their own people. They may be attracted by populist, or religious/utopian visions, or some combination of these. So they opt for the egalitarian ethos that resides in nationalism. Impelled then to resist exploitation by outside powers, they come face-to-face with the absolute impotence of their own "sovereign" nations. A next logical move will be to explore the backroads of world diplomacy (and free market bargaining under-the-counter) for weapons systems affordable by pre-industrial economies. Leaders who pursue such projects are often described as suicidal or insane. Probably they are not—at least not to begin with. By the logic of nationalism, at any rate, they would seem totally rational since there exists no other way in our current world, controlled by United States military and economic power, to resist the world-devouring domination of industrial capitalism. Thus we come around again, full circle, to the nuclear component of the crises. Had we imagined nuclear perils would vanish when the winding down of the Cold War put an end to great-power confrontations? On the contrary, it released a leakage of nuclear spare parts from great power arsenals. Even these may now be turning obsolete in the sense of being priced off the market by cheaper devices of chemical and biological liquidation.

I showed in an earlier connection that nation-states have always promoted industrial growth, the implication being that nationalism ought to be seen as part of the problem that endangers human survival. In that case, we would we be better off without nationalism. Suppose we dismantled national governments—an alternative attracting serious attention from political leaders and scholars in the social sciences—and threw ourselves into the New World Order, rationally administered, globalized, under the guidance of transnational corporations? Would such a breakthrough open the way for full-scale use of science and technology to resolve the impending crises? Here it may be worth recalling that nationalism entered its partnership with the industrializing state as a restraining force on capitalist exploitation. Nationalism steered industrial growth into competing national units. Inside each unit, nationalism (in the form of the welfare state) sought to protect its working class from reduction to the absolute level of the world market. Yet it is precisely this contradiction—between human bonding among *citizens,* and the exclusion and dehumanizing of *outsiders*; between, on the one hand, a social order grounded in moral equality, and on the other, a world ruled by the calculus of wealth—that plunged nation-states into their Hobbesian war of all against all. The crucial question, then, is not how do we get beyond nationalism, but how can we get beyond nationalism without universalizing human exploitation? Even to suggest such a question may seem hopelessly utopian. There exists today no channel for exercising global power *except* nation-states—or empires constructed by nation-states. The much-heralded American Empire may be next up, but hardly the last. What we are likely to see (in the short run) is escalating competition among regional alliances whose populations will be exhorted to save their own skins (at the expense of the rest of the world) by working faster, longer, smarter, more efficiently. Regional competition will trigger regional wars, any of which could become nuclear, biological, global. That roughly is the short run. As to the long run…

IV.

I referred at the opening to several categories of cultural institutions to which human populations under duress would be likely to turn. The first of these (the scientific/technological establishment) doubtless commands knowledge and technique needed to meet the crisis but lacks coercive power and moral authority for implementing them. The next two—nation-states and corporate industry (treated jointly because of their intermeshing historical origins)—possess coercive power and varying degrees of moral authority yet remain so locked into industrial growth as to be incapable of any initiative for restraining growth. To this point, my argument has followed the footsteps of Robert Heilbroner whose book, *The Human Prospect,* impressed me when I read it thirty years ago. My own title refers retrospectively to his. I felt Heilbroner's work was rather studiously marginalized by reviewers, and since that time the human prospect has turned bleaker than it seemed then.[5]

Perhaps because he belonged so intensely to the Age of Secularism, Heilbroner made no effort to include religion or religious institutions within his inventory of assets and liabilities. Certainly that was a mistake. No assessment of the human condition can afford to leave religion out. By 1974 (when he published *The Human Prospect*), religion's worldwide resurgence was already beginning to command headline news. Drawing my lesson from Heilbroner, I have placed religion as my central focus. We have witnessed in our own time a multifaceted revival of religious beliefs after their long winter of secularization (dated back to the Enlightenment by

many historians and most theologians). Skeptical of empirical reason, religion probably was less involved than the industrialized state or scientific/technological establishment in precipitating our present crises. Although sometimes linked (especially
through its Protestant incarnations) with industrialism, religion kept a distance from
the culture of growth and generally subordinated (in theory at least) material abundance to spiritual welfare. During the modern era, its strongest bases have been in
industrial working classes and among the multitudes of agricultural laborers and
displaced rural populations in the third world. Claiming priority over both nationalism and class consciousness, religion enjoyed a certain autonomy from forces that
shaped the age of industrial nationalism. Despite its denominational separations,
religion might be thought to offer an identification powerful enough to surmount
them. One need not suppose in pursuing this line of thought that churches would
usurp science and the state; rather, that religion might bestow upon scientists and
industrialists courage compatible with their knowledge and capacity, and upon
rulers of nation-states (or whatever forms of governance may prevail in our globalized market place) creative imagination compatible with their power. For many of
our contemporaries, religion offers the only resource through which human society can hope to survive the ecological crises and the impending threat of nuclear/bio-
logical warfare. Even Robert Heilbroner—stern secularist of an earlier era—began
making room for religion as a possible saving resource when he "reconsidered" *The
Human Prospect* for its 1980 edition.

Is there substance to such hopes?

The purpose of my book is to search for answers to this question. It will be
necessary, first, to confirm the world scope of religion and, second, to inquire
whether its divisiveness is essential or historically contingent. Divisiveness at a
surface level involves conflicting creeds and denominations, yet more important
for the crises of our era, also involves the gap that separates scientific knowledge
from religious faith. Part One of this book, after a survey of universality and divisiveness, moves to an examination of the common-law marriage that currently
governs cohabitation by our scientific and religious establishments. With this
groundwork in place, I turn in Part Two to the central question: can religion
muster sufficient moral authority to command scientific knowledge, impose social
acceptance, and inspire collective actions certain to run counter to deeply held,
seemingly indispensable interests? Such capability is by no means evident, nor is
it clear what sorts of evidence might serve to affirm or negate it. My main line of
inquiry will be historical—to seek out and examine instances in the past when

religion actually worked (or failed to work) as saving resource for particular groups, or for the human species at large. Five such critical junctures will be identified. First is the "moment" when some one of our humanoid ancestors arrived at self-consciousness (together with knowledge of individual death), and religion interposed the belief in spiritual beings as a negation of death. The second is that in which groups of those same ancestors confronted a tension between individual self-interest and collective survival; and religion defended collective survival by sanctifying it as *morality*. The third critical juncture occurred when division of labor, combined with the separations of class and gender, began to fragment the primal egalitarianism of hunter-gatherer societies. Religion then extended moral law to govern the relationships of dominance and submission imposed by gender and class exploitation. I will argue that in each of these episodes the future of our species (or its capacity to construct culture) stood at risk, and religion's intervention served as a necessary condition of survival. If we conceive of cultural history as evolutionary, religion must then appear as an adaptive attribute.[6]

There may be many reasons why religion worked for survival, but these converge at a single bottleneck; religion worked because it provided human societies with collective belief systems. Belief systems depend on *belief*: they work (or may work) when they command credibility—and this defines the last-but-one in the sequence of crises referred to above. Here the notion of a particular event, resolved one way or another in some past "moment," will no longer serve. We are dealing with a crisis that is ongoing, endemic to the history of religion, laid to rest at many times and places, reborn in new forms. This is the Problem of Evil. Human life resides in nature. Nature, according to most religious teachings, is ruled by a divine power (or powers) sympathetic to human needs. Why then is life filled with pain and why must it end in death? Some students of religion, perceiving the Problem of Evil as peculiarly Western, attempt to localize it in Western monotheisms. And indeed it has played a central part not only in theology but literature and science of the West. I make use of that centrality in Part Three to survey the problem as exemplified in the Western tradition. Given my own background, sources most readily available to me are Western, yet I am certain that to westernize the Problem of Evil is a mistake. I will argue instead for universality. The problem remains universal because it poses a question difficult (or impossible) to answer and because it confronts all believers as a credibility gap that undermines faith and subverts social order. Religions around the world have grappled with this problem since before the Book of Job. Generally they have managed to hold it in check by accentuating religion's positive values and by treating belief itself as self-evident truth. Thus my Part Three is titled, "The Will to Believe." After that come two closing chapters (Part Four), the first of which reviews the argument–at-large, then suggests conclusions (or probabilities) as to the role of religion in the upcoming crises. The final chapter—a short one—speculates on strategies and political agendas likely to be pursued, in those days, by believers and nonbelievers.

PART ONE:

Religion as an Object of Study

2

Homo Religiosus

The saving powers customarily attributed to religion refer to salvation of individual souls whereas the sort of power that would be needed for coping with nuclear/biological and ecological crises must apply to biological bodies resident on planet Earth. These two projects are not necessarily the same, although they are sometimes confused. The reason for the confusion, I think, is that both express concern for human survival and both involve a sense of some unifying essence in the human condition. Religious believers take that essence to be religion itself, an assumption supported by empirical evidence of religion's virtual universality.

Religion in this respect outreaches both nation-states and the scientific-technological establishment. While there may be individuals and groups scattered about our world who disbelieve in religion, there exists no nation, region, city, perhaps even no rural community, in which some sort of religious institution does not maintain a visible presence. With equal accuracy, the same statement could have been made one hundred or a thousand or two thousand years ago. What this suggests is that religion has been coextensive with the human species, and most scholars, including anthropologists, archaeologists, historians of religion, and theologians concur on approximations of this estimate. They thus confirm E. B. Tylor's mid-nineteenth-century conclusion, arrived at on the basis of meager and often unreliable evidence, that no trace existed of any human group totally lacking in religion. I can at least begin then by taking for granted the world scope of religion—geographical and probably chronological as well. Religion certainly is older than what we have traditionally called history. Perhaps, like language, it precedes (or begins?) human culture.[1]

The Fourth Great Awakening

Despite its impressive showing of longevity, many scholars in modern times have feared (or hoped) that religion was fading away. Intimations of decline, not so much in institutional forms as in the vigor of personal faith, have been endemic in Western culture for two centuries at least. These declinations constitute the so-called Age of Secularism referred to in the preceding chapter. The onset of secularization in the nineteenth and twentieth centuries has variously been attributed to skeptical rationalism emanating from the Enlightenment, to advances made by scientific explanation at the expense of religious doctrines, and to the breakup of traditional communities and lifestyles under the impact of industrial development and urban growth.[2] John Stuart Mill, a self-declared champion of skeptical rationalism, inquired almost a century and a half ago whether religion served any useful purpose for human welfare, or "whether that end would not be better served ... by the application of the same mental powers to the strengthening and enlargement of those sources of virtue and happiness which stand in no need of the support or sanctions of supernatural beliefs and inducements."[3] "Rationalism is the great evil of the day," John Henry Newman, a self-declared enemy of skeptical rationalism and liberal thought, wrote in 1864. "'Right Reason' would lead to a belief in God, the immortal Soul, future retribution. But we do not have 'Right Reason'—we have fallen, partial, corrupt reason with its all-dissolving skepticism of the intellect ... its tendency ... to atheism in one shape or other. ... What force can be a breakwater against the deluge?" Newman had long since abandoned any trust in rational argument (Right Reason) as defender of the faith. His answer to his own question was that faith alone conveyed power to defend the faith: "[God] cooperates with us and thereby enables us to that which He wills us to do, and carries us on, if our own will does but cooperate with His, to a certitude which rises higher than the logical force of our conclusions."[4]

One hundred years later this same debate still continued on substantially the same terms, although the tide seemed by then increasingly to favor the secularists. Thus in America, in the first full flux of America's American Century, some two hundred leading scientists and clergy gathered in the luxurious setting of a privately owned island off the New England coast to assess the relationship of their two bodies of knowledge. These sessions took the name Institute of Religion in an Age of Science. One result of their deliberations was a volume of essays edited by the Harvard astronomer Harlow Shapley, bearing the somewhat condescending title

Science Ponders Religion. The papers (all written by scientists) ranged from radical agnosticism on one side to a plea for merging Western science into the cosmic mysticism of "Far Eastern religions" on the other. The common denominator, however, was a partnership program in which science would be senior partner. To religion were left those fuzzy regions beyond the pale of clear knowledge where pastors and theologians could tinker with ethical values and spiritual motivations. Such efforts might assist at least in maintaining the orderly social structure required by science for the pursuit of real tasks in human progress.[5]

While some religious specialists doubtless resented this downsizing of religion, there were others, given the apparently irreversible thrust of secularization, who took it as realistic and necessary. Among these was a young scholar at Harvard who in 1965, to everyone's surprise including his own, authored a bestseller in theology, *The Secular City*. The author, Harvey Cox, explained that he was trying "to work out a theology for the 'postreligious' age that many sociologists confidently assured us was coming." His book became "a kind of bible for a new generation of theology students and clergy who feared their own obsolescence in the coming 'postreligious climate.' "[6] Although Cox had begun by accepting the inevitability of secularization, his tone was by no means one of lamentation. The secular city, after all, was the logical outcome of three millennia of Judaic, Greek, and Christian civilizations—maybe it ought to be welcomed for its openings to human freedom. "Pluralism and tolerance are the children of secularization. ... Pluralism is breaking out where once a closed system stood."[7] The duty of religious youth in the secular city, as Cox saw it, was not to defend obsolete and dysfunctional traditions but to search out new beginnings. As for traditional Christianity ("shorn of its political might by two hundred years of revolutions, deprived of its cultural influence by the Enlightenment ... robbed of its psychological power by the casual this-worldliness of modern man"), it might simply have to turn back "and start from scratch."[8] Doubtless Cox would have felt no less contemptuous than John Henry Newman of a junior partnership in the scientific-technological establishment. But this was not because of nostalgia for conventional religion. On the contrary, its expected collapse provided an opportunity to drive out the money changers and cleanse the temple. In the language of the 1960s, Cox's ideological allies would have been (and actually were) social critics and troublemakers in the secular city, such as Saul Alinsky or the incomparable Dorothy Day.[9]

It is therefore a double irony that Cox's rhapsody for secularism coincided with the first vital signs of a worldwide resurgence of religion. While this was exactly what he and many others who thought as he did must have been praying for, its actual advent worked to marginalize their visions of a revitalizing radicalism. From faint flickerings during and after the Second World War—ignited perhaps (as Cox had hopefully suggested) by pentecostal outbursts of "primal spirituality" among the urban poor and rural dispossessed—the revival by the 1960s was establishing its credentials as a mainline phenomenon.[10] Thus the Yale professor William McLoughlin, co-editor (with Robert Bellah) of an American Academy of Arts and Sciences symposium, "Religion in America" (1968), appraised the "postwar 'turn to religion'" as "nothing short of a Great Awakening"—the fourth, by McLoughlin's reckoning, in American, that is, American since 1492, history.[11] Statistical records verify an upsurge of religion after the Second World War and show that it leveled off in the 1970s, then resumed its trajectory during the following decade. Leveling occurred presumably because the youth counterculture of the late '60s and '70s retarded growth for Protestant denominations, and because fallout from the Second Vatican Council (1962–65) exerted a similarly negative influence on Catholics. Meanwhile various impulses described in Gallup polls as "technologies of the spirit" began to escalate; and, most important, the Pentecostals and Fundamentalists entered their high-angle growth phase. Four in every ten Americans, the Gallup Organization reported in 1995, said they had attended church or synagogue within the previous week.[12] Cox, who clearly prefers Pentecostalist speaking-in- tongues to Fundamentalist inerrancy, credits Pentecostalism as the cutting edge of the entire revival. Looking back from thirty years later, he was able to contemplate the fall of the secular city without regret. Today it is "secularity," he wrote, "not spirituality, that may be headed for extinction."[13]

Spirituality by the 1990s was riding the waves of million-dollar television programs. In October 1996, Bill Moyers celebrated the opening of his PBS series *Genesis* with a cover story, "The Resurgence of Faith," in *USA Weekend* ("39.1 million readers every weekend"). "Something is happening in America," Moyers wrote, "that as a journalist I can't ignore. Religion is breaking out everywhere. Millions of Americans have taken public their search for a clearer understanding of the core principles of belief and how they can be applied to the daily experience of life." *Time* weighed in soon afterward with an illustrated ten-page feature on the meaning of *Genesis*. And for its pre-Christmas issue in that same year *Time* brought forward a cover portrait of Jesus, long-haired and haloed, gazing gravely at prospective readers over the illuminated title, "Jesus On Line." The ensuing story, nine pages with pictures, worked up a text on "Finding God on the Web:

Across the Internet, believers are reexamining their ideas of faith, religion and spirituality."[14] As America goes—or as America in the mass media appears to be going—so goes the world. Pentecostal sects worldwide, multiplying at a rate of twenty million a year, have passed four hundred million members.[15] Mormons, once localized mainly in the Great Basin country of the Far West, now claim almost ten million adherents in 165 countries. "We're carrying the message far and wide," Gordon Hinckley, president of the Church of Jesus Christ of Latter-Day Saints, told the *San Francisco Chronicle*. "The church is growing faster, at the moment, in the Spanish-language countries, Mexico, Central America, South America. ... We've passed the point where we have more members outside ... than we have inside the United States. That's a very significant thing."[16] The statistics cited above refer only to Judaeo-Christian denominations. Similar showings can be made for Muslims, Hindus, Buddhists throughout the world, as well as for various strains of "New Religionists" mainly in the United States and Western Europe.[17] There is no need, however, to multiply these tokens of fire from heaven. Scientists, social scientists, clergy high and low, theologians, political leaders, mass media, all agree that the reenergizing of religion has altered the course of history by rolling back—perhaps forever reversing—the long secular trend that began with the scientific revolution and age of industrialization.[18]

What does such evidence tell us about the potential of religion to serve as a saving resource in the ecological and nuclear/biological crises? Obviously, it enhances the potency of that potential. If religion is coextensive with the human species—if it can be traced to a stage at the earliest beginnings of culture—if it still contains the capacity to surge back over the ramparts of the secularized modern world, then we are indeed obliged to understand our species as *religiosus* first, and only secondarily as *sapiens*. If any human resources are capable of saving us, how could such resources be mobilized and integrated except through the species-unifying power of religion?[19]

The Dialogue of Ecumenicalism and Revelation

It is true, of course, that reenergizing belief has also reenergized hostilities among believers. The inferno of the Trade Towers, the assault on the Pentagon bear witness to religious totalitarianism's lethal destructiveness. In Ireland, Central Europe, North Africa, Israel and Palestine, Lebanon, Iran, and Iraq—in

Afghanistan, India, Pakistan, Indonesia—religionists are now, or have in very recent times, been killing one another in defense of faith. Examples endemic in North America include Waco, Texas, the Oklahoma City federal building, attacks on abortion clinics, bombings and burnings of synagogues, African-American churches, and Muslim mosques. Splits within denominations, struggles among rival denominations, collisions between religious activists and legal powers of government—all appear as corollaries to the revival of religion. Nation-states are again plunging into religious warfare much as they did in seventeenth-century Europe. Are we facing a new era of religious wars? Even after September 11, this seems unlikely for the twenty-first century, yet it is by no means unlikely that religious hatreds will contribute to wars unleashed presumably for other reasons. [20]

Resurgent religion thus contains perils as well as promises. To propagate revelationist doctrine is to incite conflict. For believers whose faith rests on specific revelations, possible dangers may seem less compelling than potential gains, since revealed truth is understood to save souls precisely by this means. Yet even the most fundamental of fundamentalists will be obliged to acknowledge some form of universality, since no believer could wish to allege that the omnipotent Creator (or the creative power however conceived) had erred in creating all those other folk who choose beliefs different from our own. East and West—both in religions that purport to be monotheistic as in those that do not—the moral logic of ecumenicalism adds legitimacy to its support. Anxieties roused by religious violence tend to reinforce the ecumenical center. And because religion itself must hold religious belief essential to the human condition, believers will be impelled to speak (or even to think) favorably of ecumenicalism regardless of how little of it they suppose may enter into the Last Judgment. Sustained, then, by conscience and rationality, ecumenicalism has flourished in the post-secular era no less luxuriantly than the revelational creeds. Thus it offers neutral ground for believers who perhaps once were, and fear they may become again, bitter adversaries.

This neutral ground contains an increasing awareness of upcoming crises, together with an assumption that only religion can work as the saving resource. For ecumenicalists, then, the theological puzzle is how to authorize a unifying identity and collective agenda for believers in different belief systems without betraying the particularness that characterizes each system. What sort of identity would ecumenicalism itself proclaim? Meanings of the word have changed historically. The changes point to massive difficulties that confront ecumenicalists. Originally the word simply meant *universal* and was synonymous with *catholic*. But the synonyms diverged after the Reformation, when Catholic (with uppercase *C*) appeared increasingly unlikely ever to achieve universality. Ecumenicalism— inheriting the earlier universalist intent of "Catholic"—also took over its restrictive connotation: that is, to intend a worldwide propagation of Christian faith was to assume that only Christianity gave access to salvation. This imposed upon Christians the generous duty of opening their strait gate as wide as possible for heathen peoples who must otherwise be forever lost. Missionaries as well as empire builders enthusiastically collaborated in this undertaking, which, by the twentieth century, had become fatally tainted with the ideologies of Western imperialism and white racism. Could ecumenicalism broaden its frame of reference?[21]

Within academic circles (in the West) ecumenicalism comprises an almost autonomous division of postmodern theology. At the top of its agenda is the task of discovering a "deep grammar" of religious experience. Thus Huston Smith, an old head in this field (described by Bill Moyers as a "renowned historian of religion"), concludes his widely read text *The World's Religions* with the following parable:

> Said Jesus, blessed be his name, "Do unto others as you would they should do unto you." Said Buddha, blessed be his name as well, "He who would, may reach the utmost height—but he must be eager to learn."

For Smith, Christianity's Golden Rule and Buddhist insistence on the availability of salvation to all serious seekers comprise a common core of spirituality. He assured readers that he could quote comparable declarations from all the world's major belief systems.[22] Is there then one substance beneath the multiplicity of creeds? The late Mircea Eliade, professor of history of religions at the University of Chicago and perhaps the outstanding scholar of comparative religions in our own era, answered this question with a ringing affirmation: "The historian of religion recognizes a spiritual unity subjacent to the history of humanity.... Certainly, the unity of the human species is accepted de facto in other disciplines, for example, linguistics, anthropology, sociology. But the historian of religions has the privilege of grasping this unity at the highest level—or the deepest."[23] On this same conviction, Diana Eck, now a professor at Harvard's Divinity School, structured her career of teaching and scholarship. Raised a Methodist Episcopalian in Bozeman, Montana, Eck journeyed by various stages to Benares to study the wisdom of India. In her book *Encountering God*, she describes her spiritual odyssey as a transcendence over the parochial. All religions give partial access to the transcendent; all are limited in different ways by historical particularities. Religious believers, she maintains, ought to cleave to their own orthodoxy and tradition, yet always honoring those of others. They must strive for a "radical openess to Truth—to God—that seeks to enlarge understanding through dialogue." Dialogue, for Eck, offers the key to religion's potential as saving resource because it carries into practice the ecumenical imperative.[24]

These are all voices of the ecumenical movement. There are many such voices. Ecumenicalists occupy leading positions in theological schools and clerical hierarchies. Yet, in the West at least, they have been on the defensive. Martin Marty, a professor at the University of Chicago's Divinity School, expressed this perception almost despairingly: "The public church seems defenseless ... against the drive to form tribes whose members will see all outsiders as devils. But the odds against such a public church only increase the urgency of the need for it."[25] Why should the odds seem stacked against a "public church"—that is, against collective effort led by religious organizations to meet impending crises? American churches did as much and more in the Revolution and during the Civil War. Churches all over the world in the First and Second World Wars struggled for victory of their respective homelands. Won't the case be all the stronger when what hangs in balance is not merely which side will overthrow another in war, but survival of the human species itself? Arguments of this type seem logically compelling, and they may be so; the difficulty is that they are scarcely relevant to the problem at issue. Against such well-intentioned, basically optimistic rationalizations stands the empirically observed reality that religious revival coincides with renewal of strife. Is divisiveness inherent in religion itself, or has it somehow become contingent to the historical circumstances of our present time period? The fact that religion is coextensive with the human species (also empirically observed) offers no answer to this question since it contains no information as to the nature of religion, nor even whether religion is essentially one substance, or many. The question at this level is totally different from Diana Eck's unifying concept of pluralism. What was involved there was an assumption that different doctrinal, or even revelational, roads might all lead to a single religious truth. What we are now facing is a more mundane possibility that religion, while perhaps empirically identifiable as a particular type of human behavior, may be of such a type (like tribalism or nationalism) that it encourages discord rather than harmony.[26]

Resume

As religious beliefs have proliferated and intensified over the past half century, sectarian hostilities have done likewise. A survey of religion in the contemporary world shows a multiplicity of creeds and denominations divided internally and externally over the issue of denominational loyalty versus ecumenical cooperation. Worldwide cooperation on any issue, at this viewing, appears unlikely, but the appearance is perhaps superficial. We do know, both from the history of religion and from national histories, that great surges of enthusiasm have sometimes galvanized religious believers, obliterating sectarian and doctrinal separations. Western tradition gives us (among many others) the Crusades, the restoration of French monarchy led by Joan of Arc, and the overthrow of English monarchy led by Cromwell. In such times, religion *seemed* to be serving as a saving resource for segments of the human species, or even as a proxy for humanity at large. Yet readings from history remain subjective and impressionistic unless we can somehow separate religious belief from its inevitable entanglements with other human affiliations such as class, race, nation, language—or, in more ancient times, those of tribes, city-states, and empires. What will be needed at this point is a working definition of religion.

3

Tylor's Definition and the Social Science Stance

Edward B. Tylor, often described as "the father of British anthropology," wrote in 1871 in the opening chapter of his magnum opus, *Religion in Primitive Culture*, "It seems best ... simply to claim, as a minimum definition of religion, the belief in Spiritual Beings." Tylor had ruled out restrictive attributes that he deemed nonessential, such as worship of idols, ritual sacrifices, or the doctrine of "a supreme deity or judgment after death." Belief in spiritual beings he equated to animism, which he perceived as the first step in a progression that contained potentially all the more complex belief systems. And, as I noted at the start of the previous chapter, Tylor assumed on the basis of rather meager evidence that no society, ancient or modern, had ever been discovered totally devoid of religion as so defined.[1] His definition won wide acceptance by his contemporaries. Darwin in *The Descent of Man*, crediting Tylor, used essentially the same definition.[2] Since then, despite complaints about lack of specificity and many efforts to improve on the original, scholars have generally worked back to something close to it for their own usage. This is dramatically illustrated in recent books by Scott Atran and Daniel Dennett, based on current research in cognitive science and evolutionary psychology, which begin from, or arrive at, formulations similar to Tylor's.[3]

For religious scholarship at its beginnings in the nineteenth century, Tylor's definition established a common denominator, and consequently a realm of shared discourse, that underlay a wide range of potentially contradictory formulations. Consider, for example, two possible variants of his phrasing:

Tylor: Religion is
"BELIEF in Spiritual Beings."

1. Religion is the   2. Religion is the
KNOWLEDGE OF   IMAGINING OF
Spiritual Beings.   Spiritual Beings.

The three substantives—knowledge, *belief*, imagining—are close enough in meaning to be used sometimes interchangeably. Here, however, they express profoundly different concepts. Held by different individuals, they became icons of ideological warfare. Historically, they have exacerbated political controversy and armed conflict. Yet sometimes (perhaps most of the time) all three existed simultaneously in the minds of single individuals. Each individual, struggling for an interior sanctuary of compromise, was likely to be participating in public efforts to eradicate one of the alternatives. It was problems such as these that Tylor's definition excluded by opting for belief rather than knowledge or imagining.[4] To exclude is not necessarily to destroy. The alternatives remain as much in evidence in our own era as they were in Tylor's. Precisely by its exclusions, Tylor's definition framed the compromise that was then making possible for the first time a subjection of human phenomena, especially the phenomenon of religion, to scientific scrutiny. Both flanks—those who *knew* the truth of religion and those who *knew* that religious truths were imaginary—attacked the center. They often ignored, or bypassed, or seceded from it. Yet the flanks as much as the center had sound reasons for laboring to preserve the compromise, and so it stood, tenuously but enduringly.

From Classical Tolerance to Scientific Model

The application of scientific scrutiny to religion clearly bears on the main enterprise of this book, which is to assess religion's potential as a saving resource in the crises of ecological burnout and nuclear/biological weapons proliferation. My intent in this chapter is to bring into historical context the intellectual compromise that Tylor's definition articulated, and to indicate its bearing on my own project. Efforts to set up religion as an object of study obviously ran counter to denominational loyalties. What could any definition convey more fundamentally than truth itself—as for example the Apostles' Creed or Westminster Confession? Even to search for generic definition must appear scandalous to those who, when they spoke of religion, meant *true* religion, whereas false religion was no religion at all. Looking backwards, we might visualize a spectrum from revelationists on one side through deism in the center to nonbelievers at the opposite pole. But no such arrangement could begin to function until some sort of substratum had been identified, and partially agreed to, as underlying the multiplicity of creeds and confessions.[5] Our balkanized religious landscape harks back (in the Western tradition) to a complex history that we might be glad to forget but can never really escape. Generally, revelationist positions stem from the monotheisms of the Mediterranean basin beginning several thousand years before the Christian era. The ecumenical stance rose with the Enlightenment and remains closely linked to deism. But there is this crucial difference: whereas deism is grounded in a repudiation of specific revelations that it identified with superstition and priestcraft, modern ecumenicalism seeks to woo the various revelations by centering attention on the common ground they allegedly share. Nonbelief—probably as ancient as religion itself—showed scarcely any collective identity prior to the Enlightenment. Atheism, as a particular form of nonbelief, was endemic in the left wing of the Enlightenment. Its presumably less radical fellow traveler, agnosticism (a term coined by Thomas Huxley in 1869), came into existence only when the scientific and industrial revolutions had created a secular social base capable of sustaining it.[6]

In Western culture there has always been tension between religious doctrine and efforts at secular explanation. Conflicts occurred in Greek and Roman times and were hardly unknown during the Middle Ages. They intensified with the Renaissance and the beginnings of modern science. When the achievements of the great astronomers, culminating in Isaac Newton, made unavoidable some sort of reassessment of religious doctrine, there existed within Christian tradition not much open space for doctrinal revision. That a bit of space was actually found (or preempted) resulted from two decisive factors, one then new in European history, the other already ancient. The new factor was the extraordinary openness of the Puritan Revolution in England to secular inquiry and materialist explanation. Whether this should be viewed as a cause, or effect, or simply contingent to the beginnings of modern science, is a problem best left to historians of science. The point to be stressed here (and I will come back to this subsequently) is that it legitimized an enthusiasm for Newtonian physics that spread to the continent, gradually penetrating both the Protestant Reformation and Catholic Counter-Reformation.[7] By the end of the seventeenth century this scientific elan had fused with a second factor older than the Reformation or the Renaissance—older indeed than Christianity.

The second factor was the tradition of religious tolerance embedded in classic (and pre-classic) paganism. Tolerance had served as a building block of Hellenic and Roman empires precisely because it certified that local divinities of any city-state substantial enough to attract a conqueror's notice could not be all bad. Provided they showed respect for the sacred space of others, there would be room for them and their doctrines in the imperial pantheon. Only after the Christian God insisted on evicting his pagan counterparts did the classical age of tolerance grind to a bloody halt. A Christian polemicist might point out (correctly) that bloody repressions preceded the marriage of Roman Empire and Christian church. That of course was because Christians, who were monotheists rather than pagan pluralists, preferred death to toleration for any other divinities. When they achieved power themselves, they reversed the earlier imperial tradition by converting (or attempting to convert) the Roman Empire into God's imperium on earth.[8] We can admire the moral fortitude of generations of martyrs while at the same time recognizing that these events laid the basis for later exterminations of Christian heretics, for the Crusades, for the religious wars of the sixteenth and seventeenth centuries in Europe, and for the long, bitter saga of anti-Semitism.[9]

Pagan tolerance and the potential for critical discourse about religious doctrine—driven underground in the Christianized Roman Empire—survived to emerge again with the classical revival at the end of the Middle Ages. A component of humanism, tolerance held its ground throughout the Renaissance; then after the disasters of the religious wars, burst into full bloom as one of the brightest illuminations of the Enlightenment. To discuss religion in the mode of classical tolerance presupposed an approach that would be neither sectarian nor polemical. It would uphold as self-evident the desirability, even necessity, of *some* religious belief but grant pride of place to no particular belief. The approach must be capable of including true belief as well as others partly true or even totally false. At least that would be the ideal case, since in seventeenth- and eighteenth-century Europe the spectrum could hardly have included other than Christian denominations and occasional visitors from Judaism and Islam; only by the very end of the eighteenth century might a Buddhist or Hindu have entered the gate.

Historically it was no accident that the sum of these conditions coincided with the stance of deism and (given the differential noted above) with that of modern ecumenicalism.[10] Classical tolerance, however, still fell short of accepting nonbelievers—those at the far pole of our imaginary spectrum—into objective discourse about religion. Even Locke in the seventeenth century was opposing toleration for nonbelievers.

> Those who deny the existence of the Deity are not to be tolerated at all. Promises, covenants, and oaths, which are the bonds of human society, can have no hold or sanctity for an atheist. For the taking away of God, even in thought, dissolves all.[11]

Most religionists, like Locke, probably would have preferred to exclude non-believers, but the course of European history from the Enlightenment onward determined otherwise. While the Enlightenment moved from its focus on reason to focus on empiricism, the vital center of Enlightenment thought settled gradually upon the inseparability of these two. Reason—now somewhat bashful with respect to self-evident truths—would be applied to working up causal sequences from empirical observations both of nature itself, and of the mechanic arts which were burgeoning into a kind of second nature. For the "mechanical philosophy," as it was expounded in diverse but overlapping ways by Descartes, Bacon, Newton, Leibniz, and many of their contemporaries, causation itself (at the empirical level) was taken to be mechanical.[12]

I need to sum up here the thrust of several impressive books by Margaret Jacob, Christopher Hill, and Jonathan Israel to which I have referred in preceding footnotes. The first two authors interpret the Puritan Revolution in England as prologue to the European Enlightenment, the "High Enlightenment," of the eighteenth century. While focusing on events in England, they make clear that major causes of the English Revolution—such as the breakdown of feudalism, dislocation of rural population, rise of commerce, and increasing prominence of artisans and merchants (not to mention the Reformation itself)—were at work also on the continent. They agree that class and related doctrinal separations characterized the English Revolution (Hill speaks of two revolutions, one largely repressed, the other triumphant); and that these separations determined the shape of the subsequent European Enlightenment. And so Jacob contrasts "Radical Enlightenment" to the politically and doctrinally more conservative

"Newtonian Enlightenment," both of which were exported en masse to Western Europe, and subsequently the world. Israel, who interprets the Enlightenment as pan-European, criticizes Jacob and Hill for trying to locate its origins inside English national history; and on this point I think he is right. All three concur, however, in seeing a sharp separation between the radical and conservative Enlightenments. They are primarily interested in discovering *differences* between the two, yet by developing differences they bring out similarities; and it is in similarities (at this stage) that I am interested.

The point for my argument is that these opposite wings of the Enlightenment, both in the English Revolution and throughout the convolutions occurring on the Continent, shared an enthusiastic and dynamic openness toward the "new" science. The door may have stood wider open on the Protestant than Catholic side of Reformation, but was by no means closed on either side.[13] Thus scientific discoveries and their technological applications—validating vast regularities of natural law—rendered divine intervention diminishingly credible, perhaps dysfunctional as well, for scientific explanation. Like the Enlightenment from which it partially derived, the scientific revolution remained basically deist; yet its practice and progress favored empirical observation and secular hypothesis. Nineteenth-century science could accurately enough describe itself (in terms used later by Bertrand Russell) as "the attempt to discover, by means of observation, and reasoning based upon it, first, particular facts about the world, and then laws connecting those facts with one another and (in fortunate cases) making it possible to predict future occurrences."[14]

The "Science" of Religion

By midway in that century, young scholars, marking out disciplines that would come to be called anthropology and sociology, began to apply scientific method to studies previously gathered under the banners of humanism. Many of these new scholars centered their efforts in a grand pilot project—the "scientific" study of religion. Meanwhile, the model they tried to follow was changing shape.[15] Originally derived from celestial (and industrial) mechanics, that model was taking on—through the influence of nineteenth-century geology and biology—an overlay of organicism and historical evolution. For newly aspiring social scientists the evolutionary overlay mandated a search for origins. The mechanical model, on the contrary—Newton's solar system still being imaged in those days as virtually identical to what it had been at the instant of creation—remained relatively unconcerned with origins. Both the model and the overlay placed major emphasis on solid grounding in empirical data that could be directly observed. Taken together, these two sets of requirements raised massive difficulties for the study of religion. Religion as a human practice had to be more ancient (once the timescale of Genesis could be set aside or treated metaphorically) than any surviving empirical evidence. Moreover, if belief in divinely revealed truth were the heartland of religion (as Judeo-Christian and Islamic doctrine both proclaimed), then religion's most essential element would seem beyond reach of empirical observation.[16]

Scholars in religious studies have striven ever since to circumvent these roadblocks. Mainly they have argued that spoken words ought to be understood as conveying empirically what a believer believes and have claimed, by extension, similar privilege for written expressions, even those that may have been arrived at through long memory and oral transmission. Thus the treasury of religious documents available by the late nineteenth century could be naturalized as empirical evidence, and likewise, though with less assurance, the vast transcriptions of folklore and mythology. Labors of biblical critics, philologists, linguists, compilers of myths and legends, came to furnish the ground of the new science. Consisting of documents and manuscripts, this ground resided mainly in European archives and libraries; the science itself, however, was developing most rapidly in the backlands of colonial empires. Out of Asia, Africa, the Pacific islands, America North and South, missionaries at first, then fieldworkers in archaeology and anthropology, sent home a harvest of new and fascinating sorts of evidence: bones, images, amulets, statues, charts of pyramids and temples, on the one hand; and on the other, word-of-mouth accounts of contemporary practices and avowed beliefs of ethnic groups thought to be "primitive" because they were geographically remote (from Europe) and technologically still within the Stone Age. Artifacts and temples could be deconstructed to yield up belief systems they presumably encoded. As to the field reports of anthropologists, the presumption of primitiveness pointed to an expected correspondence between these latter-day "primitive" cultures and those of earlier primitives, as ancient perhaps as the origins of the human species. In this way contemporary field reports journeyed back to the dawn of history, then stepped forward again under the guise of empirical observation. Inevitably there were disputes among scholars over meanings ascribable to phys-

ical objects, and even more intensely over the interpretation of spoken beliefs—
abstracted, as these had to be, from interviews conducted in little-known languages and across massive cultural barriers.[17]

Pioneers in the science of religion from Tylor, Spencer, and Frazer to Durkheim and Freud all based their work on empirical data of this sort. They all were
searching for origins, but due to conceptual difficulties in applying scientific
method, and because they were stretching meager evidence across huge time
gaps, they relied heavily on speculative implants. Consequently there were variations in the origins actually arrived at. For Tylor it was animism as a first and lowest stage in the progress of Spiritual Beings. Spencer favored ghosts and ancestor
worship, and Frazer assigned a key role to magic. In Freud's view it was totemism
and the psychodynamics of sexual reproduction; for Durkheim the power and
continuity of human social organization, symbolized by totems that gradually
would be exalted to divine status.[18] These diverse speculations, obviously incompatible, rested within a congruence that looms larger in retrospect than any differences. I use the five names cited above as representatives of a tendency that dominated religious study during its earlier phases. Adherents of this tendency, ferocious partisans one against another for animism and ancestor worship, witchcraft,
or shamanism, stood in solid agreement that religion itself remained accessible to
scientific investigation. Essentially, they were secularists and I will refer to the
kinds of explanations they pushed as "secular hypotheses." Their true opponents
were scholars who questioned whether religion could ever be encompassed within such hypotheses.

Representative of this latter tendency among the pioneers would be Andrew
Lang, a student and friend of Tylor's, who even concurred in Tylor's theories
about animism. But Lang remained unconvinced that animism led progressively
to higher forms of belief. "High gods," for Lang, appeared in the most primitive
cultures in the form of creator deities as well as sponsors of social morality. And
although secular explanations of the origins of religion might seem irrefutable,
they could neither confirm nor disprove the validity of what was believed.
Historical origins of belief, he thought, moved on a different track from the content of belief. Something of a spiritualist himself, he insisted (as William James
and even Darwin's significant other, Alfred Russel Wallace, were doing at approximately the same time) that "supernormal phenomena," both ancient and modern, could serve as openings into religious understanding. R. R. Marett, Tylor's
protégé and closest colleague at Oxford, agreed with Lang (briefly at least) about

high gods. Although these remained minority voices among early anthropologists, they would be followed by important successors who comprised a transcendental countercurrent beneath the flood tide of secular explanation.[19]

It was within this intellectual context that Tylor formulated his definition. Raised a Quaker, Tylor's early years in the family brass foundry had equipped him with a merchant-artisan version of Enlightenment thought. To define religion as "belief in Spiritual Beings" corresponded at one level to the Quaker conviction of inner light. Rigorous exclusion of particular forms and attributes from his "minimum definition" served to strip away as nonessential those aspects that Quakers (and Puritans generally) deemed corruptive, such as dogma, ritual, institutionalization, and symbolic representation. These precisely were the deviancies abominated by the Reformation and (since the Enlightenment) targeted by anticlerical rationalism. Thus far, Tylor's definition can be seen as restrictive, but what endowed it with its extraordinary functionalism and longevity was its inclusiveness. "Belief in Spiritual Beings" could bracket Tylor's contentious contemporary, the Oxford tractarian and Catholic cardinal John Henry Newman, as readily as it did tribal "primitives" who assigned souls to trees, springs, and mountains. Tylor adapted the definition to his own concept of progress from animism to monotheism, yet it remained equally compatible with Andrew Lang's argument that high gods and creator deities had appeared in the earliest cultures.[20]

The Social Science Stance Toward Religion

As disciples of the new social disciplines strove to apply scientific method to religious studies, Tylor's definition provided a conceptual space within which both the secular and transcendental modes could frame and justify their sometimes contradictory undertakings. I do not mean to suggest that Tylor's definition opened the way for the social sciences. On the contrary, it was the gravitational pull of the developing social sciences that called forth a viable definition. Had Tylor's not been available, someone else would have come up with something close to it. I will refer in what follows to this modus vivendi between secular and transcendental—this free zone that first took shape in connection with efforts to make religion an object of study—as the "social science stance" toward religion.

Historically, the social science stance resulted from the enormous prestige that accrued to science during the nineteenth century. Aspirant young scholars—transcendental as well as secular—were eager to tap that prestige for their own undertakings. Conceptually, the social science stance had its footings in the boggy ground that separates belief from hypothesis. Religious believers, had they been left untrammeled by secularism, would doubtless have based their scholarship in "natural religion," that is, in "knowledge" of God arrived at through contemplating God's handiwork in the perfections of nature. This, aside from excluding secular scholars, would have discredited the new field by deviating from the scientific model because it began by assuming a conclusion not yet proven. Or we can approach from the opposite direction by inquiring whether a "knowledge" of religion composed of secular hypotheses grounded in empirical research must necessarily prove intolerable to religious believers. The answer is that it need not, and did not. An example appropriate to this discussion would be Durkheim's proposal that religion originated when humans first learned to live in social organizations. Recognizing in these a power and longevity vastly exceeding those of individual beings, they exalted this impressive social power by projection and deification. Durkheim's explanatory sequence, deriving religion itself from natural causes, is clearly secular. Yet it need not contravene belief in an omnipotent creator since the believer remains free to respond that God may have intended, indeed *designed*, precisely that sequence of events.[21]

The argument from design, long considered the strongest in the old scholastic arsenal of rational proofs for the existence of God, had always formed the core of natural religion.[22] A popular rendering of this argument in nineteenth-century British literature was William Paley's *Natural Theology* (1802), a work with which Charles Darwin as a young student had been intimately acquainted.

> Darwin was inspired by the evidence of design in nature ('adaptation,' as it is called) which Paley discussed. Later ... Darwin would turn Paley's evidence against Paley's natural theology: for in the theory of natural selection, adaptation would have a natural, and therefore did not need a divine origin. *The Origin of Species* can be read as a systematic destruction of Paley's natural theology.[23]

Yet though Darwin and Wallace may have demolished the argument from design as positive proof for God's existence, the argument itself remained conveniently available to religious believers intent on outflanking any secular hypothesis, including Darwinian theory or Durkheim's account of the social origins of religion.[24] Indeed, Wallace, more tuned to religious belief than Darwin, was soon putting it to precisely that usage. In an essay congratulating their mutual friend Charles Lyell on having come around to "the views of Mr. Darwin," Wallace wrote in 1869:

> Admitting to the full extent the agency of the same great laws of organic development in the origin of the human race as in the origin of all organized beings, there yet seems to be evidence of a Power which has guided the action of those laws in definite directions and for special ends. ... Let us not shut our eyes to the evidence that an Overruling Intelligence has watched over the action of those laws.[25]

While secular hypotheses remain subject to proof or falsification, a religious flanking statement, although no longer provable in metaphysical terms, can never be disproven by any showing of empirical evidence or logic. Hence the assertion that God created the cosmos is not falsifiable, but a corresponding limitation applies to its antithesis, that God did not create the cosmos. Upon this stalemate rests the moderate and rather uneasy inclusiveness of the social science stance. Nonbelievers fit in so long as they cast nonbelief in the agnostic mode; and believers can find accommodation provided they consent to ground their faith in reiterations of the argument from design, located just outside the perimeters of secular, or scientific, hypotheses.[26]

Neutral Zone or Contested Territory?

The social science stance has always remained contested territory. This is not because scientists are naturally hostile to religion. Probably a majority of all scientists since the Enlightenment have been religious believers. Rather, it is because the intrusion of what I will refer to provisionally as "transcendental hypotheses" disrupts the accumulation of scientific knowledge, opening easy escapes from problems that might otherwise be solved through empirical research. To take an example—again one appropriate to the present discussion—evolutionary neurologists have proposed that consciousness results from complex interactions of nerve cells whose structure is genetically transmitted. Religion traditionally explained consciousness (the soul) as an outpost of divinity planted in the body by a benevolent deity. In part for this reason, consciousness stands as one of the last components of human anatomy to come under serious scientific scrutiny. The neuro-evolutionary hypothesis certainly is subject to proof or falsification. Yet, were it proven true beyond possible question, it could still be outflanked by bringing forward the argument from design: only God can make a tree, even if the tree may also be describable in secular terms as the outcome of millennia of natural selection; and only God could synthesize a brain cell.[27]

Nonetheless, religious belief has remained vulnerable to secular hypotheses, despite the fact that religion can always outflank any particular hypothesis. Here we can turn once more to Durkheim. To the extent that Durkheim's secular account of the origin of religion commands credibility, it discredits a standard argument from the observed ubiquity of religious behavior, that such ubiquity could be accounted for only as the working of a religious sense inherent in every human being. But if the social origin of religion can be explained hypothetically through natural causes, an explanation that relies on divinely instilled intuitions will no longer be necessary and drops down to the more humble status of a competing hypothesis—and one which may be accurately described as "transcendental" because what is hypothesized is validated only by belief. So we are back to the difference between hypothesis and belief.[28]

A convenient way to sum up the intellectual thrust and historical continuity of the social science stance is to recall that it reproduces approximately the attitude recommended by classical tolerance with the important addition of a clause not quite forbidding "transcendental hypotheses," but discouraging their deployment inside the laboratory of ongoing science. Meanwhile, at the pragmatic level of daily life, the social science stance was proving useful to scientists and social scientists of all varieties. Like the Swiss Republic, it stands conveniently adjacent to otherwise belligerent powers. Religious believers—even revelationists, checking their revelational weapons at the entry—can participate in the prestigious and rewarding pursuits of science and technology. The privilege is reciprocal. Scientists and technologists share in religious observance, which in our time also conveys emotional rewards and social prestige. What they must leave at the gate is any thought of applying scientific method to the "spiritual" content of religion itself. In other words, the truth or falsity of religious belief is held irrelevant to its history and social functioning. This amounts to acquiescence in a form of dualism.[29] However, since it seems probable that a majority of scientists were (and still are) at least deistic in belief, the compromise was not one that weighed heavily on the scientific side.[30]

Tylor's Definition as Amended

At the beginning of this chapter I noted that many scholars writing on religion have managed to work their way back to something close to Tylor's definition. There are good reasons for this, and I will do likewise. My amended version runs as follows:

> Religion is belief in superhuman and supernatural but anthropomorphic spiritual power(s) functioning in (or over) nature.

The term *anthropomorphic* makes explicit what I presume is implied by Tylor's adjective, *spiritual*. In any case, I find the concept of anthropomorphic indispensable to any statement of what religion essentially is.[31] My parenthetical phrase "or over" bridges a problem on which scholarly opinion has been in disarray since the time of Tylor and Andrew Lang: Was there a "progressive" evolution from animism and ancestor worship through polytheism to pantheism and monotheism, or did religion begin with a single creator deity? I tend to side here with Lang; although I think what Lang (and contemporaries who agreed with him) meant by "single creator deity" was more like what today we would call *monism*. Monism refers not to *one* god, but to a single and undifferentiated creative force from which emerged the cosmos at-large, including multiple gods and paired contradictions such as good-and-evil, soul-and-body, spirit-and-matter. Monistic religions could be, and probably were in the beginning, animistic or polytheistic. Thus the concept of monism potentially reconciles Tylor and Lang since it allows an "evolutionary" movement from animism toward monotheism, proceeding under the aegis of a unitary creative force. These seemingly arcane distinctions become important later on, especially with reference to Eastern religions.[32]

PART TWO:

Religion and Cultural Evolution

4

The Crisis of Consciousness

Sometime in the not very distant past of our planet an animal that probably walked part of the time on two legs and scratched its crotch with its fingers became aware of its own individual existence and cognizant of irrevocable death. These two perceptions may have come separately. When the second perception was firmly in place, the animal invented religion and became the first human being.

Upon what credentials is this brief narration grounded? Alas, it claims only the credentials of myth, and a modern, jerry-built myth at that. But who says old myths are better than new ones? My newly constructed myth is shorter and simpler than culture-hero myths like Gilgamesh or Moses or Prometheus; simpler, and probably easier to believe, than secular myths such as those of Tylor, Durkheim, or Freud. Moreover it has the merit of taking us directly to what I call the "crisis of consciousness." By making religion prerequisite to humanization, it places religion as the saving resource for an animal that cannot otherwise endure the terror of self-consciousness combined with knowledge of death. Beginning in biology, the sequence ends in culture. Perhaps it records the onset of cultural evolution, certainly not the end of biological evolution. Before pursuing historical consequences, however, I need to establish a credibility rating by comparison at least with other myths, sacred and secular.

Myth and Hypothesis

All myths are dramatic abbreviations of more detailed and protracted sequences. This especially applies to culture hero myths. Prometheus in a single heroic act steals from the gods the product of millennia of random accumulation and trial and error. But it holds also for creation myths. Even if we accept the timescale of Genesis, we know an enormous amount of tiresome detail has been finessed into six days of executive decision making. And it applies equally to those parables from science earlier referred to as secular myths. Freudians are not obliged to interpret the Oedipal syndrome as imposed by a single historical patricide. Nor do Darwinians insist that natural selection can be fully grasped simply as survival-of-the-fittest, an oversimplification of which generally they exonerate Darwin himself. As to my own account of the crisis of consciousness—self-perception, awareness of death—religious construction must have developed incrementally. Or, if we follow the anthropological notion of ritual preceding doctrine, we can even suppose that resolution of the crisis had been locked in place before consciousness perceived its mortal gravity.[1] Myths, like the languages of which they are composed, speak most cogently through figures of speech.

That my myth of the crisis of consciousness was custom-built to suit a particular argument does not differentiate it from other myths. Culture hero and creation myths were similarly crafted, most in prehistoric times, but some—as Joseph Smith and the Virgin of Guadalupe remind us—deep into our modern era. Secular myths, often attributed to famous authors after whom we name mountains and lecture halls, are likewise of recent vintage and frequently polemical intent. So it is with Einstein's curvature of space-time, Darwin's origin of species, and Newton's force-acting-at-a-distance. Is there then no difference between secular and transcendental myths? There is of course a difference, and a profound one, but it does not show up in rhetorical constructions. In an earlier chapter, for convenience and no doubt from carelessness, I used the word *hypothesis* to denote what I am here calling *secular myth*, and even spoke of *transcendental hypotheses* as if *myth* and *hypothesis* were interchangeable terms. The point I was stressing was that myth and hypothesis serve comparable purposes. They often sound alike. In the narration that opened this chapter, for example, there is only one word out of sixty-six (the word is *invented*) that identifies the narrative as hypothetical rather than mythic. It is time to tighten up the vocabulary.

The difference between myth and hypothesis resides in the kinds of knowledge they purport to convey. Myths, properly speaking, contain elements of what in the last chapter I defined as religious belief—belief, that is, in supernatural but anthropomorphic power in, or over, nature. Moreover, these supernatural elements enter as prior assumptions: mythic narrative remains grounded in supernatural belief.[2] The term "transcendental myth," then, is redundant, while "secular myth" is a contradiction in terms. Myth, by this definition, cannot be part of scientific discourse and has no place (except as an object of study) inside the social science stance. "Hypothesis," on the other hand, is not so easily dealt with. A hypothesis poses a statement to be tested by scientific methods of verification or falsification. Technically, verification can never be absolute since the possibility remains that new scientific developments might falsify the hypothesis. Any assertion subject to scientific verification (and not internally contradictory) can be stated as a hypothesis. But this includes all sorts of transcendental assertions, such as, for example, "God created the cosmos," which might conceivably be verified by experiment or empirical observation but hardly could be proven false. Thus the term "transcendental hypothesis" is neither redundant nor internally contradictory, and the thing itself enters legitimately into scientific discourse. Newton's relegation of the Law of Universal Gravitation (inexplicable in terms of the prevalent "mechanical philosophy") to ongoing divine will is perhaps the most famous example.[3] Transcendental hypotheses, then, can hardly be excluded from the neutral enclave I refer to as the social science stance, although there has existed (as noted in the preceding chapter) a generally accepted protocol to discourage such hypotheses because they offer easy escape routes from problems otherwise amenable to empirical research. For this reason they are usually located just outside the perimeters of established secular hypotheses. There they function as part of that outflanking apparatus that keeps scientific pursuits open to religious believers and religious belief open to secular scientists.

With respect to vocabulary, I will henceforth avoid speaking of *myth* when I mean *hypothesis*, and banish not only *secular* but *sacred* or *transcendental* myths from my vocabulary. To *transcendental hypotheses*, however, I may need to make continuing reference, and for that reason also to differentiate *secular hypotheses* from the transcendental variety.

The Dark Night of Consciousness

Because our ancestors gathered in social groups before they became human beings, the crisis of consciousness is inconceivable except in social context. Yet since the primary thrust of the crisis is psychological (what induced it was awareness of individual death), I will examine it first as an inner event, introspectively experienced. "Fear, first of all, produced gods in the world." Religious sentiment, according to the anthropologist Paul Radin, begins in terror of the uncontrollable environment. The vulnerability of early human societies in relation to nature expressed itself in "reflective consciousness" as a conviction of helplessness. "With fear man was born. ... It is but natural," Radin wrote, "for the psyche, under such circumstances, to take refuge in compensation fantasies."[4] If Radin's attribution of hope ("fantasies") to the nature of the human species is correct, it would seem more accurate to place the onset of religion not in terror alone, but in the counterpoint of terror and hope. For most animals, terror would be occasional and instantaneous, triggered by immediate threats to life. Between such life-threatening occasions would lie intervals of placid feeding and recovery. "We may wonder," writes Walter Burkert, "how herds of African zebras and gnus are able to graze in the presence of lions. The lions will attack ... but only at the moment of immediate danger does an animal take flight; the others save their energy and go on grazing, and before long so will the animal that escaped the predator this time—what else can they do? But humans, as they consciously seek to control their environment, storing recollections and anticipating the future, cannot forget the presence of lingering lions." Consciousness must render instances of terror—together with the desperate responses they evoke—continuous and unrelenting. Endlessly protracted, the terror and response would prove lethally dysfunctional to any organism cursed with consciousness.[5]

But is it reasonable to speak of consciousness as a curse? Ought we not rather celebrate it as culmination or triumph? The brain evolves to a level of neural complexity that permits (or compels) self-observation. The animal that acts in the real world while observing its actions, and observing the mental sequences that prepare and execute those actions, gains a competitive advantage over all other creatures. Consciousness, to an animal hitherto lacking it, would come like illumination, like gazing out over a new landscape—like Balzac's rapacious Rastignac over the jungle of Paris rooftops. Or like "stout Cortez" with eagle eyes and so forth; but we must add one other simile: like the son of Daedalus when the apex of his ascent marked the beginning of the Fall. Paraphrasing Genesis, we might say that consciousness gave to human beings dominion over the good things of earth, yet because it also conferred knowledge of individual death was more like punishment for a crime than an invitation to generous living. Consciousness, storming the gates of heaven, plunges simultaneously into the abyss.[6]

But evolution already had anticipated this impasse by impressing on some of its selected species—particularly on predators whose limited progeny requires extended parental care—the gift of bonding.[7] Bonding begins with maternal nourishment that gives life. For predators this might seem an ironic gift since their biological situation is defined by imposing death on other live creatures. For them, however, bonding serves as an antidote to death. And if, for human predators, consciousness renders inescapable the terror of death, it must render the hunger for bonding continuous as well. Parental bonding, like all sexuality, opens into elaborate sublimations. It was this psychological process that Paul Radin referred to as "compensation fantasies." Fantasies are not made of nothing. They are made from the remembrance of familiar voices and powerful warm bodies projected with desperate anxiety across a glittering sky. To self-conscious observation, that terrifying sky would soon be known as the reality behind false, temporary skies of balmy nights and summer days. Imagination, then, could people the nearby world and distant sky with anthropomorphic images. Were they real? Could willed belief *realize* them? Here is a sequence that comes to us from the epic of Gilgamesh, already ancient when it was incised in clay tablets now three thousand years old. Exhausted by his Promethean struggle to claim immortality for human beings, Gilgamesh cries out,

> What can I do, Utnapishtim? Where can I go?
> A thief has stolen my flesh.
> Death lives in the house where my bed is,
> And wherever I set my feet, there Death is.

Utnapishtim the Remote, a demigod residing on the far side of the River of Death, replies by ordering Gilgamesh back to his boat, to return over the river he had defiantly crossed, and live out his mortal life with whatever consolations human culture and terrestrial religion can afford him.[8]

Writing of religion as contemporary experience, Peter Berger, a sociologist who is also a religious believer, made his governing metaphor the mother's gesture of reassurance to her frightened child. Nightmare and darkness represent chaos and death. The reassuring gesture asserts life and love. "Is the mother lying to the child?" Berger asks. "The answer, in the most profound sense, can be 'no' only if there is some truth in the religious interpretation of human experience. ... Every parent (or, at any rate, every parent who loves his child) takes upon himself the representation of a universe that is ultimately in order and trustworthy. This representation can be justified only within a religious (strictly speaking a supernatural) frame of reference. ... The parental role is not based on a loving lie. On the contrary, it is witness to the ultimate truth of man's situation in reality." In his role as social scientist, Berger accepts the protocol of religious neutrality within the social science stance and defends the need for secular hypotheses. Here, however, he is declaring allegiance to a "reality" beyond the scope of empirical science. Religious believers, he tells us, will discover "'in, with and under,' the immense array of human projections [i.e., secular hypotheses] ... a reality that is truly 'other' and that the religious imagination of man ultimately reflects." How might such an ultimate reality be arrived at? By acts of "inductive faith." The "social construction of reality"—that web we endlessly spin through our everyday lives—is salted with clues, "signals of transcendence," like the mother's spontaneous gesture of reassurance. Such clues point the way that "inductive faith" must turn in its great leap to religious affirmation. The adjective "inductive" signals an analogy between such transcendental leaps and the secular process of induction by which hypotheses are said to be derived from (or bear some relation to) empirical observation.[9]

Berger was of course not discussing the discovery of religion in the dawn of human history, which is the point at which I introduced the notion of the crisis of consciousness. I quote his work (despite disagreement with most of his key assumptions) precisely because he presents that crisis contemporaneously—*existential* in the sense of a continuous component in the ongoing life of our species. Such a rendering of the crisis, as both an archaic episode in human evolution and an ongoing strategy of survival, permits me to introduce the only sort of psychological evidence that seems conceivably relevant. "The truth is," Mircea Eliade warned us, "... we ignore everything of which prelithic man thought during many hundreds of thousands of years." On the other hand, we do have access to what men and women actually think and feel in potentially comparable situations if we take advantage of the resemblance between the crisis of consciousness as sketched above, and experiences of mystics within that mental abyss named (by John of the Cross) "the dark night of the soul." Here again *Gilgamesh* proves illuminating. The editors of a recent translation (whose perspective is historical and literary, not mystical) divide their text into two sections. The first, which portrays the hero in full sunlight as king and cultural leader, is presented as "Apollonian," whereas the later part, recounting the hero's hopeless struggle to outflank death, drifts down into "Dionysian" darkness. "From the triumphal journey outside the city that marks the first half of *Gilgamesh*, the narrative turns to terror, the dark night of the soul."[10]

Narratives of mystic experience seem particularly relevant to distant gods. Perhaps they are as old as language, but their persuasive power will certainly be enhanced by literacy, a latecomer in cultural evolution. Within this later setting, I will now argue, mystic experience recapitulates the crisis I placed at the starting point of human history. Mysticism in the modern world thus represents a repetition, a continuing reenactment of the crisis of consciousness under the later circumstances of institutionalized and intellectually sophisticated belief. Religion, having once installed a god on the altar of the secular temple, belongs as much to the realm of transience and death as any other worldly phenomenon. The success of religion removes its gods to a vast distance. What is then at issue is their openness to human contact. Craving reassurance against death, mystics must now break through barriers of dogma and ritual even to reach a starting point. Their journey begins in terror of death, or of being abandoned by the divine power, and terminates in ecstatic claims of possession and love. "That which this anguished soul feels most deeply"—quoting John of the Cross from late-sixteenth-century Spain—"is the conviction that God has abandoned it ... . The shadow of death and the pains and torment of hell are most acutely felt, and this comes from the sense of being abandoned by God." "Do not think I am exaggerating," wrote Teresa of Avila, who was both friend and teacher to John, "... that which I say is less than the truth, for lack of words in which it may be expressed. ... The pain thus grows to such a degree that in spite of herself the sufferer gives vent to loud cries, which she cannot stifle, however patient and accustomed to pain she may be, because this is not a pain which is felt in the body, but in the depths of the soul."[11]

Reassurance, to prevail over such despair, must carry the emotional impact of immediate experience. Like their predecessors of the archaic crisis, mystics turned to the bonding powers of mortal love. "All things I then forgot." John recalled of his moments of ecstacy,

My cheek on Him Who for my coming came,
All ceased, and I was not,
Leaving my cares and shame
Among the lilies and forgetting them.

"This utter transformation of the soul in God," Teresa of Avila reported, "continues only for an instant: yet while it continues, no faculty of the soul is aware of it, or knows what is passing there." "So deep and intimate, so vivid and penetrating," an eighteenth-century French woman wrote of her mystic experience, "that it was easy for me to judge that Thou was but hidden from me and not lost." "We must remember," Evelyn Underhill admonished readers of her monumental work on mysticism, that "the mystic life is a life of love ... [its] final quest ... is an object of adoration and supreme desire."[12] Underhill quoted Islamic poets and also quoted copiously from the *Song of Songs*[13]. She endorsed Saint Bernard's famous sermons on the *Song of Songs*.[14] "There are several excellent reasons [here she was citing one of her contemporaries, also a historian of religion] why the mystics almost inevitably make use of the language of human love in describing the joy of the love of God. The first and simplest is ... they have no other language to use."[15] Although making no claim of her own to mystic insight, Underhill was clearly a celebrant of mystic tradition, which she presented as "the highest form of human consciousness." Thus it seems appropriate to consult her directly on the question—crucial to this discussion—of mysticism's involvement in the anthropomorphizing of divine power. Mysticism, she declared in her first preface, expresses "the innate tendency of the human spirit towards complete harmony with the transcendental order," and in her final chapter claimed for mystics the Christ-like role of cosmic redeemers and unifiers:

> The mystic act of union, that joyous loss of the transfigured self in God, which is the crown of man's conscious ascent toward the Absolute, is the contribution of the individual to this, the destiny of the Cosmos.[16]

Underhill's *Mysticism* was published in 1911. A second preface was added for the twelfth edition in 1930 and there have been other editions since. Now, at the beginning of the twenty-first century, one reads the work in astonishment that its vision of human destiny can have moved so far from us in so short a time. Underhill's cosmic optimism took for granted what to us poses problems requiring research and study; that is, whether religion commands the power to serve as a saving resource during the upcoming nuclear, biological, and ecological crises. She also took for granted that mystics, far from being deluded by their compensation fantasies, had grasped intuitively the real nature of divinity. Relying on this *a priori* assumption, she tended, I think, to underestimate the weight of terror and uncertainty in the mystics' dark night of the soul; yet nonetheless portrayed that experience, from *their* recollections, with impeccable scholarship.

From Pseudo-Myth to Hypothesis

This chapter began with a pseudo-mythic narrative of the crisis of consciousness. The narrative had been arrived at conceptually in the sense that a notion of self-consciousness necessarily contains knowledge of individual death. How would a conscious organism react to that knowledge? Radin, the anthropologist, speculated that it would naturally seek "refuge in compensation fantasies."[17] Berger, the sociologist, invoked the image of a mother shielding her child from terror of death by projecting maternal love into the cosmos. Both responses are hypothetical in form, although both remain devoid of any empirical evidence to back them up. Berger's, however, has shifted the starting concept from a single episode at the dawn of history to that of an event reenacted as part of the ongoing human condition. His alteration, by making the crisis "existential," opens it to comparison with later and more fully recorded experiences of mystics. It seems doubtful that Berger, who is not sympathetic to mysticism, intended such a comparison, but the definition—almost identical to Underhill's—invites precisely that: "Mysticism, broadly speaking, is any religious practice or doctrine that asserts the ultimate unity of man and the divine. ... The depths of the human soul are identical with the depths of the universe."[18] The definition works equally well for the existential phase of the crisis of consciousness, as conveyed, for example, in Berger's metaphor of the protective mother. Thus, thanks to mystics themselves and the work of scholars like Evelyn Underhill, we possess voluminous accounts of the psychodynamics, introspectively recorded, of mystic experience. These I am suggesting can be pressed into service (analogically) as empirical grounding for my "myth" of the birth of religion, which bears restating in the guise of secular hypothesis:

> When the advent of consciousness imposed knowledge of individual death, our ancestors sought solace from this terror by projecting anthropomorphic images into nature and imputing reality to those images as spiritual beings.

If such images then permeated the depths of the universe, it would obviously be possible to discover identity between the depths of the universe and the depths of consciousness.

Images of spiritual beings, however, must first have been projected within intensely local situations. That rock, that water source, this cave, this slippery ledge—and thus the objects become animated. They make themselves habitations for invisible beings with whom we establish familial contacts, both of bonding and hostility. This is animism. Its psychological service lies in its absolute immediacy. Spirits evoked by it live within touch and call. But how could such localized spirits permeate the depths of the universe? To ask this question is to drop back into the controversy between Tylor and Lang, which in my amended definition of religious belief I attempted to reconcile. Animism yields throngs of local spirits, close enough to dominate daily life, too small to control (or ever to have created) the multiplicity of nature. Imagination then skirts the edge of some vast, shadowy creative force, and draws back.

> Who then knows whence it has arisen? ... Perhaps it formed itself, or perhaps
> it did not—the one who looks down on it in the highest heaven, only he
> knows—or perhaps he does not know.[19]

And this is monism. One might think of it as the flip side of the coin of animism. The two sides are indivisible but in tension. Starting from animism, a sequence of conceptualizations moves toward larger, more powerful spiritual beings. Why? We have several explanations of this progression. Tylor reads it simply as upward intellectual progress. Sociologists like Durkheim and Weber see it as a function of larger, more effective units of social organization—band to tribe, tribe to city-state, and so on. I will be focusing on this outward aspect of cultural evolution, but here I need to bring out the internal logic of the sequence. What first motivated the discovery of Spiritual Beings was psychological craving for reinforcement against the terrors of nature—that is, against death. Animistic spirits are contained inside nature. Eventually any spiritual being conceived as inside and subject to nature must prove conceptually impotent in defending humans *against* nature. This is the dynamic that drives concepts of divinity away from animism, to polytheism, to pantheism, ultimately to monotheism—which is (perhaps) as close as any personalized spiritual being can approach to monism. Even pantheism—although it holds many other attractions—cannot satisfy the desire for defense against nature because pantheistic divinity, being equal to nature, remains *in*, rather than outside and *over* nature. Thus the search for psychic security reaches a logical stopping point in monotheism, the idea of a personal Creator God.

But there also is a reverse movement. The concept of Creator—even when portrayed as the familiar white-bearded patriarch with magic finger out-stretched—remains an intellectual abstraction. Such a deity is too far removed to be much concerned with *this* cave and *that* water source, with my arthritic knee or my husband's infatuation for the witch next door. So we move back through the pantheon, to animism again, to local saints and roadside shrines, to amulets and prayer wheels. In part such a return seeks to escape the monopolizing by pro-fessional clergies and institutional churches, which—in history—accompanies "progress" toward monotheism. Religion (by this hypothesis) began from an emotional bonding to spiritual beings felt to be within immediate grasp. The god whose hand orders the cosmos, however, will not be an easy one to touch; espe-cially so, historically, when that deity has withdrawn, seemingly, behind estab-lished churches and possessive clerical hierarchies.[20] This hidden god is also the god pursued by mystics. But the deepest level, I think, is conceptual. Reverse movements may repopulate heaven and earth with angels and demons; these—as in Christianity and Islam—being regulated by their monontheistic king; or—as in Hinduism and Buddhism—contained within the force field of a monist Creator.

I return now to the crisis of consciousness and its cultural evolution.

Religion and Cultural Selection

Here, and (with one exception) in the chapters that follow, I will be speaking sole-ly of *cultural* evolution—although it is quite possible to bring forward a biologi-cal account that might reinforce and partly overlap the cultural sequence. For the biological argument, those psychological factors to which the earlier part of this chapter was devoted remain irrelevant. This is because the biological focus—given our knowledge that religion did in fact develop—can assume that some-where within the reaches of evolutionary time some combination of genetic fac-tors installed patterns of ritual behavior that moved adaptively toward religion.[21] If, on the other hand, we suppose the beginning of religion occurred inside the domain of cultural evolution, the timescale may seem insufficient to justify a solu-tion arrived at largely by chance. Psychological explanation thus provides a causal sequence in lieu of chance and unlimited time. On the other hand, if the begin-ning (or "beginning" of the beginning) occurred during biological evolution, that event in itself would have determined the opening date of cultural evolution. For these reasons the psychological account may be unnecessary in explaining the crisis of consciousness; yet I find it absolutely necessary for establishing the crisis as *existential*—that is, as an ongoing component in the human situation. Since my project relates primarily to the realm of cultural evolution, I will postpone discussion of biological evolution until chapter13.

Once religion, by whatever route, locks into place as a resolution of the crisis of consciousness, there will be at least one individual believing in supernatural but anthropomorphic power in (or over) nature. Because this individual experiences friendly voices and intimations of harmony with natural phenomena—perhaps even assurances of special protection and direction—her or his behavior will tend to grow more purposeful, more integrated, more effective than behaviors of other members in the same band or tribe. The believer wastes fewer calories in terror and despair. He or she copes more patiently with the repetitiveness of primitive technology, endures more courageously the dark nights of bloody predators. Small margins accumulate into larger advantages of hunting and gathering, mate selection, tribal leadership. Belief enhances the begetting of offspring and life expectancy. Spouses, children, close relatives, will be more likely to absorb the sacred teaching than any others. So the family flourishes; yet since transmission remains largely untrammeled by genetics, the new knowledge spreads through example and imitation, through teaching and learning, by all the multiple channels of cultural diffusion. Religion is epidemic within the band. It becomes indispensable to individual success. "Animism has something for everyone," the anthropologist Marvin Harris writes, using animism as prototypical of all religion. "Whether they live in bands or villages, chiefdoms or states ... who does not like to be reassured that life has purpose and meaning and that it does not end with the death of the body?"[22]

The focus thus far has been on the margin of advantage that religious belief confers on individuals in social groups. But as religion becomes a factor of personal achievement and prestige, it quickly permeates the group. One band of true believers now confronts other bands that have not yet learned to believe. Which is better fitted for survival? Advantages of individual belief will be multiplied by emulation, social solidarity, above all by a shared sense of purpose seemingly larger than the band or tribe itself. Other factors being equal, the believers will prevail, but their success proves self-liquidating since conquest and diffusion result in raising the competitive level to a new stage, at which all bands and tribes will be composed of believers. Different tribes, however, march to different revelations. Competitive advantage now attaches not to belief itself but to refinements of belief. Some may prove more adaptive than others. Gods will be likely to stand above animistic spirits; tribal gods (in nomadic and pastoral economies) over deities of location and place.

> And the Lord said unto me, Fear him not: for I will deliver him, and all his people, and his land, into thy hand; ... And we utterly destroyed them, as we did unto Sihon, King of Heshbon, utterly destroying the men, women, and children, of every city. But all the cattle, and the spoil of the cities, we took for a prey to ourselves.[23]

We here see in operation the driving dynamic, the self-powered spiral of innovation, diffusion, and cultural survival that replicates (or at least resembles) processes of natural selection.

Cultural historians, understandably, are prone to emphasize cultural modes of transmission. They focus on language and oral tradition, teaching and learning, the importance of commercial exchange. They debate the merits of diffusion versus multiple discoveries. What they are less likely to dwell on are the Darwinian aspects of cultural evolution. While culture certainly includes the benign sharings and borrowings of intellectual and aesthetic dissemination, it includes also conquest and domination, pillage, rape, enslavement, genocide. The quotation above, from Deuteronomy, tells us that those not yet fitted for cultural survival are likely to go to the slaughter field. The tribal chief who at God's bidding destroyed all the men, women, and children of an opposing tribe, was laboring to extend his own particular culture (and religious belief) into new territory. If successful, he would be in line for reincarnation later as a culture hero, one of Joseph Campbell's heroes with a thousand faces. " 'The blood of the martyrs is the seedbed of the church'—a striking metaphor of biological growth. ... In an analogous way, even religions that proclaim self-sacrifice may be basically adaptive. Because on the whole the history of religions has been a story of success, a good strategy for survival in the long run must have been at work. In other words, a certain survival fitness of religion has to be granted."[24] Cultural evolution, in which religion plays so prominent a part, functions through causal sequences totally different from those of biological evolution and on a time scale that differs astronomically. Yet for both systems many of the mechanisms of change, involving competitive survival by selected individuals or groups, remain impressively similar in their lethal impartiality.

Conclusion

Concluding this chapter, I need to stress again a distinction between psychological aspects of the crisis of consciousness and its social manifestations. At the psychological level, the crisis does not immediately involve competition. It centers on the confrontation between individual consciousness and the certainty of death that consciousness entails. Since consciousness, presumably, and knowledge of death, are generic to the human species, the crisis must be lived through by each individual, and in this sense anticipates what will be universal in religious experience and potentially unifying for the species at large. Our ancestors, however, gathered in groups long before the advent of consciousness. The social setting came first. The social setting was necessarily divisive since it required individuals and groups to compete for survival space inside the species. Competition involved multiple overlapping relationships: cooperation and resistance, dominance and subordination, growth or dissolution. Thus the psychological and social aspects of the crisis of consciousness differ profoundly. It is the social aspect that points toward historical change, and brings forward the Darwinian characteristics of cultural evolution.

5

Morality, Gender, and Class

The claim is often made that religion institutes and maintains morality. Since, as ethologists inform us, no social species can survive without codes of reciprocal behavior, and since humans comprise the social species *par excellence*, the claim, if accurate, would identify an instance of major importance in which religion served humanity as a saving resource. The claim has two parts: to institute and to maintain. It is best to examine them separately, but first we need to unpack some of the meanings and connotations with which the term *morality* is overloaded.[1]

Mores in Latin means customs—specifically human customs—and corresponds approximately to the Greek word *ethos*, the two words in English remain partly at least synonymous, and both imply that moral codes may be studied systematically and that definitions of ethical, or *moral*, behavior can be determined or agreed on. Morality is necessarily social. It involves relationships among individuals. (Honor thy father and thy mother. Thou shalt not kill. Thou shalt not commit adultery.) It also involves the relation of individuals to groups with which, by birth or choice, they find themselves identified, as well as relations among such groups. Morality, then, consists in codes of social relationships. But the codes may come into conflict since obligations vary with different social identifications. Thus a parent's obligation to care for children may conflict with the citizen's duty to serve the nation at war; religious identifications run counter to ethnic, or national, identity, and so forth. Solutions to moral conflicts may be simple, although often difficult to carry out, or they may become outrageously complex.[2]

The Social Construction of Morality

How are such codes constructed? If temporarily at least we accept Judeo-Christian scripture as inerrant, the claim that religion instituted social morality seems clearly mistaken. The earliest moral code to appear in the Old Testament is the Ten Commandments, transmitted from God to the world by Moses. But the Hebrews had already been leading a social existence for many generations before that event, which they could hardly have done had they not possessed some sort of moral code. Their earlier code, in part at least, must have resembled the one brought down by Moses, so at most the Ten Commandments may have reinforced or modified an already functioning morality. The same applies even more cogently to Christ's Sermon on the Mount, often credited as the origin of the Golden Rule.[3]

In other religious mythologies, law-giving gods and morally instructive culture heroes also play prominent roles, but since (like Christ and Moses) they are generally portrayed as dealing with already established human societies, their efforts would have had more to do with maintaining morality than instituting it. One could of course argue—since the survival of societies without moral codes amounts to a contradiction in terms—that the deity who created the first two humans must have simultaneously instilled moral sentiments that would enable them to love and reproduce rather than cannibalize one another. But this amounts simply to saying that a god who created the universe *ex nihilo* must also have created everything in the universe including codes of social morality. God in that case becomes the indispensable saving resource for the human species. Defenders of religion could hardly disagree with this conclusion, yet its formulation is too reductionist to serve their purposes. If God implanted morality in the minds and hearts of his creatures—and that was all there was to it—religion would then be unnecessary for the practice of morality. This is exactly what atheists and agnostics assert, and comes perilously close to reproducing the viewpoint which, since the Enlightenment, has characterized anticlerical deists (Thomas Jefferson, for example), but it reverses the message most religious believers would wish to endorse. For them, the essential question cannot be whether God serves as saving resource (which they take for granted), but whether religion, as practiced and transmitted in human societies, could furnish such a resource. This puts us back into the middle of the social science stance, since the question concerning the historical functioning of religion will remain unchanged regardless of the truth content of the religion. Is there something about religion *per se* that institutes moral behavior?[4]

Having circled back to the social science stance, we are at liberty to invoke whatever may be gleaned from the secular disciplines of anthropology, archaeology, geology, paleontology, and all the rest. And there is indeed a lot to be learned that was unknown a few years ago. We can now date approximately the earliest fire rings, the earliest stone axes, the earliest signalings of what we presume to be religious belief as conveyed by artifacts arranged for burial with the dead. We can correlate these cultural traces to geological time recorded in ice ages and to evolutionary time marked out in changing postures and cranial capacities of primate fossils. While once we conceived biology and culture as irreducibly separate realms we now know them as deeply interlaced. "Conscience is not some disembodied concept that can be understood only on the basis of culture and religion," writes the zoologist and primatologist Frans de Waal:

> Morality is as firmly grounded in neurobiology as anything else we do or are. Once thought of as purely spiritual matters, honesty, guilt, and the weighing of ethical dilemmas are traceable to specific areas of the brain. It should not surprise us, therefore, to find animal parallels. The human brain is a product of evolution.[5]

Humans share the earth with many other social beings, from ants and wasps to porpoises, coyotes, and lions. These species too must possess codes of reciprocal rights and obligations. Are they moral codes? They often refer to the same relationships dealt with by human morality, including parental nurture of offspring, dominance and submission, and rights and obligations of individuals within groups. No yeoman of the guard dies more cheerfully for the queen than a soldier ant. Yet the heroism of ants is customarily described as instinctive. Our own species, attributing human behavior to moral sensibility, ascribed all other social behaviors to instinct.

Since ancient times, instincts have been seen as fixed in nature. Instincts defined the *nature* of animals, and in Judeo-Christian cosmology at least, formed part of the original creation. Until Darwin, they remained as changeless as the stars. Humans, of course, also possessed instincts that constituted the animal side of human nature, but in humans these governed only the biological functions, such as ingestion, excretion, sexual reproduction. Instincts, however, were imperialistic and required a willful vigilance by morality to keep them in their proper sphere. Morality, residing in the higher organs (the brain, the heart), expressed man's spiritual nature. Only occasionally could it express female spirituality, because the female role in procreation was perceived as instinctive and natural whereas the male role would be willed and spiritual. In somewhat the same way that instinct represented each man's animal side, woman represented the animal side of the species. Thus it was especially through morality that the human (male) animal claimed kinship with those spiritual beings in whose existence it had long since learned to believe.[6] All this makes a poor case for the initiation of morality by religion. It seems more reasonable to suppose that the great continuities of human history such as family, social organization, language, religion (all previously ascribed to divine gift or the sacred intuitions of culture heroes), were in fact adumbrated before the beginnings of culture—carved out by the slow processes of biological adaptation. In any case, codes of social reciprocity must have come into use at the same time that group living began, while both of these could only have developed prior to language and long before the advent of any animal much resembling our current human species. In the light of such paleontological reconstructions it seems superfluous to insist that religion, even as defined by Tylor's lowest common denominator, could somehow have penetrated the brains of primary primates to teach the rudiments of social morality they would need for survival in family groups and hunter-gatherer bands.[7]

Recent evolutionary science makes the foregoing conclusions inescapable; yet it is important to remember that similar conclusions could have been arrived at by different routes. Religion is not conceptually necessary to explain the origin of social morality. Ants and bees, even coyotes and wolves, practice social morality although we have no evidence that they believe in spiritual beings. The fact is that any brain capable of the simplest act of imitation would be capable of extending parental bonding to other members of a mutually dependent band. Or, if we leap forward a few millennia in the evolutionary scale, it would seem that a brain capable of learning how to kindle fire or chip scraper blades from flintstone would have little difficulty mastering the concept that reciprocity might pay off in group living. Do unto others as you would have them do unto you. Darwin wrote in *The Descent of Man*:

> Any animal whatever, endowed with well-marked social instincts, the parental
> and filial affections being here included would inevitably acquire a moral

sense or conscience, as soon as its intellectual powers had become as well developed, or nearly as well developed, as in man.[8]

We may suspect that the Golden Rule among Neanderthals was more honored in the breach than observance, but as much can be said of human society in our own era. Individual advantage derived from violating social reciprocity has always been as obvious as the collective benefits of enforcing it. In paleolithic times as in our own, social groups possessed moderately efficient enforcement powers. Religion would subsequently enhance those powers by promising damnation to transgressors and salvation for the obedient. Belief in spiritual beings may well have encouraged moral behavior, yet persuasive though such threats and promises might prove to be, they stand at a long distance chronologically and conceptually from the origins of morality. The problem of how moral codes were first instituted has always been mystified because religious enthusiasts tend to confuse morality with other sorts of codes that religion probably did initiate, such as those prescribing belief and governing rituals for worshipping or propitiating the gods. The latter sort could only be of religious origin; the former could not have been.[9]

Religion and Morality Maintenance

Religion, then, as saving resource for the human species cannot gain much mileage from the origins of morality. But the second part of the claim, that relating to maintenance of social morality, remains more persuasive. Let me begin by stripping our conceptual model down to its absolute minimum. We imagine a hunter-gatherer band, small in numbers, marginal in food supply, innocent of class differentiation or division of labor beyond the apparently aboriginal separation attaching to gender. Members of the band understand reciprocity and appreciate its benefits. No one goes without eating so long as food remains to be shared.[10]

Early one morning a young woman who has walked out on the beach looking for shellfish is delighted to discover parts of an oyster bed washed up by recent storms. Her first impulse is to eat the oysters herself, a second is to take them home to her children; her third is to share them with the band. How will she choose? The band doubtless disposes of various sanctions for enforcing reciprocity. The woman, however, may think she is safely out of sight. But suppose some incipient shaman among her peers has experienced the "crisis of consciousness" (my first myth, in the preceding chapter) and shared a newfound belief in spiritual beings with the band at large? This introduces a third, and perhaps uncertain, participant into the woman's deliberations. Spiritual beings might have sharper vision than ordinary folk. Which side will they come down on? Will they protect her secret? Or will they punish her disloyalty to the band by jinxing her good fortunes as food gatherer? In terms of the argument set forth in the preceding chapter, this amounts to asking whether the anthropomorphic spiritual beings so fortunately discovered in the external world will function as saving resources by strengthening each individual separately, or by fortifying the group. Of course, they must do both; but for the young woman on the beach, I think the probable outcome is that, imagining such beings as larger and more powerful than herself, she will identify them as guardians of the collective interest. Her decision, then, must be to share the oysters with the band.[11]

What I have sketched above in this second (and last but one) of my prefabricated myths is an early performance by religion in its premillennial role, not as initiator, but as maintainer of social morality. The service of religion to humanity, thus far, remains pure in the sense of still being untainted by special interests of gender, class, clerical hierarchy, or royal power, on the one hand; or bribery and bargaining with individual believers on the other. The spiritual beings made no promises to the young woman; they merely watched with the austere and judgmental gaze of a disembodied collective conscience. Religion here functioned as direct mediator between the self-interested individual and the collectively self-interested social group. It condemned private transgressions against the collective and sanctified whatever penalties the group might decide to impose. "A hunter-gatherer society is above all a moral community with a strong sense of right and wrong ... in general, 'right' coincides with group welfare and 'wrong' coincides with self-serving acts at the expense of other members of the group."[12] At this stage, social morality could scarcely have been involved in *external* conflict. Ishi, last survivor in his band of Northern California Indians, had no name for human beings at large, other than that of the tribe Yana to which his own band belonged; and this appears to have been typical of hunter-gatherer identities. Collisions with more distant groups would have seemed not so much moral conflicts as part of the ongoing struggle to survive in nature, against death.[13]

Morality and Social Order

Changes of this opening scenario followed the accelerating pace of cultural evolution as it raised structures on the prior accretions of genetic adaptation. "Over the past 13,000 years," Jared Diamond writes in *Guns, Germs and Steel*, "the predominant trend in human societies has been the replacement of smaller less complex units by larger more complex ones." Bands became tribes; chiefdoms, city-states; kingdoms, nations. "Ordinary folk took it for granted," Norman Cohn tells us, describing the ancient Nile Valley, "that, just as the priests strove to sustain and strengthen *ma'at* [cosmic and social order] through ritual, so they themselves should do so through their social behavior. ... Although their preoccupations did not coincide with the concerns of those who watched over the well-being of the state, they harmonized with them. For ordinary folk the supernatural world was always present. Little gods and beneficent spirits surrounded one, watching over one's everyday occupations and preoccupations, while harmful spirits, or demons, hovered nearby, awaiting their chance to inflict injury or sickness or death. Separate minor gods and goddesses supervised the marshlands bordering the Nile and the hunting and fishing that took place there; weaving and the making of clothes; the production of wine."[14] From the egalitarian reciprocity of hunter-gatherer bands, emerged—with agriculture—multiform divisions of labor and separate standings based on control of land and accumulated wealth. Tribal shamans proliferated into sorcerers, healers, diviners, astrologers and priests, theologians, bishops, popes. Gilgamesh, warrior-king of Uruk, could report back from his journeys to the borders of mortality that while all human spirits fared poorly in the netherworld, kings and warriors, elders and priests fared better than common folk who had left behind no affluent mourners able to intercede with gifts and offerings. The epic ends on a broken clay tablet containing these fragments of dialog:

The one who was slain in battle: have you seen him?
"I have. His father raises his head and his wife tends the corpse."

The one whose body was thrown into the wasteland: have you seen him?
"I have. His spirit does not rest in the underworld."

The one whose spirit has no one left alive to love him: have you seen him?
"I have. The leftovers of the pot, the scraps of bread thrown into the gutter, he eats."[15]

To negotiate protocols between human communities and spiritual beings demanded new skills; and because in agrarian societies so much rested on these protocols, the experts who negotiated them must be persons of influence. Influence, then as now, translated readily into lands and wealth. Priesthoods attached themselves to power. Priests served as advisers to chiefs and lawgivers; thence, by higher ratchetings of labor division, to their familiar role of spiritual counselors to kings and emperors, prime ministers, presidents.[16]

Thus cultural evolution fragmented the moral bonding of the early social order. Religion (or religion's vicarious priesthoods) could now no longer mediate directly between individuals and the collective at large. Collectives broke down into arenas of conflicting interest as inequality and exploitation replaced the egalitarian mores of marginal survival. Those at the upper levels, appropriating social morality, transformed it into gender and class morality. They invoked religion to legitimate this change. From rights and duties of each with respect to all, moral obligation expanded to include what common folk owed their social superiors. But any morality that embraced class and gender would be obliged to reach beyond common understandings of the collective good, since what seemed good to domestic servants and laborers in the brick kilns might prove unacceptable for kings and warriors. Some abstract denominator would be needed; and especially—as deterrence and enforcement came to the heart of the matter—some supernatural definition of misbehavior. Social deviance was thus transformed into sin. Priesthoods, following this shift, tapped their transcendental connections for rewards and punishments in this world, and in the one beyond. Still, there must have been gaps and regressions. The old egalitarian ethic, neither forgotten nor totally abolished, survived as moral grounding for the entire social enterprise. Religion thenceforth functioned both to maintain morality at its collective, social level, and to sanctify and defend class and gender exploitation.[17]

To the questions posed at the opening of this chapter, I now offer several responses.

1. Codes of social reciprocity—moral codes—essential to the survival of any social species, may accurately enough be described as saving resources; but religion could not have instituted them. Whatever the genealogy of primates, their forebears must have acquired reciprocal behavior patterns at the same time they adopted group living. These two traits interlocked. Neither could be transmitted without the other. When and how such a junction actually

occurred remains irrelevant to the present discussion since it had to have been long before the entree of *homo sapiens* or the beginnings of religion. Consequently no claim for religion as saving resource can be made with respect to morality.

2. The case for religion as maintainer of morality is different. If reciprocal behavior became instinctive among early primates, it seems likely that the arrival of individual self-consciousness, by converting the band into a company of prima donnas, could have undermined social solidarity. Groups with obsessively egocentric members would tend to disintegrate into units too small for survival.[18] I argued in the preceding chapter that the psychological crisis of self-consciousness would have proved lethal to the human species had not a discovery of belief in spiritual beings intervened as *the* saving resource. I am now proposing a parallel and reinforcing argument: self-consciousness would (again) have destroyed the species through weakening the cohesiveness of hunter-gatherer bands. But here, too, the discovery of religion, which sanctified group solidarity, served as saving resource.

3. Religion worked initially as mediator between individual self-interest and the general interest of the band. I described this above as the pure phase in religion's maintenance of social morality. Human history, cultural evolution— divergent gender roles, labor division, poverty and wealth, class hierarchy and enslaved labor—terminated the pure phase. Law and order imposed by gender and class would now be equated to social morality itself, and at the crux of this process lay the transformation of social deviance into sin against the gods. The first, bad though it might be, was at least understandable as human miscalculation, or misdirected self-interest; the latter, because spiritual beings were alleged to hate and punish it, took on a spiritual character of its own. Passing beyond ordinary social controls, it demanded the special attention of spiritual authority. Ruling classes in symbiotic alliance with their priesthoods demonstrated the terrible efficacy with which religious belief could be marshaled to justify class and gender domination.

Was this usage of religion a disservice to humanity? Despite my own heritage of anticlerical sympathies, I am obliged to answer, No, it was not. On the contrary, it proved beneficial. Given the marginal situation of human societies through most of history, exploitation and class hierarchy have been essential to survival of the species. Without such inequalities there would have been no elites liberated from the daily grind of food production and thus privileged with leisure and resources to construct culture. Humanity, had it survived at all, could have done so only at the level of marginal egalitarianism defined by Thomas Hobbes. Life under such circumstances must have been "nasty, brutish and short."[19] But here I am repeating the same argument I summarized in my opening chapter, that separations of class mainly developed between minorities with the leisure to pursue religion, art, literature, technology, science and the majorities that labored to support these privileged superiors. Often referred to in American history as the "mudsill theory," the argument was made famous by James Hammond, John C. Calhoun, and other champions of the Old South as a justification of slavery. In European history, its best-known exponents probably were Marx and Engels who grounded their materialist explanation for the triumphant complexity of human culture on it. In any case, the argument has the recommendation of multiple uses and endorsement from opposite ends of the ideological spectrum—not to mention its own hard-nosed persuasiveness as historical explanation. It cuts close (I think) to what must actually have happened.[20]

Ruling-class power was never easy to maintain. We know that class rule has been sporadically resisted from down under through all recorded history.[21] The strength gained from support of religious institutions with their power to consign opponents and dissenters to the Kingdom of Evil—to punishment on earth and eternal damnation thereafter—may well have supplied the margin by which ruling classes maintained themselves, and by which, when they crumbled, they could periodically be reconstituted. If that is true, then in large measure we owe to religion those achievements of civilization now endangered by ecological crises and the imminence of nuclear-biological warfare. And if this is true, we have no choice but to conclude that religion at this historical juncture proved (once again) a saving resource of our species—if not for its biological existence, certainly for its ongoing life in culture.

6

The Evil Empire

When as a child I used to go to mass on Sundays I recited a prayer from which I recall the following fragments:

Saint Michael the Archangel, defend us in the battle ...
Be thou our protection against the wickedness and snares of the Devil ...
Drive into Hell Satan and all the other Evil Spirits
Who wander about the world seeking the ruin of souls.[1]

Most religions have discovered evil as well as benign spiritual beings. Christianity, within which I was raised in the Roman Catholic communion, doubtless contributed its share in this respect. I visualized demons more readily than angels and supposed it natural that heaven and hell would have their own teams of champions just as rival nations have armies and generals. I don't know exactly what I understood then by *natural*, but it would have been along the lines of "the way it has to be," as when seasons change or one moved up a grade every September. At approximately this level of wide-eyed curiosity is how I will open this chapter. Does belief in beneficent spiritual beings compel, by some interior logic or external necessity, reciprocal belief in a spiritual power of evil? If religion is indeed universal to the human species, must the spiritualization of evil also be universal?

Who Begat Satan?

I can best begin with the tradition closest to hand. The Book of Genesis in its third chapter sets out the definitive Judeo-Christian account of how evil entered

the world. This is the story of Adam and Eve, in which the Serpent, "more subtle than any beast of the field," plays the part of seducer. Both Jews and Christians
would later understand the serpent as Satan incarnated, but no such connection
appears in the original. Actually, the Old Testament runs rather light on evil spirits.[2] It gives us Satan in various capacities, mainly as God's agent or messenger,
occasionally, as in the Book of Job, a malevolent special prosecutor. Satan
throughout the Old Testament remains *spiritual* in the sense of *angelic* yet by no
means autonomously evil, since he always acts under God's authority. Lucifer, the
fallen angel who indeed acted autonomously by rebelling against God, enters
Judaic scripture only as a Babylonian king, thoroughly mortal in his descent from
power. But Lucifer would not be spiritualized and wedded to Satan until well into
the Christian era.[3]

In Christian scripture, on the other hand, Satan's advent as a fully spiritualized, one-on-one adversary of Jesus occurs in the fourth chapter of the first book,
the Gospel According to St. Matthew. Given the relative absence of an Evil One,
or any autonomous prince of darkness, from the Old Testament—by contrast to
the prominent role Satan immediately undertakes in the New—it might be supposed that Judaism differs fundamentally from Christianity with respect to con-
ceptualization of evil. But this would be a misreading: the pattern is continuity,
not difference. During three centuries approximately bracketing the birth of
Christ—the so-called Apocalyptic period—Judaism developed an extensive folk
literature about evil spirits in general, and the Evil One in particular.[4] Jeffrey
Burton Russell, a historian of religion at Cornell who has devoted much of his
professional career to tracing the guises and disguises of the Evil One, describes
the sequence as follows:

> A wealth of names of different origins—Belial, Mastema, Azazel, Satanail …
> and Satan—congealed during the Apocalyptic period around one figure, that
> of the Evil One. … The Devil—the personification of evil itself—is to be dis-
> tinguished from the demons, the evil spirits who serve as his henchmen. What
> is most important is the development of a single principle—or, better, princi-
> pal—of evil. … New Testament ideas of the Devil derived primarily from
> Hebrew thought, especially the Apocalyptic tradition.[5]

Russell's explanation rests on an assumption that religions were generally
monistic in origin. The term *monism,* as noted in an earlier chapter, refers not to

any single deity but to an undifferentiated creative force from which springs every-thing there is, including multiple gods and nature's mind-boggling diversity.[6]

Monistic religions probably began as animistic or polytheistic. Genesis, for example, conveys hints of earlier polytheism, and the far more ancient Vedic "Creation Hymn" speaks directly of the coming of "gods": "Whence is this creation? The gods came afterward, with the creation of this universe. Who then knows whence it has arisen?"[7] Good and evil in animistic or polytheistic systems would be intermingled as they are in nature and human nature, or parceled out as they must have been among tribes with which "we" were sometimes in alliance, sometimes at war. Certain religions, however (for reasons Russell does not specify here), evolved toward monotheism. Taking Judaic religion as his ideal type, and, since Judaism already had arrived at monotheism before the opening chapter of Genesis, Russell perhaps considers explanatory accounts of that transition redundant, or beyond the scope of historical research. In any case, the crucial point for him is that when monistic creeds mutate from polytheism to monotheism, their now singularized deities must assume sole responsibility for such distasteful aspects of the human situation as suffering and death, flood and famine, social immorality inside the group as well as lethal competition outside. A monotheistic creator must supposedly have created everything creation contains including "evil" in both its natural and social forms.[8]

Writers and compilers of the Old Testament had experimented with various openings for introducing intermediaries or demiurges who might shoulder some of the blame for evil. Satan appeared first in such intermediary roles. The logical next step would be to elevate the intermediaries to self-governing status—in order to protect the perfect goodness of God, that is, by assigning his burgeoning "evil empire" to a separate chief. This step was already being taken in the contiguous religion of Zoroastrianism in which sibling deities of good and evil, Ahriman and Ohrmazd, strove together in dubious and endless battle. Zoroastrianism deeply penetrated Judeo-Christian tradition. But because that penetration reached effective levels only during the Apocalyptic period when Judaic scripture had already been culled out and canonized, Satan's coming of age goes largely unrecorded in the Old Testament. It is in Christian scripture (the New Testament) that Satan steps out fully dressed. Russell here follows approximately the transition sketched in more general terms by Max Weber in *Sociology of Religion.*[9]

But who created Satan? Or did the Devil (and evil) always exist? Thus the effort to preserve God's goodness undermined God's reputation as omnipotent creator. No good god would create Satan and no god could be omnipotent if Satan came into existence simply on his own recognizance. The Judeo-Christian tradition has always been preoccupied with this exercise in logic. Does contradiction signify defect? Russell writes:

> Far from being a defect this ambiguity was a great virtue; it was founded in a creative tension. ... God is good; evil exists. There is no easy resolution to the dilemma, and the difficulty of the Hebrew view testifies to its deepness. It was the Hebrews, loving God with such intensity, who first faced the problem of evil with such poignancy.[10]

Without necessarily embracing Russell's proposition that conceptual difficulty points to theological depth, I pose the dilemma somewhat differently. The gods of polytheistic pantheons are never powerful enough individually to have created the cosmos in which they reside, nor sufficiently at ease with one another to have done so collectively. In this respect, as in many others, they resemble human beings. Creation in polytheistic religions is usually relegated to shadowy background figures such as the Greek Chaos and Gaea, or to unknown forces, as in the Vedic hymn cited above with its suggestion that the gods had come aboard only during, or *after*, creation.[11] To move from polytheism to monotheism, however, wrenches this question out of the shadows. If there is only one God, that God must either have created the cosmos or be contained inside it.

The first alternative places God over nature, as in the opening line of Genesis: "In the beginning God created the heaven and the earth." The second makes God equal to nature, as in pantheism, or ultimately subject to nature in the same way that humans are subjected. But a God who *is* nature, or subject to nature (even if more powerful than humans), can hardly be relied on for defense *against* nature. The compulsive logic of this sequence works to push conceptualizations of spiritual beings from animism to polytheism, and eventually to monotheism and the first of the two alternatives referred to above. Since it is precisely that alternative (God as omnipotent creator) that triggers a psychological and intellectual need to exonerate God from responsibility for evil, it would seem that any adequate explication of belief in autonomous evil spirits ought to include an account of the transit from polytheism to monotheism. I have already offered such an account in chapter 4, "Crisis of Consciousness," and later in this chapter we can see how it works (or *if* it works) as opening gambit for an explanation of the evil empire. First, however, it is important to inquire whether the developments traced in Judeo-Christian belief are also found in other religious traditions.[12]

Demons of the World, Unite

Judaism is one in a consortium of religions native to the Mediterranean Basin and its North African and West Asian hinterlands. Interlaced by long cultural exchanges, religions of this region developed intense family resemblances. Their pantheons overlap. All of them exhibit belief in spiritual beings totally or partially dedicated to evil. Thus the red god of the Egyptian desert, Seth, represented violence and death against the salutary, fertilizing powers of Osiris and Horus. Far more dangerous, however, was the monster Apophis, an endless serpent dwelling in waters beneath the earth— "an embodiment of primordial chaos ... [having] no sense organs ... could neither hear nor see ... [but] only scream ... [and] operated always in darkness."[13] In the Mesopotamian epic, *Gilgamesh*, which developed through many variations over a thousand years, the "late" version (ca. 1600–1000 BCE) offers an adumbration of its hero/ demigod as champion of cosmic justice against a chaos-monster who, if not yet cosmic, is at least thoroughly evil. The Mesopotamian cosmos was awash with demons, some of whom, like the sperm-devouring Lilitu (Lilith), migrated into Judeo-Christian belief. Canaan had Mot, a prince of death counterpointed to Baal, the champion of springtime and regeneration. Islam, developing in the same hinterland many centuries later, contained, despite its intense monotheism, an impressive menagerie of demons (*jinn*) as well as principal spirits of evil.[14]

The Greco-Roman gods, already several generations downhill from creator deities, remained closer to human scale. Products of mimesis more than abstraction, they individually acted out the moral ambiguities of the human condition. Among them, however, were specialists and abstractionists—the Erinyes, for example, who exalted vengeance as the highest obligation of moral law, and others, like Charon the boatman, totally in service to death. Was death evil? It was Charon who, through his Etruscan incarnation, furnished what would become during the Middle Ages and on into modern times the standard Christian representation of Satan.[15] More generally, the Gods of Greece and Rome—doubtless reflecting the politics of city-states that became empires—favored pluralism, as did many of their regional contemporaries. Yet there were powerful tendencies toward monotheism in all these religions, briefly emergent in Egypt, dominant in Judaism, Christianity, Zoroastrianism, and Islam.[16] Russell's argument that monotheism generated efforts to protect the purity of creator gods by allocating evil to separate, progressively autonomous principalities, although constructed in reference to the Judeo-Christian sequence, serves equally well to explain the emergence of satanic figures in Zoroastrianism and Islam, in the Essene creeds of Apocalyptic Judaism, in the Zoroastrian spin-off of Mithraism and in the enormously powerful, recurrent Christian heresies described by Max Weber as "the great ideas of Manicheanism." No less a founding father of Christian doctrine than Augustine was Manichean before he became Christian. Augustine's conversion to Christianity hinged on his deeply studied rejection of the Manichean teaching that evil existed independently of God. How could a god unable to control evil in his own kingdom find power enough to save human souls? After he became Christian, Augustine would be obliged to devote a share of his theological labors to the riddle brought forward by denying Manicheanism: Why would a god thought to be omnipotent tolerate evil in the kingdom he had himself created?[17]

Turning now to the world beyond the Mediterranean hinterlands, we can start off, at least, on solid ground. Two of the Mediterranean religions, Christianity and Islam—in part, perhaps, because of their commitment to monotheism—proved extraordinarily successful evangelists and colonizers. As Christianity spread across northern Europe and the Americas, as Islam expanded into Africa and through the Middle East to Asia and the Pacific Islands, Satan traveled with them so that his potential dominions encircled the earth. Christianity and Islam together comprise currently about 53 percent of our species, all of whom (if we follow Russell's argument) will be driven by the logic of their beliefs to the construction of satanic deities.[18] Beyond this point answers become increasingly tenuous. The two next-largest belief systems, Hinduism and Buddhism—2,500 years after they parted company in the Ganges Valley—account for slightly over 19 percent of the human population. Whether these religions are monotheistic and whether they ascribe authorship of the cosmos to a creator deity are questions that still remain debatable—an ambiguity paralleled by uncertainty as to whether either of them contains a clearly-identified CEO for evil enterprise. According to Norman Cohn, the struggle narrated in the *Ṛg Veda* between Indra and the demon chief Vritra is actually a combat myth of cosmic order against chaos derived from the same Indo-European origins as Zoroastrianism. And once we step down from high theology to popular belief, it seems clear that both Hinduism and Buddhism have generated intermediate deities thought to be working both sides of the street, as well as an astonishing profusion of localized demons and evil spirits.[19]

Beyond the four world-class religions, some 15 percent of human population adheres to smaller creeds localized on all the continents but especially in Africa, the Americas, and the Pacific Islands. Several of these are monotheisms (Judaism, for example), but the majority are polytheistic; some have produced principal spirits of evil and most, doubtless, have generated devils and demons. A remaining 13 percent (according to the presumably authoritative *World Christian Encyclopedia* recently published by Oxford Press) is composed of nonbelievers of various types, approximately one-fifth of whom are said to be "atheists." Due to the difficulty of distinguishing between denominational membership and personal belief (the latter being virtually impossible to ascertain) it would be unwise to take these estimates too seriously. I assume, for simplicity's sake, that people who *dis*believe in benign spiritual beings are not likely to believe in evil ones, although such an assumption is far from self-evident. Obviously statistics are not taking us far into the problem of evil. Yet they convey important information which can be summarized as follows: More than half the people in the world are socialized into belief systems that assert the existence of evil empires ruled by semi-autonomous spiritual beings such as Satan or Lucifer. Approximately 87 percent of world population engages in some sort of religion and almost all religions acknowledge demons and evil spirits, at least on the lower levels. Statistics indicate that fundamentalist sectors of monotheistic religions—within which spiritualized evil apparently commands higher credibility than elsewhere—enjoy the highest growth rates of the current religious revival. Statistics, then, confirm that religion is almost universal, that satanic figures are widely, though not universally, believed in, and that evil crops up as a "problem" in virtually every religion.[20] Yet statistics tell us little about the problem itself and nothing whatever as to the nature of evil presumably underlying it. For that we need to pursue a different line of inquiry.

Absolutizing the Relative

Are asteroids evil? Some of us think one particular asteroid carried evil tidings for dinosaurs and great lizards.[21] But the same news would have been good news for humans (had there been any then to receive it), since the downfall of dinosaurs contributed a causal factor favorable (eventually) to the rise of the human species. Good and evil in this example are relative. The example suggests that every event or phenomenon in the cosmos may be described as good, bad (or indifferent), relative, say, to the proliferation of icebergs in the Bering Sea—or the interests of dinosaurs or human beings. As soon as we attempt to absolutize good (or evil) we run into difficulties. An absolute good could be only a good that was relative to the cosmos in its entirety. But such a good might be indifferent (or even negative) relative to human destinies. The only way to unite cosmic good and human good would be to anthropomorphize the cosmos, which is precisely what belief in spiritual beings begins to do; and what the movement from animism to creator-god monotheism carries conceptually to completion. For practical purposes, however, all of us—believers and nonbelievers, revelationists and ecumenicalists—assign cosmic importance to the human species by simply ignoring the otherwise inescapable relativity of good and evil. For the time being at least I will do likewise. Gentle, nourishing rain is good, floods are evil; yeast that makes the bread rise is good, virus infections are evil.

Good is what seems beneficial in nature, but a big part of nature is not beneficial to human beings. This is the usage that corresponds to the crisis of consciousness in which one of our primate ancestors, appalled at nature's neutrality with respect to the life or death of a now self-conscious human animal, discovered anthropomorphic spirits in the natural environment. Their assigned task was to bring forward beneficial elements and ward off the destructive powers of nature. In many ways it would be easier to anthropomorphize nature's destructiveness than its benevolence. Indeed this might have been done first in an effort to explain the seemingly supernatural malevolence often displayed by nature, or to collude with, and control it. Benevolent spiritual beings would then be even more desperately longed for. Either sequence will do. Either one shows a mimesis by which social relations are projected as pantheons of spiritual beings, subsuming the goods and evils of nature and converting nature into a mythic representation of human bonding and social conflict. Both help to explain the hordes of demons still operating at lower echelons in most religions—even religions that apparently contain no principal figures of evil. But these are adumbrations of future developments. The immediate point is that evil was found *in* nature.

Yet this account differs sharply from the one arrived at in the preceding chapter. That evil, consisting in transgressions against social morality, was of human origin; this evil resides in the *nature* of nature—in nature's colossal indifference to human affairs, its identity with death. To call both by the same name seems mistaken, yet the two have been joined through so many centuries of theological speculation as to be now inseparable. We can refer to them as different kinds of the same thing—natural evil and social evil—and begin by discussing them separately.[22]

Natural Evil

Natural evil is earthquakes, tidal waves, floods, locusts, famines, disease—death. It was terror of natural evil that evoked the crisis of consciousness. The crisis found a partial solution in religion, but since the solution was psychological it had no direct impact on natural evil itself. Indirectly, by making people feel stronger and more confident, it enhanced their powers and contributed, perhaps decisively, to the unfolding of cultural evolution. Human population circled the globe, forms of social organization moved through their *cursus honorum* from bands and tribes to city-states and empires. Meanwhile concepts of divinity traced a parallel sequence from animism toward creator-god monotheism. Yet earthquakes, famines, and all the rest continued unabated. For belief systems like the Judeo-Christian and Islamic, which had already arrived at monotheism, this required holding the divinity—now conceived as one, omnipotent and perfectly good—responsible for all evil in the cosmos. "The more the development tends toward the conception of a transcendental unitary god who is universal," Weber tells us in his *Sociology of Religion*, "the more there arises the problem of how the extraordinary power of such a god may be reconciled with the imperfection of the world that he had created and rules over." The next step, as in Russell's studies of satanism, was to amalgamate privateering devils and demons into confederations ranged against the Divine Power and ruled by increasingly autonomous princes who, presumably, would absolve the creator God of responsibility for evil.[23]

Thus the conceptual drive to monotheism triggered a rebound toward dualism (as exemplified in Western theology by Zoroastrianism), yet that project could never complete itself because an actually autonomous evil empire would have denied *omnipotence* to the creator God.[24] This leads us into a conceptual morass. It would be better to say that monotheism vacillates between two dualisms. One is the dualism just referred to—that of the benevolent creator versus a god of evil—which can be unified only by stressing the absolute preeminence of the creator. What then results is a new dualism of creator and created, since whatever was created must somehow contain evil, and the two appear to be moving on separate tracks. A logical escape from this second dualism is to conceive the creator God and the created cosmos as comprising a single substance (as Spinoza did, perhaps Milton also).[25] But this amounts to pantheism. Judeo-Christian and Islamic orthodoxies have always rejected pantheism, maintaining (as in the second of the two dualisms above) that the created must be less perfect than the power that creates. Since only God can be omnipotent and eternal, the world God created remains dependent and time-bound. Pantheism, by contrast, imbues the world we live in with divinity and brings God as close as our own existence in nature. For these reasons pantheism has always proved attractive to religious believers. Why the Judeo-Christian and Islamic orthodoxies reject pantheism is explained (I think) by the psychological and intellectual need for a spiritual being powerful enough to protect human consciousness against nature, and against death.[26]

On the other hand, a God conceived as totally *other* than nature offers little in the way of psychological sustenance.[27] To avoid so stark a separation of the creator from creation (which of course includes *us*), the so-called Western monotheisms while denouncing pantheism have also dallied with it by permitting certain degrees of immanence for their God, *in* nature. One such dalliance is the concept of providential intervention, as when God, in order to clean up the mess human beings had made on earth, intervened by sending the flood. Another is to be found in the intricate Neoplatonic constructs of *emanation* in which creation is conceived as emanating from God in a descending hierarchy with spiritual entities (angels) inhabiting the upper levels while material objects (including human bodies) exist at the lowest. Divinity, pure self-existing Spirit, enters most fully (yet never totally) on the higher levels; less fully or not at all on the lowest. Evil—already gravitating toward matter since the days of Zoroaster—can now be explained simply as the deficit of good between pure Spirit and those lower levels of emanation.[28]

The contradictions just summarized are often said to have been called into existence by Western theology's addiction to abstract logic and rational discourse. Thus, for example, the French philosopher Luce Irigaray proposes that meditation "starting from practices and texts of Eastern cultures, especially pre-Aryan aboriginal ones, can show us how to carry on our history. ... Unfortunately," she adds, "Westerners retain above all [the] post-Aryan aspects, which are less disorienting for them than the more feminine aboriginal cultures."[29] What is implied by such accusations is that other religions, intuitive and experiential rather than cerebral and intellectualized, perhaps more vaginal than phallic, may be spared from floundering through such conceptual bogs.[30] This I think is mistaken, and I will attempt to show in the next chapter that similar contradictions beset any belief system that engages anthropomorphic spiritual beings in explanations of the problem of evil.

Social Evil

If it was terror of natural evil (hunger, disease, death) that triggered the crisis of consciousness, what then becomes of social evil? Social evil is like a paraphrase of natural evil. In the same way that "natural evil" derives from a relationship between the human species and nature at large, social evil derives from that between individual humans and the social groups to which they adhere. From any point of view other than human, natural evil would not be evil at all, but simply natural. And social evil—from any perspective other than that of the immediately relevant social group—would not appear as "evil," but as self-serving or instinctual. The fact is that every individual, and every group of individuals within some larger set, is likely to harbor desires and aspirations potentially in conflict with the collective interest. This relationship gets further complicated by the fact that individuals share in, and actually depend for life and well-being on group membership. Individual dependency, socialized into each new generation, arms the group at large with powerful sanctions. It can disapprove, hold up to shame, ostracize, banish, or kill. Yet despite such restraints, individuals constantly press their own agendas, testing to see how much they might get away with. What is at issue thus far is relationships among human beings who live together collectively but whose interests and desires often collide.[31]

When spiritual beings through the crisis of consciousness become part of group dynamics, they will take the side of collective interest. Thus they bring religion to support social morality and, as I have already suggested, our species may owe its survival to this intervention. Religion at first speaks an egalitarian rhetoric, proclaiming general welfare over acquisitive individualism. That moment of innocence, however—if it ever existed—cannot last long. Cultural evolution creates more complex units. In gender-and class-divided societies, ritual and doctrine become the specialty of professional clergies whose skills give them entry into the upper echelons. Claiming special expertise in communicating with spiritual beings, they reinterpret social morality to include the privileges and obligations of gender and class. Earlier perceptions of moral offense as violation of the common interest will now no longer serve because the common interest has fragmented into many interests, separate and unequal. Codes of moral behavior, once dictated by the demands of collective survival, must now be ascribed to some outside source, presumably above and beyond the group. It is at this juncture that religious leaders (like Moses) discover the stone tablets and social evil is transformed into sin against the laws of God, or gods.[32] Social evil stems from *intra*-group conflict. Social groups, regardless of size, are defined by shared moral identities. The earliest groupings of the human species are now thought to have been small hunter-gatherer bands. Since these depended on foraging and lived in sparsely scattered communities, moral identity was likely to have been limited to the members of each band. Other bands, which they sometimes came in deadly conflict with, would appear not so much fellow humans struggling for survival as elements of nature, wielding terror and death. They were like predatory animals but more dangerous. Thus from the very beginning, for each particular group, the vast majority of human beings belonged already to the alien realm of natural evil.[33]

Spiritualizing Evil

Under the influence of religion, social evil slides into natural evil and both together drift toward absolute evil. There is a borrowed logic to this movement because it follows the conceptual sequence that impels spiritual beings from animism toward creator God monotheism. A single creator God must be thought to create not only nature, but human beings in nature. As natural evil is part of nature, social evil must be part of natural evil. Believers who believe that a spiritual being created the universe elevate spirit over nature. Spirit to them is supernatural. Since evil emanates from nature, good must emanate from spirit. Humans— believed to partake of both nature and spirit—have their bodies from nature, their spirit from spiritual beings. Evil invades through their bodies, good resides in their spirits, or souls. This line of thought, abbreviated and oversimplified though it may be in my rendering, corresponds to the pattern of Western monotheisms and (although perhaps more distantly) to that of Eastern religions as well. Severing good and evil from their natural and social matrices, the effect is to reify them as universal substances, reflected in microcosm inside each human consciousness. Then, because a benevolent God cannot be held responsible for it, evil must be deified and given its own anthropomorphic chieftain—the Devil, Angra Mainyu, Satan, Lucifer.[34]

Spiritualizing evil and escalating it to the cosmic level raises the stakes for antagonists in social conflict. With respect to *intra*-group conflict, it reinforces defenders of social morality and vastly expands the arsenals available to entrepreneurs of gender and class domination. That was the aspect brought into focus at the end of the last chapter. Equally important, however, is the role of spiritualized evil in *external* conflict. Foreign wars—wars, that is, in which bands, tribes, city-states, nations, seek to destroy one another—have provided a major dynamic of cultural evolution. Religion shares in this process by empowering each contestant to perceive human adversaries as dupes, agents, conspirators in the evil empire. The immediate effect will be to escalate political conflicts into holy wars. Since war stimulates technology and technological development expands the general culture, a longer-range effect will be to enhance the global hegemony of the human species. Religion and war, yoked together, have functioned adaptively throughout cultural evolution. This linkage is deeply embedded in history. Compiling a historical checklist, say, in reference to the Crusades, or European conquest of the Americas, although doubtless laborious, would not be conceptually difficult. To do so in our own era becomes even easier. Historians customarily analyze the Second World War (1939–1945) in political terms, yet the Second World War unleashed a revival of religious faith and triggered a firestorm of conflicts (the Cold War), which for the United States (in the opinion of its then commander-in-chief) amounted to a holy war against the "evil empire." Scarcely had the evil empire in its Soviet incarnation been safely deconstructed than a new Islamic evil empire rose from the ruins, becoming, in turn, a target of military high technology. What this more recent history tells us is that crusades and holy wars, even in modern times, can effectively revolutionize culture. And since the revolutionary changes have proved "adaptive" with respect to human domination over nature, they tend to confirm widely held expectations that religion will be our fortress, as always, in the crises that lie ahead. On the other hand, it might not be unreasonable to fear that human domination could change nature in ways that would make domination self-destructive. Yet these are low-energy signals. Delivered to the message center by way, as it were, of an unauthorized digital code, they remain (for the time being) marginal.[35]

Next Up

Remembering ancient times before the Great Depression and Second World War, when, as a child in a Catholic family I was attending mass on Sunday mornings, I wonder sometimes how much credence I allowed for those demons and evil spirits. I give them credence now, but in a metaphorical way that would have struck me as stupid when I was a child. They seem real to me now, or at least meaningful, because they call attention to the most intractable problem of human culture: the problem of evil. The problem of evil is older than religion; indeed, it was this problem that inspired religious belief, not the other way around. Its crux is the relation of consciousness to nature—and death. Theologians have labored over this since before the Book of Job, but the difficulty transcends theology. It boils over into culture and politics. Because religion endorses social morality— and especially because it so consistently justifies gender and class exploitation— religion appears in most historical circumstances to be declaring God's approval for the existing economic and political establishment. Churches function as parts of that establishment. Thus the problem of evil, by mocking and discrediting religious authority, tends to subvert established social order itself. If, as I have been arguing, religion's essence is belief in spiritual beings, then its essential role in human culture must be the defense and propagation of belief. Part Three, which comes next, begins with Hume's famous definition of the problem of evil, a text that Hume prudently withheld from publication until after his death.

7

The Problem of Evil

Our most succinct statement of the problem of evil comes from David Hume:

> Is he [the divinity] willing to prevent evil, but not able? then he is impotent.
> Is he able, but not willing? then he is malevolent. Is he both able and willing?
> Whence then is evil?[1]

Repetition of the (masculine) singular pronoun suggests that Hume saw the problem as one pertaining especially to monotheism. Jeffrey Russell in his genealogies of Satan shows that monotheism pushed the problem of evil to a dominant role in the development of Western culture. Does this mean that non-monotheistic or non-Western religions might offer ways, unavailable to monotheisms, for evading, or resolving the problem of evil? The question holds immediate relevance because many people, in the West at least, have come to believe that non-Western religions are more natural, more pantheistic, more "spiritual," than the rigidly intellectual belief systems of the West. Ecumenicalists, and those seeking to reconcile the hostile establishments of science and religion, tend to place their hopes in a marriage of West and East. Since my long-range goal is to arrive at generalizations reaching beyond the parochially "Western," I need to dispose of this question before turning to the problem of evil itself, which provides the main focus of the present chapter.[2]

Is Any Religion Exempt from the Problem of Evil?

Religious scholarship on this issue remains in disarray. What I take to be the standard opinion, I quote from the opening pages of *Evil and the God of Love* by John Hick, a professor of theology at Princeton Theological Seminary and the University of Birmingham (England):

> The problem of evil does not attach itself as a threat to any and every concept of deity. It arises only for a religion which insists that the object of its worship is at once perfectly good and unlimitedly powerful. The challenge is thus inescapable for Christianity, which has always steadfastly adhered to the pure monotheism of the Judaic source in attributing both omnipotence and infinite goodness to God.[3]

Jeffrey Russell is almost (though not quite) as proprietary as Hick:

> I have pursued the idea of the Devil in the Judeo-Christian-Muslim context ... because it emerges most sharply in these monotheist religions in which the existence of evil contrasts with the idea of a single, good, and omnipotent God.[4]

Ronald Green in *The Encyclopedia of Religion* expressed a similar view, locating the problem of evil primarily in "ethical monotheisms" and concluding that efforts to resolve that problem would find "little room for development" in either Hinduism or Buddhism. "For Hindu thought there is no problem of evil," Allan Watts declared; and the late Mircea Eliade—professor of history of religion at the University of Chicago as well as general editor of the *Encyclopedia of Religion*—wrote that in "fundamental Indian doctrine ... good and evil have no meaning or function except in a world of appearances."[5] Max Weber, on the other hand, found the problem of evil worldwide; and Wendy Doniger O'Flaherty, a specialist in Hindu religion and philosophy (who now holds the University of Chicago's Mircea Eliade Chair) agrees not with Eliade but Weber on the ubiquity of the problem. Its most cogent expression, she explains in her massive study of Hindu mythology, is to be found in myths and folklore; scholars, Eastern and Western alike, often missed it because they looked in high theology, whereas at the mythic level, according to O'Flaherty, the problem suffuses Indian thought.[6]

The two sets of opinions sampled above appear as if in direct contradiction. Actually they are not. They pass like vehicles on a divided highway. Moreover, neither set is cohesive; authors in each set are packing ideological baggage that brings them together at this point but separates them on others. For posing the key question, their comments are collectively illuminating, not so for constructing a response in the form of historical explanation. I need to begin further back. One of the earliest efforts at "Natural History" of religion comes to us from Hume. Hume proposed something like animism as a starting point for an intellectual progression that moved from animism through polytheism to monotheism. Tylor, writing a century later (and after Darwin), added a loosely evolutionary sequence. Durkheim and Spencer attached both to social evolution, arguing that spiritual beings widened their jurisdictions as human societies expanded from bands to tribes to city-states and so forth.[7] A fourth explanatory sequence, essentially psychological (see chapter 4), links religion to the advent of self-consciousness with its necessary awareness of death and the overarching terror of nature. Thus to explain the "natural" origins of religion, four separate accounts might be invoked. Since all four run parallel in the sense of being noncontradictory, each can serve to reinforce the others. Two of them ("loosely evolutionary" and sociopolitical) require development through time. The other two (intellectual progression and psychological) need no time sequence for themselves but are not incompatible with such a sequence. Finally worth noting is that only the last of these provides any sort of dynamic or driving force. The dynamic is human consciousness, which—craving reassurance against nature (and death)—pushes concepts of spiritual beings toward forms that can seem powerful enough to cope effectively with nature. The logical sequence, then, must be to promote local spiritual beings toward the status of high gods and creator deities.[7]

If we now glance back through our series of "natural histories" we recall that among early anthropologists, Lang—who resisted evolutionary explanations (and Marett who came briefly to his assistance)—continued to insist on the immediate knowability of high gods. This position was partially confirmed by field reports of "primitive" groups that believed in high gods or even creator deities and sometimes believed simultaneously in intermediate and local spirits as well. In such cases monotheism seemed capable of coexisting with polytheism and animism. Precisely that possibility is suggested in biblical narrations that portray Moses and other prophets, long after their flock has acknowledged Jehovah as the one and only God, still struggling against tribal impulses for returning to graven images—for turning back, that is, to polytheism and animism.[9]Why should there be impulses working against the logical and psychological drives toward monotheism? Part of the answer can be found, I think, by applying class analysis to the social structure of bands and tribes. Since that undertaking lies beyond the scope of this book, I will simply note its possible feasibility and move on. The other part of the answer, the conceptual part, is that high gods and creator deities operate in a realm too far away to permit much involvement in local affairs, psychological or otherwise. Traditionally such gods preside over sunrise and the aurora borealis and stellar movements.[10] Could they be expected to expend cosmic resources on purely local issues? If division of labor proved helpful to human enterprise, must it not be essential to labors of the gods? Thus there were (and obviously still are) social and conceptual counterforces to monotheism. Pantheons (the Greek and Roman, for example), even after they have elevated one of their number to kingship, stop short of conveying total power. Whereas monotheistic gods, even after having arrived (like the god of the Old Testament) at omnipotence, busy themselves creating flocks of subordinate spiritual beings or (like the Christian god) divide up their own sacred oneness into multiple "persons." Weber commented that only Judaism and Islam remained true monotheisms, Christianity having forfeited its claim when the Council of Nicea voted for the Trinity. I think Weber was correct about Christianity, probably mistaken with respect to Judaism and Islam.[11]

Going beyond Weber, I would suggest that no true monotheism could sustain a broad popular base, nor could any religion totally devoid of monotheism do so, since the psychological empowerments of religious belief push simultaneously in both directions. The historical pattern, then, is not progression through time from animistic beginnings to a monotheist conclusion, but rather a continuing oscillation between partly contradictory (yet powerfully attractive) alternatives. Thus we see that "pure" monotheisms can tolerate worship of saints, even devil worship, while avowed pluralisms, for all their gods and demons and prayer wheels to quantify spiritual communication, still display monotheistic traces. The high gods of Hinduism, for example, sometimes wielded ruling power; and in certain Buddhist traditions a supreme spirit incarnated itself through generations of messiahs (Bodhisattvas) who after fulfilling their terrestrial missions would be reabsorbed into the spiritual source. This much suffices to call into question the "standard opinion" (with which I opened this discussion) that the problem of evil resides only in Western religions. If tendencies toward monotheism encircle the world, so must the problem of evil.[12]

In what has been said so far, I have summarized roughly the history of "natural histories" of religion as it developed in the West after the Enlightenment. But because those natural histories focused obsessively on monotheism, I need now to bring forward two other concepts drawn mainly from the comparative study of mythologies including those that surround major Eastern religions. The first of these again involves *monism*, discussed earlier in different contexts. Monism supposes an undifferentiated creative force that somehow produced multiplicity. The other concept I will refer to is that of *pre-secular time*. Since, in the Judeo-Christian-Muslim account, monism merges immediately into monotheism, that account contains no pre-secular time, time having begun with creation and all time since then has been secular. The creator God of course existed before creation, but existence in those days was timeless. Other belief systems, here, especially the Eastern, push the beginning (if there was a beginning) deep into the background by means of vast cycles of pre-secular time punctuated by monistic creations, destructions, and re-creations. Perhaps all this resulted from efforts to escape the dilemma of eternal existence versus creation *ex nihilo*. In either case, the gods, when they do come into existence, remain subordinate to that nameless force out of which it all began. The same applies to pantheism and to the so-called process theology of our own era in which divinity is supposed to be maturing and growing wiser through some sort of evolutionary partnership with the human species. Spiritual beings in these systems must be conceptualized not as creators but *creatures*—latecomers in a cosmos that existed before them and will endure after they have gone.[13] Such gods (or God, if there is only one) are contained within nature in the same way that spirits and demons, humans and animals, are thought to be contained, all more or less equally vulnerable.[14]

To hold such beings responsible for good and evil seems pointless. They would lack the power either to initiate evil in the first place or protect us against it. This, however, is not an escape but merely a distancing. Obscured behind complex time cycles and delegations of power, the problem of evil may seem less crucially posed than in creator deity monotheisms, yet remains basically unchanged. There are minimalist traditions in Buddhism, for example, that reject anthropomorphic images of creator gods, although they retain a sense of spiritual power as somehow permeating, or underlying, the universe. Yet spirituality itself can be seen as an anthropomorphic projection. Somewhere must be a (conceptual) starting point, whether as a beginning from nothing or self-generating eternity. We can cut through these mental complications by asking what sort of monistic force stood (conceptually) at the starting point. Was it a spiritual force? In that case, no matter how many eons of pre-secular time are thought to have intervened, we wind up with a belief system to which the problem of evil remains irrevocably attached. Or was the force non-spiritual—like volcanic eruptions or fields of force such as gravity or maybe even the Big Bang?[15] In these cases, we can certainly escape the problem of evil but will have jettisoned religion in doing so. Christian theologians of the early modern era targeted Spinoza and his follow-ers for precisely this reason. If God and nature are the same, and if nature (as Spinoza wrote) "has no end set before it, and all final causes are nothing but human fictions," then God himself would be only a fiction.[16]

It is time to return now to the original question: Is any religion exempt from the problem of evil? The answer, I think, is No.

Job

If the answer is no, the problem remains inescapable and the next question must be: Can we resolve the problem by confronting it? Religious literature is full of such confrontations. One of the most ancient is the Book of Job, compiled in the fifth century BCE, after the Babylonian captivity, but containing older elements, perhaps of Babylonian origin. The prose narrative that frames the discursive chap-ters of Job is especially thought to be more ancient than the rest. Often described as an earlier folktale, this narrative offers what seems at first a traditional and non-problematic account of the problem of evil. Job's afflictions represent a test (and demonstration) of his devotion to God. Job enters the folktale as a man of wealth and power, already famed for piety. Job is pleasing to God, and God, conferring in heaven with his counselors, calls the attention of one of them—Satan—to Job's admirable behavior. "A perfectly upright man," God says boastfully, "one that feareth God and escheweth evil."

Satan suggests that it is easy for a man blessed with such good fortune to make a show of piety.[17] God takes up this challenge. He empowers Satan to test Job by destroying "all that he hath"—an order Satan executes with impressive efficiency, even demolishing Job's children (seven sons, three daughters) along with his flocks of goats and herds of camels. Job, crushed by this turn of fortune, rends his garments, throws himself on the ground, but his piety remains untainted. "Naked came I out of my mother's womb and naked shall I return thither; the Lord gave and the Lord hath taken away; blessed be the name of the Lord." God, having won the first round, chides Satan at the next meeting of the heavenly council, where-upon Satan replies that for human beings the ultimate test of dedication is bodily pain. Again God accepts the challenge; this time Satan assails Job with "sore boils from the sole of his foot unto his crown." Even Job's wife turns from him. "Dost thou retain thine integrity?" she demands. "Curse God and die." But Job rebukes her: "Shall we receive good at the hands of God, and shall we not receive evil?"[18]

At this point Satan vanishes from the narrative, his cruel counsel seemingly repudiated. Job has submitted himself without protest or question to God's will. We are now scarcely two chapters into the Book of Job and it remains only for God to reveal to Job that his faith has been triumphantly vindicated (Job, of course, did not know it was being tested) and perhaps also to make some amends for the agonies suffered in the process. This is precisely the way the book will end and less than half a chapter (when we reach the ending) will suffice to wrap it up. Thus a grand total of two and a half chapters tells the entire story of Job's trial by ordeal, which is the substance of the more ancient folktale referred to above. These two and a half chapters, however, have been separated so that thirty-nine and a half quite different chapters lie between their beginning and end. The effect is to establish the folktale as boundary, or framework, for the longer and presum-ably more complex writings contained inside.[19]

The interior chapters are discursive rather than narrative. They include poetic invocations and dramatic dialogue. They bring forward a different cast of characters. Satan disappears, as does Job's wife, while a quartet of "friends" invade Job's privacy, perhaps to commiserate, perhaps simply to enjoy the spec-tacle of his downfall. The most important difference, however, is the altered behavior of the two central characters. Job, having suffered in silence ("with the patience of Job") during the folktale, turns abruptly into a loquacious complain-er, whereas God—whom we had heard conniving with Satan as any landlord might with his overseer—now withdraws into the austere silence of the *Deus Absconditus*. These transformations make explicit a full-dress confrontation with the problem of evil. Job, as he now protests his innocence over and again, is chal-lenging God to show why he deserves punishment. Yet the reader knows that God had earlier certified Job as "a perfectly upright man." Why then must he be tormented? God offers no answer.[20]

Meanwhile, Job's four "friends," instead of helping to ease his pain, obliging-ly offer assistance to God by trying out various possible explanations. One invokes the doctrine of original sin: "What is man that he should be clean? and he which is born of woman that he should be righteous?" The second suggests that even so upright a man as Job may have sinned secretly through overweening pride in his own virtue. Another thinks affluence and success are likely to generate scorn for persons less fortunate. The fourth accuses Job of *hubris*, an arrogance so gigantic that it claims for mere creatures an accounting from their creator. What these sev-eral proposals have in common is that they put the onus on Job. His best strate-gy, then—knowing God is just—must be to repent his sin, whatever it may have been, and throw himself on God's mercy. This Job has done twice already, and will do once again, but only after his repeated demands for justification have pro-voked God into a thunderous tirade exalting power but saying nothing whatever of justice or love. Reduced to his final and most abject submission, Job declares that his own words have overreached his understanding. "Wherefore I abhor myself and repent in dust and ashes."[21]

A great deal—not all—of later efforts to explain God's treatment of Job is adumbrated in the comments by Job's four "friends." Still, to most readers I think their arguments appear self-serving and hypocritical. Partly this is because both Job and God obviously resent their intrusion. Job several times urges them to shut their mouths and hear what he is actually saying. And God, in a curious episode at the very end of the intervening chapters, turns angrily on the four who presum-ably have been speaking in his behalf and accuses them of misrepresenting him. The implication is that at the level of God's ultimatum to Job logical argument becomes irrelevant. Immediately after chastising the "friends," God reinstates Job, returning to him all he had previously possessed. His ten children (seven sons, three daughters) are gone beyond recall but God provides ten new ones. Was Job rewarded for his lifelong devotion, for his brief and purely verbal recal-citrance, or for his blind repentance?[22]

The Orthodox Reading

I turned to the Book of Job as an early example of confrontations with the problem of evil that recur in Western religious literature. Job certainly is that. Its eloquence, its dramatic intensity, its appalling dissonances, have fixed the attention of readers through two and a half millennia. The question now before us is what Job offers in the way of resolving that problem. There are two principal readings, or types of readings, that can be derived more or less logically from the text, depending on how the framing folktale and the chapters contained inside it are balanced against each other. The folktale, which specifies the beginning and end, will govern the reading of Job unless the interior chapters generate power sufficient to explode the folktale. Since for most readers this has not been the case, the folktale with its constraining framework has remained dominant. I call this the orthodox reading. The other, which has tended to be recessive, I will call the Promethean reading, to be discussed in the next chapter. Here I must deal first with the orthodox version.

The orthodox reading is summarized by Augustine in the opening book of his *City of God*:

> There is a further reason for the infliction of temporal suffering on the good, as is seen in the case of Job—that the spirit of man may be tested, that he may learn for himself what is the degree of disinterested devotion that he offers to God.[23]

Actually, Augustine gives the notion of testing a broader moral scope than that of the Job folktale in which the test served only the needs of the Grand Inquisitor. Testing—in Augustine's sense of spiritual improvement—would be meaningless without some belief in an ongoing existence after death. During the long interval between Job and *City of God*, intimations of immortality had gradually coalesced into various salvation creeds, one of which was Christianity. Augustine, projecting Christian belief back into earlier scripture, could now interpret testing as a means of self-improvement for those who were tested. To inflict suffering on the good certainly is evil, yet without it there would be no test. Evil, whether in its natural forms of famine and disease or its social guises as "Vanity Fair" and "Slough of Despond," furnishes the resistance against which pilgrims must measure their progress toward the City of God. Thus construed, testing subordinates evil to God's benevolent purpose.[24]

Augustine, eager to construe it in this way, ignored the discursive chapters of Job. Perhaps he had no problem with those chapters in any case. If Job's accusations against God might be condoned as temporary aberrations due to excessive suffering, then God's bad-tempered response could be seen as a fitting rebuke to Job's *hubris*, prior to his restitution. Nor could Augustine really have dissented from the charges of guilt brought forward by the four "friends," since in *City of*

God he employed almost identical guilt trips to explain the murder and rape of innocent matrons (including many Christians) during the sack of Rome by the Visigoths. One might easily suppose he took them directly out of Job. Arguments from guilt remain essentially negative. They explain why certain persons, or groups of persons, may deserve punishment, but not why God tolerates evil-at-large. So in the larger question of why a benevolent and omnipotent God would permit such a disaster to human civilization as the fall of Rome (and Rome recently Christianized at that!), Augustine gave precedence to the concept of testing. This is the orthodox reading, and virtually all rational explanations of evil—including theories of original sin and redemption as well as those of reincarnation and karma—can be contained within it.[25]

Augustine

Basic to testing in any form is an assumption that some will pass while others fail. In human affairs, tests are normally justified as serving either educational or personnel selection needs. For educational purposes, those who fail are prompted (presumably) to continue their studies and try again. Personnel selection examinations identify those best qualified to serve while returning without prejudice (presumably) other applicants to their previous situations. Both forms may be reconciled readily enough to reason and common sense. In religious affairs, however, the personnel selection form of test takes on quite a different aspect since those who fail go back not to their former status but downward into torment or death. Augustine in his interpretation of Job had favored the softer, educational variety of testing; and a parallel line of thought might have led him to cosmic extensions of educational testing such as the doctrines of reincarnation and karma. That he was aware of these conceptual possibilities is clear from his discussion of purgatory.[26] Venial sins, he conceded, could be cleansed through tests and ordeals imposed while the sinner still lived or during limited time periods after death; more serious offenses, however, were so seeped in evil that only eternal damnation could expunge them. Augustine ridiculed the belief (held by some Christians in his time) that no sin could ever be so heinous as to merit eternal punishment:

> Now if this opinion is good and true, just because it is compassionate, then it
> will be the better and the truer the more compassionate it is. Then let the

fountain of compassion be deepened and enlarged until it extends as far as the evil angels … [as far as] liberation of the Devil himself!)

Augustine was here using classic *reductio ad absurdum* to refute the idea that educational or pilgrim's-progress modes of testing might be extended broadly enough to achieve universal salvation. Earlier, with respect to Job, he had endorsed this mode and obviously relied on it for Christian redemption including his own. Yet to extend it to all humankind, he argued, would be equivalent to redeeming the Devil—therefore absurd, since the Devil is the very evil that corrupts a majority of our own species beyond hope of redemption. For them, the only appropriate test will be the one that separates saints from devils and sheep from goats—the Last Judgment.[27]

Augustine assigned to Satan major responsibility for splitting God's creation into hostile cities. At the beginning, however, Satan had not been evil. Like all other angels created by God as pure spirit, Satan was originally good. In a sense he was too good since it was pride in his own perfection that led him to imagine himself equal to God. When Augustine had turned from Manicheanism to Christianity he abandoned the doctrine that a spirit of evil could equal God in substance and power. Instead, Augustine believed, Satan, having been *created* by God, was of a lesser order. Satan of course knew this too, but his pride led him to overlook it. Pride furnished the cause of this error, yet the error was self-inflicted because Satan had chosen of his own free will to exalt self-esteem over devotion to God. Satan's rebellion, for Augustine, foreshadows and predicts that of Adam and Eve. It serves to mitigate their guilt to the extent that Satan, having already embraced and spiritualized evil, brings that enormous power to bear on their corruption. Thus Adam can blame Eve, Eve blames the serpent, and the serpent will turn out to be one of Satan's many guises. All this provides a loophole of credibility for redeeming some at least among the progeny of Eve and Adam while rejecting utterly Satan and his fallen angels. Satan has only himself to blame, and this brings us to the nub of Augustine's efforts to resolve the problem of evil.[28]

Given that Satan was created pure spirit by a benevolent and omnipotent God, why would he choose freely to turn away from God? The question is loaded with theological complexities. Free choice offers an attractive hypothesis for explaining the origin of evil for two reasons. The first is that it resembles the moral choices humans are constantly making in relation to their social milieu (family, community, tribe, and so forth) and so imparts a moral tone to the relationships of humans to spiritual beings. The second is that if evil emanates from choices made freely by God's creatures (Satan, Adam, and all the rest) this *might* serve to exonerate God from the authorship of evil. But in order to do so, the free choice must be totally *un*-caused, since any chain of prior causation would necessarily emanate from God. "If you try to find the efficient cause of this evil choice, there is none to be found. For nothing causes an evil will. ... The truth is that one should not try to find an efficient cause for a wrong choice. To try to discover the causes of such defection ... is like trying to see darkness or to hear silence."[29] These are muddy speculations in contrast to the usual lucidity of Augustine's explanations. Moreover, they lead to a dead end between contradictory alternatives. If the free choices of evil (or good) were left totally free, what would become of God's omnipotence? The will, Augustine wrote, "can turn away from good to do evil—and this through its own free choice; and it can also turn from evil to do good—but this can only be done with the divine assistance."[30] Of what use, then, was free choice to God's creatures if they could make only the wrong choices? And why—knowing this; and knowing the disasters that would flow from those choices (which had to be foreseen by an omniscient deity)—why had God chosen to impose on Satan (and on Adam and Eve's progeny as well) the "freedom" to choose evil instead of good?[31] Was God somehow constrained (as Leibniz would argue thirteen centuries later) from doing otherwise? But this alternative Augustine rejected indignantly.

> Who would dare to believe or assert that it was not in God's power to ensure that neither angel nor man should fall? But God preferred not to withdraw this issue from their power, and thus to show the magnitude of their pride's power for evil and of God's grace for good.[32]

So God insists on freedom of choice in order to show—Augustine apparently is saying—how stubbornly sinful his creatures have become and how gloriously merciful God's proffer of grace to some of them will then be. Augustine's God here seems scarcely less punitive than Job's, and the human condition has gotten worse. Job at least could look forward to death whereas Augustine's contemporaries are now locked into the terror of eternal punishment.[33]

The problem of evil stands as alpha and omega of Augustine's religious journey. His mother, Monica, was Christian, his father pagan. The son became an inventor, synthesizer, and brilliant borrower.[34] Perhaps he took his perception of the human condition from Job. Certainly it was from pagan Neoplatonists (who presided over his education) that he borrowed the vision of a creator endlessly spinning out the splendors of our universe, yet separated from that universe by the difference in rank between the two realms, that of creator on one hand, and of created beings on the other. Whatever God made was beautiful and good in its own right, yet because it was created and created out of nothing (nothing existed before God), remained transient and corruptible. Evil arose necessarily within this default, this deficit between the two realms. Neither divine substance nor created being, evil was simply an emptiness, a deficiency.[35] Augustine tells in the *Confessions* how this explanation—by enabling him to escape the Manichean doctrine that evil exists independently of God—brought him back to Christian belief.[36] Yet the Neoplatonist theory remained always cool and abstract. By contrast, the sense of evil as physical power, as a counterforce unleashed and unrestrained in the mortal world, Augustine drew from his own experience with sexual passion; nor ever quite relinquished the somber view of the Manicheans, with whom he had sojourned during the hot days of youth, and later repudiated. When Augustine returned to the Christians, he used Christ's human trial and ordeal to assert those attributes of justice and love he must have found wanting in God's ancient encounter with Job. So we see him struggling through the pages of *City of God* and all those thousands of other pages, like Sisyphus rolling stones uphill. No sooner has he lodged one securely in place than it nudges another that rolls downhill and Augustine comes down to fetch it up. Sometimes he gave up hope of arranging the pieces in any coherent pattern.

> I examine myself and remember what the Scripture says, "What human being can know the design of God? Who will be able to think what God intends? For the thoughts of mortals are timorous and our speculations uncertain. For the corruptible body weighs down the soul." [37]

Resume

At the beginning of this chapter I endeavored to show that thinking the problem of evil relevant only to Western monotheisms is mistaken. I can now be bold enough to assert that it pertains to all forms (and all stages) of religion. Here again I am following Weber: "The problem belongs everywhere among the factors determining religious evolution and the need for salvation."[38] The starting point of Weber's "religious evolution" might then correspond to my pseudo-myth of the crisis of consciousness (chapter 4) in which the menace of nature (and death) was partially controlled by discovery (or invention) of spiritual beings. Yet animistic spirits and local gods cannot (conceptually) be potent enough to protect against nature—a disability that becomes increasingly evident as human societies expand and local spirits escalate into pantheons of intermediate gods. Surely an omnipotent creator ought to be strong enough; the same logic, however, fastens on such a creator all the evils contained in the universe.[39] I have dealt in some detail with Job and Augustine because the line between them, which I refer to as the "orthodox reading," establishes a pattern that will prove recurrent in efforts to resolve the problem of evil, without at the same time undermining God's power.

But an alternate set of readings, which I describe as "Promethean," tends to favor justice and benevolence over power. These make for radical criticisms and encourage demands for doctrinal change. It is notable, for example, that Job expressed no expectation of life after death, whereas for Augustine such anticipations were all-important. The contrast points to the fact that even doctrines understood as revealed truths, and therefore ultimate, can often be seen to have altered through time. The next chapter examines Promethean criticisms as modifiers—and sometimes deconstructors—of orthodox belief.

PART THREE:

Religion and the Will to Believe

8

Promethean Readings

Since death is the primary evil that confronts conscious beings, no religion can fully engage the problem of evil without venturing into speculations about life after death. Ancient religions offered hopes in this direction. Indeed, our earliest empirical evidence of religious belief consists in packets of provisions for spiritual journeys found in Stone Age burial sites. Yet these intimations of immortality remained diffuse and noninclusive. There seems to have been powerful resistance to any general concept of immortality. Even such a hero as Gilgamesh held no assurance of crossing the river. Valhalla might furnish a resting place for great warriors and *illustrados*, but what of the common folk who toiled in the brick kilns?[1] One way to approach the Book of Job is to read it as expressing the difficulty posed by the problem of evil for a belief system which, having arrived at monotheism, had not yet embraced individual afterlife. Job, in the framing folktale, lived long enough to be recompensed for the evil he had suffered. Had he died (as most of us do) from Satan's lacerations, God's treatment would have seemed intolerably unjust. The problem of evil demands some assurance of divine justice. Since it is obvious to any observer that scoundrels flourish in our mortal sphere while persons as virtuous as Job often perish unrecognized and unrewarded, no such assurance would be credible apart from a promise of life beyond death.

From Doctrinal Drift to Theodicy

Salvation cults, worldwide in modern times, have existed probably as long as human culture. We know they flourished in the Mediterranean Basin during the

Hellenic period, gradually penetrating traditional belief systems just as Christianity penetrated Judaism. Augustine believed in immortality before he became a Christian. In the *Confessions* he explained that he opted for Christianity because—among the several belief systems available to him—it offered the most satisfactory response to the problem of evil. This it could not have done without a clear commitment to individual afterlife. Taking that commitment for revealed truth, Augustine could read Job as a parable of the tests Christians must surmount on their toilsome way to the City of God. Evil, construed as testing, was thus transformed into the means by which God's grace worked for the salvation of those who could be saved.[2] From the foregoing it seems evident that religions tend to "evolve" in directions that facilitate coping with the problem of evil. Such alterations could hardly be deliberate. Dogma is usually thought to rest on God's direct word or on sanctified renderings of that word invulnerable to human revision. Nonetheless, inspired readings by seers and prophets may reveal meanings previously unperceived even in sacred texts. Christian theologians (Augustine, for example) were able to discover adumbrations of immortality in Job as well as coded previews of Christian teachings scattered through the entire Old Testament. Allegedly these were not revisions but discoveries (or rediscoveries) of what had always been there.[3]

Apart, then, from the incendiary impact of new revelations, there appear to be two distinct ranges of doctrinal change. The long range, involving gradual assimilation of many commentaries and popularizations, works at a distance beyond individual intent. It takes the apparent form of an unfolding of inner meanings. I will refer to it as doctrinal drift. A short-range process, involving deep readings of traditional texts, is individual and certainly purposeful but not deliberately innovative.[4] Augustine, when he opted for Christianity, was receiving what the slow process of doctrinal drift had set before him. Writing *The City of God*, he engaged purposefully in the short-range process. Let me show you, he was arguing, how a particular body of doctrine which I now hold to be true, will, if properly interpreted, render harmless the problem of evil.[5] At least by Western scholars since the eighteenth century such purposefully directed arguments have been called theodicies. Theodicy's purpose is polemical. Milton put the point bluntly in *Paradise Lost* when he invoked both the "Heavenly Muse" and the "Spirit" to fortify his powers for the "great argument" through which he hoped to "assert Eternal Providence and justify the ways of God to men." The term itself we owe to Leibniz, who published his *Essays of Theodicy* in 1710. It derives from the Greek, *theos*, plus *dik* (justice) and means exactly what Milton identified as the purpose of his epic: an argument for, or defense of, the justice of God. So why does God's justice need defense? Because of the problem of evil. Theodicies in Western literature customarily reach back, as did Augustine, to the Book of Job. In the last chapter I referred to Augustine as exemplifying an orthodox reading of Job. In the present chapter I turn to the more radical polemics of Promethean readings.[6]

Fast Forward

Midway into the final decade of the twentieth century, Jack Miles, a Jesuit scholar turned professor of humanities at Claremont Graduate Center in California, published a book titled *God: A Biography*. To Augustine this would have seemed not only impious (since no human creature could pretend to such knowledge) but self-contradictory, because God (or more precisely the Judeo-Christian God about whom Miles claimed to be writing) does not live and change through time like subjects of biography but exists eternally unchanged. Miles defended his project by arguing that although unchanging divinity may be theologically correct, that is not in fact the way God appears in the Old Testament. On the contrary, God alters his behavior (and presumably his character) as profoundly as do heroes in Shakespearean tragedy or romantic fiction. Miles then insists on the legitimacy of treating sacred scripture as literary text. Given this argument, it may seem peculiar that he titles his work "biography" when novel, or even *bildungsroman* might be more appropriate. Yet that was the author's choice; and it won him a Pulitzer Prize, not to mention high praise in critical journals.[7]

Predictably, Job furnishes the keystone of Miles's "biography." He writes in his introductory chapter:

> God's last words are those he speaks to Job. … Within the Book of Job itself, God's climactic and overwhelming reply seems to silence Job. But reading from the end of the book of Job onward, we see that it is Job who has somehow silenced God. God never speaks again, and he is decreasingly spoken of.

Later on, assessing possible interpretations of Job, Miles suggests that writers who have been drawn "intuitively … to Job as to a yawning abyss" were by no means mistaken. They were right, that is, in seeing Job as subversive because the question it raises with respect to divine justice remains unanswered. To escape this subversive impact, Miles brings forward his literary interpretation, which shows us God being educated and fundamentally altered in character (just as heroes of *bildungsroman* are educated) through painful experience. In God's case, the experience emanated from his vexed relationship with humans and especially the controversy with Job. This of course amounts to heresy in terms of the orthodox reading since it makes God less than totally powerful. How can eternal omnipotence be modified by experience? But we need to recall that our original turn to the Book of Job was to consult an early confrontation in Judeo-Christian scripture with the problem of evil. What I referred to as the orthodox reading attempted to control the admittedly troublesome tendencies in Job by stressing its enclosing folktale, which ends with Job's confession of sin and reinstatement by God. But Miles will have none of this. Insisting that Job spoke truth to power, he concludes that God must either relapse into total evil by slaying Job, or somehow absorb the truth Job has dared to utter. Perhaps no longer a Jesuit though still a believer, Miles chose the latter alternative.[8]

At the Brink of the Abyss

And that essentially is the Promethean reading. By validating Job's criticism of God, it invites all sorts of other criticisms. It cuts through the old dilemma of revealed truth versus doctrinal drift by acknowledging either that human knowledge of divinity is constantly changing or that divinity itself may be in process of alteration. Since criticism of God erodes faith, as does any concession to uncertainty in what is believed, the Promethean reading has always contained a left wing that moved toward agnosticism and disbelief. I presume this is what Miles referred to when he warned that readers, drawn "intuitively" to Job, would find a "yawning abyss." On the other hand, what I meant when I described the Promethean reading as recessive is that it has always provided a return route by which religious rebels could find their way back to belief, sometimes even to orthodox belief. Precisely because the Promethean reading incited radical attacks on the problem of evil, it served Western religion as an almost established channel of doctrinal revision.[9] I need to emphasize how vast a territory this account of the Promethean reading takes in. Job and Prometheus, embedded in distinctly different cultures, show no prior linkages in mythology or religious belief. What they share is simply their response to the problem of evil. Both stood against divinity that used divine power in support of humanly unjust purposes. If it is accurate to describe Judeo-Christian doctrine as an amalgam of Hebrew and Greek, it can be no less so to speak of a Promethean reading of Job in the same terms. Western religions (perhaps all religions are similar in this respect) display a galaxy of innovations, heresies, schisms, breakaways, and persecutions. While there were multiple causes of such conflicts, the one that primarily concerns us here is dissatisfaction with orthodox treatments of the problem of evil. Thus, in the Western sequence, belief in individual immortality developed mainly after Job and served partially to correct the injustice Job had made glaringly obvious. The same can be said for Christianity itself, which emerged as a Judaic version of salvation cults that proliferated during the Hellenic era through communities centered around the Mediterranean.[10]

Christianity sought to bring the old creator God of thunder and cataclysm into human dimension by ascribing to him a son begotten more or less in human style. The Son thus figures as an exception to creation-ex-nihilo, which had been the route of all previous creations including (with such disastrous results) those of the angels and Adam and Eve. Against the evil of death (represented metaphorically by eternal damnation), the Son offers salvation to all who "freely" choose Christian belief. The Son of course is also free, yet with no risk of choosing evil (as Adam and Eve and the rebellious angels had done) because as *begotten* son he shares the "substance" of the father. Founders of Christian doctrine, seeking to make these innovations persuasive to orthodoxy, declared the Son (whose birth date marks year one of the Christian era) to have coexisted from eternity with the father. Augustine and his colleagues (as I noted earlier) were even able to discover intimations of the Son scattered through Judaic scripture (including Job) and argued rather speciously that Christian doctrine, far from altering older revelations, revealed for the first time their true meaning.[11]

Christianity, a breakaway that launched a world religion, offers the most famous case in the Western sequence. But there were others—among them Gnosticism, driven underground by Augustine's predecessors; Manicheanism, against which Augustine himself struggled; the Manichean heresies of the Albigensians and Cathars in the early Middle Ages, presumably obliterated by papal crusade and inquisition; and through all European history from Hellenic times to the Renaissance and Protestant Reformation, that underground river of ancient heresy often referred to as the Hermetic tradition. Doubtless in formal terms the Protestant Reformation centered on questions of church structure, yet one need only recall Protestant denunciations of the papacy as Antichrist (Satan), or the Whore of Babylon, to realize the problem of evil was not far from the heart of the matter. Details of these controversies are not requisite to my argument. What I need simply do is establish their relevance to the collective mind-set I have been speaking of as the Promethean reading. I can best make this point by turning to an exemplary work of scriptural interpretation often thought to stand near the brink of the abyss—Milton's *Paradise Lost*.[12]

Milton: In Search of Promethean Heroes

Many years ago in Mexico I met a young professor of philosophy (aesthetics) just beginning his career as a teacher and scholar. He visited Cuba after the Castro revolution to help, if he could, in reconstructing their university system. From Havana, he wrote me describing the revolution as *"la cosa la mas linda."* I thought of Wordsworth's remembrance of the first years of the French Revolution:

Bliss was it in that dawn to be alive
But to be young was very heaven![13]

I suppose Milton experienced the English Revolution in the same way. He had grown up in a Puritan household. At Cambridge, he mingled in the Puritan faction led by the so-called Cambridge Platonists, who became his intellectual and political associates. Saturated in classics and Judeo-Christian scripture, these young men were extraordinarily open to the new science—as Newton's career at Cambridge, only one generation later, would demonstrate. Milton, on his grand tour of the continent in 1639, had visited Galileo, then under house arrest in Florence. I think Milton viewed Puritan reform as a kind of Enlightenment, liberating the human species from ancient bondages. By sweeping away corruption from the Church it would not only restore religion to its original and pure sources, but open up God's natural world to scientific study; and at last perhaps illumine even the dark chambers of governmental power.[14] With these grand projects on the horizon, why would a young and revolutionary poet consider such a topic as the problem of evil? The English Revolution was religious before it became political; to resolve the problem of evil Milton probably thought was essential to its completion. In the early years, at least, this could have seemed within grasp. Milton stood near the end of a long tradition of religious realism in Western culture (the end would be Leibniz, born about forty years after Milton). Accepting the world as real, religious realism asserted that *natural religion* (that is, science) points directly to God and that God's existence is knowable by "infallible proofs." Given this starting point, one might reasonably suppose "the ways of God to men" could be "justified" in terms of a moral logic accessible to Milton's contemporaries. Nor could there be much hope of building a godly commonwealth in the absence of such understanding. If we take seriously Milton's declaration of intent, we must suppose his initial strategy would be to make the God of Christian scripture his protagonist—since Puritan revolution was grounded in Christian scripture—and portray that protagonist as a sovereign who ruled with perfect justice.[15]

Paradise Lost was completed five years after the Restoration, when Milton was old, blind, and in danger of having his head chopped off. We do not know exactly when he began to think about writing *Paradise Lost*. At the opening of the Long Parliament he was in his early thirties, and must have wondered, as the Commonwealth ground down to its bitter end twenty years later, how God could permit so splendid a human undertaking to be crushed by evil. Why had God not aided God's partisans? Was he unable? Or unwilling? How could Jerusalem, the City of God, be built here if God averted his eyes? One might think God would have dominated the opening scenes of Milton's epic, but it is Satan who makes the grand entrance. Several generations of critics, in fact, have classified Milton as a satanist, in praise or blame depending on whether they favored the deist or trinitarian establishments. As for Milton himself, given the resemblance of Satan's role to Cromwell's (or his own), he must have been tempted to make Satan a Promethean hero—Lucifer, bearer of light—freely rebelling against power corrupted by evil. But this analogy (impossible in any case for political reasons, since it ends by identifying King Charles with God) was unsustainable because of its scriptural context. Satan hardly figures as a bearer of light or champion of human liberation.[16]

Obviously Milton was not planning to exalt Satan, yet *Paradise Lost* begins as if that were his intent. Many of his grandest lines are given to Satan. These, for instance, as Satan lies writhing in the pit of Hell:

The mind is its own place, and in itself
Can make a Heaven of Hell, a Hell of Heaven.
What matter where if I be still the same
And what I should be, all—

But these are heroic; they assert the power of mind—or spirit?—to transcend physical circumstance. Milton himself might have spoken them—struck blind, writhing in political defeat. Christopher Hill writes, "It was in defeat that Milton set about justifying the ways of God to man."[17] But this would not be my interpretation. I think Milton must have seen solving the problem of evil as a necessary element of Puritan Revolution; it was defeat that brought him to doubt the possibility of any solution within Christian orthodoxy. Obviously these *are* Milton's lines: he identifies here with Satan. Yet not for long. By the beginning of Book Three (of twelve) we arrive at what may have been the conceptual starting place. And here the story unfolds in more traditional style. We behold God on his throne with the Son—whom trinitarianism requires to be eternally coexistent with the Father—seated on the Father's right side. The Son then leads Heaven's loyal angels ("in dubious battle on the plains of Heaven"), hurling the rebel angels down into Hell. Satan, as we know, recuperated and counterattacked with his famous infiltration of Eden. By planting his own evil spirit into the serpent that seduces Eve, Satan brings about Adam's "free" (and fatal) choice, from which stem all the appalling consequences of original sin. God (we are told), although foreseeing these events, chose to permit them free rein. But God now demands just punishment. The Son—eager to temper justice with mercy—volunteers to incarnate his own divine spirit into mortal flesh; to suffer death for redemption of Eve's children; or for those of them at least who, by their own "free" choice to follow Christ, show themselves worthy of salvation.[18] Thus far, Milton has reiterated Augustine's account. Free choice has been identified as the occasion of evil. Testing with its grievous ordeals establishes the strait gate that offers escape from evil. The fallen children of Eve and Adam, free though they certainly are to choose evil, remain powerless to choose good except by virtue of divine Grace, dispensed through the medium of the Son's sacrifice. In formal— one might say *legal* terms—Milton could claim that his epic asserts "Eternal Providence" and justifies "the ways of God to men." On this basis it was accepted, even canonized, in post-Restoration England, not to mention Puritan New England, as well as Protestant America. [19]

The poetry of *Paradise Lost*, however, sends a message different from the plot line. There is a curious shift, in focusing the role of protagonist, from Satan at the beginning as Jobean challenger of God's justice to God himself, presumably the just Sovereign, then to Christ as purveyor of mercy and grace, and finally in the closing section to Eve and Adam, somehow set free by their own expulsion from paradise. Before coming to rest, then, on Eve and Adam, the focus has moved from Satan—to God—to Christ. Yet Milton's poetry works to disqualify each of these potential protagonists from actually filling that role. Satan first. When Satan wings his way through chaos to spy on God's newly created world, he is stunned by its beauty and deeply moved at the affection Eve and Adam show each other. By his sympathetic response we know he once really *was* good. But his rage against God overpowers him. Melt, as I do, he laments, at their "harmless innocence," still my right revenge "compels me now to do what, else, though damned, I should abhor."[20] Satan then gets on with his cruel scheme of deception and betrayal, upon which Milton comments:

> So spake the Fiend, and with necessity—
> The tyrant's plea—excused his devilish deeds.[21]

Nothing Milton might say of the devil could be worse than comparing him to a human tyrant. So the spotlight moves on to the next potential protagonist.

> High throned above all highth ...
> About him all the Sanctities of Heaven
> Stood thick as stars ...
> And on his right
> The radiant image of his glory sat,
> His only Son.[22]

God knows immediately that Satan has entered the Garden of Eden. Being omniscient, he knew this beforehand, and knows how it all will turn out. To the Son he says:

> For man will harken to ... [Satan's] glozing lies
> And easily transgress the sole command—[God's command, that is,
> not to eat the forbidden fruit]—

Sole pledge of his obedience: so will fall
He and his faithless progeny. Whose fault?
Whose but his own? Ingrate, he had of me
All he could have; I made him just and right,
Sufficient to have stood, though free to fall.
… They themselves decreed
Their own revolt, not I. If I foreknew,
Foreknowledge had no influence on their fault.[23]

The Son then makes his offer to suffer crucifixion in order to redeem mankind and God grants approval—to the thunderous applause of the angels.

No sooner had the Almighty ceased but—all
The multitude of Angels, with a shout
Loud as from numbers without number, sweet
As from blest voices, uttering joy—Heaven rung
With jubilee, and loud hosannas filled
The eternal regions. [24]

For seventeenth-century Christendom, Protestant as well as Catholic, the doctrines set forth by God in the speech just quoted were mainline orthodoxy, and to Milton's contemporaries would scarcely have seemed unusual. Nonetheless, there is a lingering irony in the contrast between God's cold legalism toward his creatures and the spontaneous warmth earlier shown by Satan. The contrast serves to darken the splendor of the angels' fanfare. All this of course is in the poetry, not plot line. If Milton—as poet—seems now to have disqualified both God and Satan for protagonist of his epic, perhaps that role might be played by the Son?

I think no one (certainly not Milton) can fail to notice that when Christ volunteered for the *via dolorosa* of passion and crucifixion he could not (even had he willed to do so) have chosen spiritual death, since that was precluded by his status as eternal Son of God and Second Person in the Trinity. Christ suffered mortal death, but rose quickly from the dead to reclaim his customary place on the right hand of the Father. This celebrated sacrifice (to one who had lived through the civil war in England) might seem trivial compared with that exacted from human defenders of the City of God—Christian martyrs, for example, or soldiers

his epic, which he knows by this time has failed of its declared purpose. Expelled on God's orders from "the eastern gate" of Paradise, Eve and Adam stumble down the hill to the ordinary world below. There they pause gazing back for a moment at the heights behind them, "with dreadful faces thronged and fiery arms," then on, and out, through the marvelous closing lines of *Paradise Lost*:

> Some natural tears they dropped, but wiped them soon;
> The world was all before them, where to choose
> Their place of rest, and Providence their guide.
> They, hand in hand, with wandering steps and slow,
> Through Eden took their solitary way.[28]

The phrase "and Providence their guide" may seem out of place in this passage. I would describe it as a safety–line, but also bitterly ironic, since Milton has already made clear how unreliable he deems providential guidance to have been for Adam and Eve.

In Deepest Consequence

Like many of his contemporaries (Isaac Newton among them), Milton remained deeply involved in theology. His theology tended to be symbolic rather than literal and provided a means of communicating with fellow travelers. He took pains to set up signposts bearing witness to his own crises of belief. The Book of Genesis in its first verse declares that at the beginning God created heaven and earth. Since that was the beginning, nothing except God had existed previously. The second verse, however, speaks of "earth" as "without form and void." This implies that the act of creation required imposing form on something—(earth? matter?)—till then formless. In the interest of simplicity, I will refer to the something as *matter*. Where did matter come from? Christian orthodoxy has always explained it as created by God out of nothing, thus preserving the Neoplatonic concept of a *gap*, or *deficit*, between an absolutely perfect creator, on the one hand, and the less-than-perfect beings of the created world on the other.[29] In *Paradise Lost*, when God sends the Archangel Raphael to explain creation to Adam, the Archangel delivers his message as follows:

O Adam, one Almighty is, from whom
All things proceed, and up to Him return,
If not depraved from good, created all
Such to perfection, one first matter all,
Endued with various forms, various degrees
Of substance.[30]

We note the angel seems not only to be subordinating substance to matter, but leaves out the point that matter is supposed to have been created out of nothing. Has he misremembered his lines? Not exactly. While he may not have followed God's script here, he certainly was following Milton's. One could easily interpret this passage as saying that all the less-than-perfect beings of the created world are composed of the same "first matter" as God himself. The effect is to bridge the gap between creator and created, between God and nature. But nature is the habitat of death and evil; how can God save us from these if nature and God are the same? Thus Raphael's speech undercuts the traditional explanation of evil as originating in that gap, that *deficit*, through the inherent transiency and corruptibility of beings composed from nothing. Lacking such a conceptual account of evil, it will be difficult not to hold God responsible for all the evil uses to which the faculty of free will has been put—by fallen angels as well as human beings.

Unless, that is, one chose to exonerate God by denying his omnipotence. And this, I think, is the alternative Milton is being driven to by failure of the Puritan Revolution. During the same years in which he completed *Paradise Lost*, he was writing (in a separate and private manuscript) the following speculation (as if from the brink of Jack Miles's abyss):

Many visible proofs ... have compelled all nations to believe either that God—or that some evil power whose name was unknown—presided over the affairs of the world. Now that evil should prevail over good, and be the true supreme power, is as unmeet as it is incredible. Hence it follows as a necessary consequence that God exists.[31]

I will make no attempt to sort out the involutions of this passage, but simply say that it reveals a painful and strange interlude in the consciousness of its author. The private manuscript (prudently unpublished at the time of the Restoration) was then "lost" and rediscovered more than a hundred years later.

In it Milton rejected creation out of nothing and declared (far more explicitly than in *Paradise Lost*) his belief that God created the universe out of his own divine substance. We in the twenty-first century are not greatly agitated by such theological infighting, yet it may behoove us to ponder the intellectual and social implications of failing to resolve the problem of evil. For Milton—since one can scarcely imagine that he could have abandoned religion any more than he could have denied the revolution—the outcome apparently is to loosen his bonding to Christian orthodoxy. He appears to be moving from the traditional concept of a separate, sovereign, creator toward a riskier notion of divinity as somehow immanent in nature. This would be a form of pantheism. We know Milton paid close attention to the radical theologies with which revolutionary England was awash, and pantheistic visions were rife among them. Typically, he denied tampering with revealed truth. Thus in *Paradise Lost* he reaffirms (with Augustine and all the others) that the Son indeed coexisted from eternity, timeless and unchanging, with the Father. Yet *Paradise Lost* reads more like a narrative of development through time: a *history*. When one protagonist fails, another steps forward to take the lead. If God forsakes his human partisans in the crunch of revolution (and if that was not because he was himself evil, or willingly tolerated evil), then it must be because he lacked power, or wisdom, to prevail over evil. And yet, while that might have been his situation then, he need not be constrained by what he once was, or might be now. Has he not as much freedom to undertake new ventures as humans beings, said to be made in his image? A God residing in nature (as humans do) would come closer to the human situation. He might even love human beings, and try to help them; although this at best would be a faltering sort of help, because—instead of commanding nature from above—an immanent (or pantheistic) deity lives inside nature, and remains subject to it.[32]

Pantheism is certainly as ancient as religion itself. But the pantheism hinted at in *Paradise Lost* points in a strikingly modern direction. It suggests a notion of partnership: God and his creatures moving hand-in-hand into a future that remains unknown to any of them. We find expressions of similar ideas in works of John Stuart Mill in the nineteenth century, and especially Alfred North Whitehead early in the twentieth. More recently, bearing titles such as "panentheism" and "process theology," they constitute an important component in postmodern religious ideology. This would require an evolutionary view of divinity. From our own perspective it seems obvious that such theologies stem partly out of Darwin, which will explain their proliferation in the twentieth century.[33] Yet

Paradise Lost warns us to look out for more ancient origins. Milton, had he been required to explain the identity shift in the protagonist role of his epic, would have taken us to a teleological sequence atop which stood the idea of the Good, as final cause. Good, conceptualized in such a way, would necessarily be separate from God. God—along with his multiple offspring (one among them begotten, all the others created out of God's own substance)—would be seen groping toward the Good through slow stages of a cosmicly progressive evolution. Evil, gigantic although (perhaps) diminishing, corresponds to the gap that separates God's children from Paradise.[34]

So what is Paradise? Paradise is nature purified of evil. And since evil comprises whatever in nature is foreign or hostile to human aspiration, an evolutionary progress to Paradise would amount to humanizing nature. Yet that could hardly be possible unless nature itself were constructed along anthropomorphic principles. Are we not back, then, to imposing on the cosmos (nature) an anthropomorphically harmonious spiritual force? If so, the problem of evil confronts us again, totally unscathed by the detour we have just made through pantheist, or process, or *bildungsroman* theology. I don't know that Milton actually entertained such a scheme. Yet something like it seems implicit in *Paradise Lost* and might have restored—if not Christian belief—at least some hope in spiritual beings during his last difficult years. The next chapter takes us again to the main line of orthodox theology.

9

Theodicy

The two most luminous theodicies of European literature are Milton's *Paradise Lost* and the *Divine Comedy* of Dante.

> My guide and I entered that hidden road ...
> We climbed, he first and I behind, until
> Through a small opening ahead of us
> I saw the lovely things the heavens hold
> And we came out to see once more the stars.[1]

Thus Dante, ending his tour of the evil empire, testified to the supremacy (and beauty) of heaven. Since for him beauty and reason were inseparable, this amounted to an affirmation of the rightness of evil. That these two epics always stand near the top in rankings of European poetry tells us that theodicy has long been central to the high culture of the West. Milton's *Paradise Lost*, discussed in the previous chapter, offers a stellar example of theodicy in the Promethean mode. For the mainstream of Western theodicy I turn now to Dante and Leibniz.

Dante

Separated by four centuries and totally different in their gifts, these may seem odd companions, but they were alike in commitment to an omnipotent creator and in

their strivings to untangle the problem of evil by focusing on the interlocked concepts of free will and testing. Both, to that extent, followed in the agile footsteps
of Augustine. Dante of course had never heard of *theodicy* (a word invented by
Leibniz) and would probably have disapproved on the ground that God's justice,
already known by faith, needs no defense. I think many of Dante's modern cele-
brants, persuaded that poetry occupies a realm more exalted than theological
argument, would indignantly reject the term. Yet since faith was precisely what
was at issue in Dante's journey, and since Dante himself maintained that poetry's
highest achievement would be to make tangible the beauty and perfection of
God's creation, it seems not inappropriate to view his work under the aspect of
theodicy.[2] Testing provides both the central theme and narrative structure of the
entire *Divine Comedy*. The first lines of the opening canto bring Dante up against
his crucial test.

> Midway in our life's journey I went astray
> > from the straight road and woke to find myself
> > alone in a dark wood.[3]

He determines to save himself by breaking through to the hilltop that rises
beyond the forest in the last glow of setting sun. But this proves beyond his powers. He is in terror of total loss. Then comes the intervention by Beatrice, who
sends Virgil to be his guide for the descent into Hell and the long climb up the
Mountain of Purgatory to the Garden of Eden.[4] The journey is at once a second
chance for Dante and an allegory of the tests that face all pilgrims on the road to
salvation.

In Hell Dante sees multitudes who have failed the tests: there but for the grace
of God go I. In Purgatory he observes testing in its more benign form of remedi-
al self-improvement. Dante experiences Purgatory as both observer and participant. Himself a marginal sinner, he shares in ordeals of purgation and endures the
trial by fire that precedes entry to the Garden of Eden. Beatrice, in the Garden,
waits to be his guide through Paradise; first, however, she must impose her own
test, which requires him to confess that after her death on earth he betrayed her
by dallying with fleshly loves. Only after Dante has acknowledged in tears his
dereliction can she lead him upward through the heavenly circles of Paradise.
And here still another trial confronts him: like a scholastic candidate he must
withstand oral examination before Peter, James, and John—demonstrating to

these formidable keepers of the keys that he grasps intellectually the meaning of what he has felt and seen. Altogether, then, it would seem impossible to read the *Divine Comedy* without knowing that Dante believed human suffering was ordained by God in order to test out souls worthy of salvation.[5]

What is being tested in these multiple ordeals is the power to make right choices through free exercise of the will. Right choices are those that select faith and obedience to God. To make right choices requires standing against the temptations (and terrors) of the flesh. Were such choices easy there would be no merit to making them. Consequently there must also be easier choices that lead down primrose paths to damnation and Hell. Thus while Paradise rests on free will, even more so must the evil empire. Dante is at pains to make this point. As the case of Augustine suggests, it will not be an easy package to put together, and Dante perhaps wisely avoids any attempt to frame it in logical discourse. He relies instead on metaphor and on the contrasting images of darkness and cosmic illumination that his poetry evokes.

During the tour of the Inferno, Hell's teeming population rivets our attention on the wrong choices made by free will. The earliest direct reference to free will occurs midway into *Purgatory* and comes as an abrupt interruption in what seems at first a casual encounter. Dante, with a kindred spirit from northern Italy, is exchanging lamentations over how everything in the real world has gone downhill since the days of their youth. Then he interposes an urgent question: "The world is indeed thus wholly barren of every virtue, as thou declarest to me ... but I beg thee to point out to me the cause that I may see it and show it to men, for one places it in the heavens and another here below." His countryman replies, "Brother, the world is blind. ... You that are living refer every cause up to the heavens alone as if they moved all things with them by necessity. If it were so, free choice would be destroyed in you and there would be no justice in happiness for well-doing and misery for evil. ... To a greater power and to a better nature you, free, are subject, and that creates the mind in you which the heavens have not in their charge." The translator, John Sinclair, points out in a footnote to this passage that the question remained "in debate then as ... now, and Dante's answer ... is that of Augustine and Aquinas."[6]

Nonetheless, the answer seems not to have carried total reassurance for Dante, since a few steps farther up the steep slope of Purgatory, he raised the same question with his mentor, Virgil. Dante's Virgil, poet laureate of triumphal Rome, symbolizes in the *Divine Comedy* the highest pinnacle human reason (by itself)

can attain; but because Virgil lived before the advent of Christianity he is precluded from entering Paradise, where Beatrice must replace him as Dante's guide. "As
far as reason sees here," Virgil says, "I can tell thee; beyond that wait only for
Beatrice, for it is a matter of faith." Meanwhile he can explain that all reasonable
creatures are moved by nature to pursue what they love, yet not all loves are equally good and the power to choose resides within ourselves. "That noble faculty,"
Virgil admonishes, "[is what] Beatrice means by free will ... therefore see thou
have it in mind if she would speak of it to thee."[7]

Beatrice, who turns out to be impressively articulate in scholastic discourse,
does indeed speak on that subject: "The greatest gift that God in His bounty
made in creation, the most conformable to His goodness and the one He accounts
the most precious was the freedom of the will, with which the creatures with intelligence, all and only these, were and are endowed." This is a strong statement. But
instead of going on to show how free will might elucidate the problem of evil,
Beatrice digresses to a lesser problem—that of whether the Church ought to bar-
gain with persons who make vows in expectation of favorable responses to their
prayers. We need not follow her into this subordinate argument. I had hoped (as
I suppose the fictional Dante must have been hoping) that she would find her way
back to the central topic; yet Dante, the poet, doubtless arranged these matters for
his own purposes, and she does not, never at least in words.[8] Thus both Dante
and Beatrice avoid the non sequiturs that Augustine fell into when he wrote,
"Nothing causes an evil will." To avoid conceptual problems, however, is not necessarily to solve them. The task of making evil the outcome of free will remains as
intractable in the *Divine Comedy* as it was in *City of God*. If God had freely given
the gift of free will (as Beatrice assures Dante he did), then the gates of Paradise
must stand open for any human creature who wills to enter and God's omnipotence would be accordingly reduced. But Dante can no more accept this corollary
than could Augustine. In the opening canto of his epic when he spoke of his own
situation as "lost in a dark wood," Dante was describing metaphorically the helplessness of a sinner to effect by right will his own salvation. Unable to find a way
through the "dark wood" toward the sunlit hilltop he sank into terror from which
he was rescued only by the loving zeal of Beatrice—whose luminous figure symbolizes the grace of God.[9]

Lest any reader miss the significance of this parable, Dante went out of his way
to incorporate a truncated version of one of the most widely known journeys of
classical (pagan) antiquity. In the lower depths of the Inferno, Dante conversed

with Ulysses engulfed in his own torturing flames. Ulysses recounted that he and his shipmates, lured by "lust to experience the far-flung world," had set forth beyond Gibraltar "on the high and open sea" (that is, the Atlantic) steering westward and south. "We made wings of our oars for our fool's flight." Five months into the trackless southern sea, rose "dead upon our course ... dark in space a peak so tall I doubted any man had seen the like." Any reader of Dante who reads on to *Purgatorio* will recognize this as the Mountain of Purgatory, which no living creature can approach from the seaward side. So Ulysses and his crew perish, sucked down into the maelstrom.[10] According to the "real" story (which we have from Homer), Ulysses, wisely turning homeward from Gibraltar, eventually reached Ithaca—where after cleaning up the mess left by his enforced absence—he savored life's twilight wrapped in the loving embrace of Penelope. These two versions of Ulysses' journey stand as diametrical opposites. In Augustine's time, Neoplatonist philosophers (among them Augustine's teachers) often made use of the Homeric version as an analog of the soul's outward journey and return to heaven. Neoplatonists taught that since human souls were eternal, heaven was in a sense their birthright and all they needed to return there were the human qualities of wisdom, prudence, and good will. These were the gifts that defined Homer's Ulysses. Dante's Ulysses, on the other hand (like Ahab), chose a fool's journey into trackless seas. Thinking himself skillful enough to sail to Purgatory, he imagined he could go there of his own free will, and for this God struck him down. Both versions circulated in the medieval Catholic culture in which Dante was raised; he chose the version that favored grace over free will.[11]

Dante, then, differed from Augustine not in the answers he offered to the problem of evil (both designated testing and free will; both stressed special grace as indispensable to salvation) but in his ways of presenting those answers. Unlike Augustine, Dante minimized discursive argument. Testing, conceptually simple, could be displayed directly through mimesis and narrative structure; special grace personified in Beatrice. Free will, however, required more complex strategy. Dante began with repeated assertions. First the penitent spirit he met on the slope of Purgatory identified free will as the necessary source of evil. Virgil then made the same assertion and so (several times) does Beatrice. None of these discusses the implications of free will. But Beatrice prays to the Virgin Mary to grant Dante the gift of transcendent vision. So as he rises with Beatrice into the highest circle of heaven, he finds himself visualizing Christian doctrine as if it were pure light. To make the faculty of vision a metaphor of intellectual understanding was as commonplace in Dante's culture as our own; he pushed this metaphor to its maximum setting. In the famous thirty-third canto of *Paradiso* (which concludes the opus) Dante described what he had seen as follows:

> O abounding grace by which I dared to fix my look on the Eternal Light. ... In its depth I saw that it contained, bound by love in one volume, that which is scattered in leaves through the universe, substances and accidents and their relations as it were fused together in such a way that what I tell of is a simple light. I think I saw the universal form of the complex. ... In the profound and clear ground of the lofty light appeared to me three circles of three colors and of the same extent, and the one seemed reflected by the other as rainbow by rainbow, and the third seemed fire breathed forth equally from the one and the other.

Dante is here telling us that he "saw" in celestial light the mystery of the Trinity and the true relationship of good and evil ("substances and accidents and their relations"). Claiming mystic vision, he came up against the difficulty reported by all mystics, that of "ineffability"—the inadequacy of human language to convey transcendent experience:

> From that moment my vision was greater than our speech, which fails at such a sight, and memory too fails at such excess. Like him that sees in a dream and after the dream the passion wrought by it remains and the rest returns not to his mind, such am I; for my vision almost wholly fades and still there drops within my heart the sweetness that was born of it. ... O Light Supreme that art so far exalted above mortal conceiving ... give my tongue such power that it may leave but a gleam of thy glory to the people yet to come.[12]

Of this final canto, John Sinclair, the translator, wrote: "In the end the scholastic from very faithfulness in his thinking, becomes the mystic, and thought is wholly surpassed and superseded in vision."[13] The context suggests that Sinclair intended this remark as high praise; in any case, I take it to be an accurate summary of Dante's theodistic strategy. Whether it was the best strategy for that purpose remains debatable. Leibniz, who came long after Dante but shared his religious beliefs, would hardly have opted for a strategy that "surpassed and superseded" thought. To come to Leibniz after Dante is a disservice and something of an anticlimax; it is like matching a tortoise against a hare. We know who won that race, but since here neither is likely to come in the winner, I should begin by giving Leibniz his due. If Dante was a world-class performer in the realm of poetry, Leibniz was no less so in the realms of mathematics and philosophy. He sought to establish a theodicy on the same level of precise reasoning that informed the calculus he developed (and published) three years before Newton.

Leibniz

Leibniz stands near the end of a line of religious realism starting somewhere before Augustine and descending through such eminent predecessors as Aquinas who is often identified as Dante's intellectual role model.[14] At the heart of this realism was a commitment to the reality of the created world and to the validity of rational proofs for the existence of the creator God and of that God's necessary attributes.[15] Leibniz published his *Essais de theodicée sur la bonté de Dieu, la liberté de l'homme et l'origine du mal* in 1710. He wrote in French for the purpose of reaching readers of Pierre Bayle's famous *Dictionaire historique et critique* (1702), which Bayle had made into a compendium of rational criticisms of Christian doctrine. Most of these criticisms pointed to the problem of evil by suggesting that a god who permitted so many evils within his own kingdom must be lacking either in power or goodness. Bayle protected himself from accusations of heresy by insisting that the questions he raised simply proved again what always had been maintained by the Church fathers—that faith held precedence over secular knowledge and human reason.[16]

During the early decades of the Enlightenment, however, to exalt faith in such terms amounted to an invitation to deism or outright disbelief. Leibniz, no less a champion of Enlightenment than Bayle, believed his duty as Christian philosopher required him to show that no necessary conflict existed between revelation and reason, provided one understood reason (as he understood it) in the dual sense of *a priori* reasoning and rational induction from scientific observation. Theodicy, for Leibniz, must be both orthodox and scientific; its starting point would be to prove formally what he already took to be self-evident: the existence of the omnipotent creator.[17] Many well-grooved arguments were available and Leibniz chose the venerable proof from first cause. Clearly he considered this argument "infallible" since, after summarizing it, he wrote: "There in a few words is the proof of one only God with his perfections, and through him of the origin of things." Such a deity, while possessing power to construct "an infinitude of possible worlds," would select only "the best, since he does nothing without act- ing in accordance with supreme reason." Thus we can rest certain the world God created is the best world possible, and theodicy's task will be to explain why this world contains ingredients that are, or to human perception appear to be, evil.[18]

For humans the greatest good is salvation of the soul. Salvation, which depends on choosing good in preference to evil, entails suffering; yet "one has no cause to complain of the fact that usually one attains salvation only through many sufferings, and by bearing the cross of Jesus Christ. These evils serve to make the elect imitators of their master, and to increase their happiness." The choice of good over evil is moral choice. Moral choice requires freedom to choose. "Freedom is deemed necessary," Leibniz explained, "in order that man may be deemed guilty and open to punishment. ... Now we can seek with confidence the origin of evil in the freedom of creatures." If the soul's salvation depends on making right choices through the exercise of free will, then human life functions mainly to cull out makers of right choices from those who make wrong ones: it becomes a series of tests. Thus evil serves the high purpose of God because, first, it gives meaning to moral choice, and second, because it is essential to testing. "God made man in his image; he made him upright. But also he made him free. Man has behaved badly, he has fallen; ... man is delivered up to the Devil by his covetous desire: the pleasure he finds in evil is the bait that hooks him." "In this sense," Leibniz conceded, "... we may say with Augustine that being subject to sin we have the freedom of a slave." We are always free, that is, to make wrong choices yet too weak to stand for good against evil except through the direct intervention of God's grace.[19]

Since God is omnipotent and knows the course of all events beforehand, his grace benefits only those he has predestined to be saved. We must not, however, take this as contrary to justice or reason. "For if we were capable of understand- ing the universal harmony, we should see that what we are tempted to find fault with is connected with the plan most worthy of being chosen; in a word, we should *see*, and not *believe* only, that what God has done is best." Granting certain reservations—such as infant damnation and the denial of salvation to virtuous pagans—Leibniz found through all these doctrinal convolutions that he could generally endorse the Augustinean "system." This concurrence brought him eventually to Augustine's key questions: given that human souls are creatures of an omnipotent and loving God, why do they so often use their gift of free will to select evil over good? Why do they need special grace in order to pursue what ought to be their natural and inevitable preference?[20] The traditional Christian response is original sin. Leibniz made less of original sin than Augustine, the reason being that Leibniz never shared Augustine's fixation on sexual passion as the incarnation of evil.[21] Yet original sin offers only an intermediate answer; after we have blamed Satan for the downfall of Eve and Adam, we still need some explanation for Satan's turn against God. Answers brought forward by Leibniz were those that Augustine and his colleagues thirteen centuries earlier had adapted to Christian usage from their Neoplatonic teachers. The creator deity, who is author of all that exists (including his own eternal existence) necessarily inhabits a realm more exalted than that of created beings; otherwise creatures would equal their creator. "For we must consider that there is an original imperfection in the creature ... whence ensues that it cannot know all, and that it can deceive itself and commit other errors ... properly speaking, the formal character of evil has no efficient cause, for it consists in privation." "Evil," Leibniz wrote, echoing Augustine, "is therefore like darkness."[22] Darkness is absence, or deficit, of light. God said in Genesis, "Let there be light," but never said let there be darkness.

In his effort to defend rational orthodoxy against Pierre Bayle, Leibniz largely reproduced Augustine's "system" including its muddiest and most irrational backwaters. Yet it is fair to point out that for Leibniz all this remained of secondary importance. One might take it or leave it. He was not so much telling believers things they ought to believe as showing them ways in which they could attach semblances of rationality to things they did believe. What carried primary importance for Leibniz was the scientific turn he was seeking to impart to religious belief.

> The ancients had puny ideas on the works of God, and St. Augustine, for want of knowing modern discoveries, was at a loss when there was question of explaining the prevalence of evil. It seemed to the ancients that there was only one earth ... the remainder of the [the universe] was, according to them, a few crystalline spheres. Today ... it must be acknowledged that there is an infinite number of globes as great as and greater than ours. ... Thus since the proportion of that part of the universe which we know is almost lost in nothingness compared with that which is unknown ... haply it may be that all evils are almost nothingness in comparison with the good things which are in the universe.[23]

From his opening premise, which he believed rested on "infallible proofs" of reason, Leibniz had deduced the master builder of the universe—capable of projecting "an infinitude of possible worlds"; able to compare and evaluate these worlds by cosmic calculus—and then select "the best, since he does nothing without acting in accordance with supreme reason." If this best contained elements that to our limited vision appeared evil, we could rest assured they were the minimum possible and only as much as might be necessitated by the overarching good of God's grand design.[24] Leibniz was adapting rationalist theodicy to the era of scientific revolution. His work won acclaim early in the eighteenth century, especially in Germany. More enduring fame, since then, has stemmed not so much from its cosmic calculus or scientific *mise-en-scène* as from that single phrase, "of possible worlds ... the best." Seized on, brilliantly expropriated by Voltaire, this was the formulation that set up theodicy for ridicule—and immortality—in *Candide*. Even should we fail to recall the *Essays of Theodicy* we are not likely to forget Voltaire's Dr. Pangloss, who in the throes of unbearable suffering finds all for the best in the best of possible worlds.[25] What had made Leibniz's treatise vulnerable to ridicule was that Enlightenment thought was already undermining its initial premise—that of an omnipotent creator known by infallible proofs of reason.[26] And this, at longer range, would bring the project of an orthodox and scientific theodicy to its terminal moraine. The outcome, beginning in the West, will be the famous Era of Secularism, accompanied by an intensifying crisis of belief, to which I turn in the following chapters.

10

Empiricizing the Spiritual

Theodicy is an ancient enterprise. In preceding chapters I sketched its development from Job, approximately fifth century BCE, to Leibniz in the early Enlightenment. The driving force of theodicy has been the problem of evil, which demands to know why evil exists in a world presumably governed by benevolent spiritual beings. This point needs to be made sharply: what drives theodicies are anxieties generated by the recurrent difficulty of responding to the problem of evil. Such anxieties erode religious belief, and this—given the degree to which human consciousness stands mortgaged to spiritual beings—works to disrupt both individual psychic structure and social cohesiveness. Theodicy's mission is universe maintenance, but the mission remains problematic because the universe to be maintained is one grounded on religious belief, which, simply, is *belief*—belief in spiritual beings; whereas theodicy's work, that of justifying God's ways to man, must be carried out in terms accessible to human reason.

What may be accessible to reason changes, of course, with the human condition; we need not expect the social construction of reality to confront hunter-gatherers in the same way it does computer programmers. But changes result also from partial successes of theodicy itself. Persuasive responses to particular aspects of the problem of evil establish themselves as orthodoxies; at first seemingly flawless, they gradually reveal gaps and shortcomings that beget protests (as in the discursive chapters of Job) and these in turn through slow processes of doctrinal drift become integrated into new and more far-reaching orthodoxies. Thus there is a directional movement that reflects cultural evolution and the cumulative tech-

nology that accompanies it—as well as sequences of thought about these phenomena. Science and religion now appear as if harnessed in tandem. Especially in
the West, the spectacular success of empirical science imparted to theodicy the
semblance of an irreversible march toward Truth. That was what Leibniz intended to convey when he faulted Augustine for ignorance of eighteenth-century
astronomy. Telescopes, calculus, universal gravitation—these would be the steps
by which reason approached God. Asserting that whatever world God chose to
create must be the best world possible (and therefore free from *arbitrary*, or
unnecessary, evil), Leibniz brought religious realism to its fullest expression. His
conclusion about God rested on an assumption that human reason would be able
to know the existence and essential characteristics of God. Inherent in Western
theodicy since before Augustine, such an assumption worked to bridge the dis-
juncture between belief itself and thinking rationally, or instrumentally, about
belief. It proposed knowing spiritual beings in the same way that calculus or the
law of universal gravitation are known. Even Locke, who seems so empirically
minded in other lines of thought, insisted on the logical and necessary knowability of God.[1]

During the Enlightenment, rationalism (for which Leibniz was a leading
spokesman) seemed at first to be reinforcing this assumption. Yet also during the
Enlightenment, rational thought (as in Hume's *Dialogues Concerning Natural
Religion* or Kant's more systematic approach in *Critique of Pure Reason*) entered
into alliance with skepticism. Rationalism, pursuing its skeptical mode, exposed
the infallible proofs to criticism. The proofs, as we know, failed to stand, and it
was this disclosure of fallibility that brought Western religion to a crisis in its
efforts to contain the problem of evil. I am not suggesting that theodicy came to
an end at this point, but that it assumed radically different form. The purpose of
the present chapter is to assess the consequences of the alteration. But first, I need
to inquire whether such an assessment will be parochial or global in its reference.

East of Suez, West of the Galapagos

If no religion is exempt from the problem of evil one would expect to find theodicies in every religion; and we have found them abundantly represented in
Western monotheisms. What about the rest of the world? The question proposes an encyclopedic answer, but for present purposes it will be sufficient to focus

on the two great Eastern religions, Hinduism and Buddhism. Here, as with respect to the problem of evil itself, the scholarship is divided. Logically enough, those who found the problem of evil irrelevant to Eastern religions found little in the way of theodicy, whereas those reaching an opposite conclusion discovered a great deal of it. Having already enlisted against the first contingent of scholars, I turn directly to the latter.[2]

Wendy Doniger O'Flaherty, in her study of concepts of evil in Hindu mythology, examined mythic materials that spanned almost three thousand years. Of "Hindu theodicy," she wrote, "... the sheer volume of the material is in itself a significant fact. ... The number of myths that the Hindus told about this subject says, as no brief summary could, how deeply troubled they were by the problem." "When logic fails, and theology fails, irrational resolutions are offered by other modes of religious thought—notably mythology—and these, proving psychologically satisfactory, are acceptable to members of that faith, however inadequate they appear to professional philosophers." O'Flaherty concurred with Max Weber that Eastern religions were no less deeply engaged in the problem of evil than Western monotheisms, and that theodicy was to be found in both sets, though they disagreed in their evaluations of reincarnation and karma.[3] "Hindus often behave as if they did not believe in karma," O'Flaherty wrote, and in her final chapter asserted that "myths of karma were widely rejected in India and hence cannot be regarded as 'dominant,' despite the efforts of Western scholars to force them to play this role." That the accusation against "Western scholars" targeted Weber is indicated by a reference on the following page to his having "praised the theory of karma."[4]

This Weber did indeed do. Standing beyond the end of the long Western tradition of realist religion (and having perhaps abandoned belief himself), Weber deeply admired the rationality with which the doctrines of reincarnation and karma addressed the problem of evil. "*Karma* doctrine," he wrote, sets forth a "strictly rational, ethically determined cosmos ... the most consistent theodicy ever produced by history."[5] Contrary to O'Flaherty's (much later) conclusions, he thought most Hindus believed in karma, that they accepted caste status as irrevocable, dreaded punishment in future incarnations for any dereliction from caste ritual or obligation in the present, and hoped, on the other hand, that karma would reward their adherence to caste ethics by dispatching them to higher social (and spiritual) levels in the next incarnation.[6] Weber seems to have linked his sense of karma's rationality to his perception of its social role. Like all religious ethical systems it would simultaneously support both the egalitarian morality of group membership and the hierarchical obligations of gender and class. In Hindu societies karma functioned to sustain the caste system, which in turn worked to render class domination more complex and impenetrable. Paraphrasing Marx, he wrote that although Hindus of low caste might have little to lose but their chains, they had a "world to win"—and more. They could win both upward mobility and spiritual liberation. They might be reborn as Brahmans, gaining access to heaven and thus become gods—"only not in this life, but in the life of the future after rebirth. ... So long as *karma* doctrine was unshaken," Weber concluded, "revolutionary ideas or progressivism were inconceivable."[7] With expressions such as these Weber was pitching camp next door to religion-as-opiate-of-the-masses. It is well known that he devised other, perhaps subtler, uses of religion, but all of these were sociological and profoundly secular. We catch here the tension between the Age of Secularism in which Weber was immersed and the work of a post-secular scholar like O'Flaherty, who by no means rejects social history and sociology but focuses primarily on the pursuit of spiritual experience. Weber, famous for his analyses of charisma in religious history, could hardly be thought to have denied spiritual experience, but his primary allegiance was to the intellect and its rational constructs; "spirituality" he viewed agnostically as a phenomenon of human behavior.[8]

O'Flaherty's work is more recent by almost a century than Weber's and based on more reliable evidence. She is doubtless right that he exaggerated the ideological role of karma in sustaining the caste system. Yet one need not for this reason abandon his appraisal of "Karma doctrine" as a supremely rational theodicy. We might indeed describe it as the epitome, the "ideal type" of that genre. Buddhism, which in ancient times derived its doctrines (including reincarnation and karma) from the Hindus, languished in India but flourished in other regions where the Hindu caste system never developed. We have thus an opportunity to observe reincarnation and karma in settings largely separated from caste (although by no means separated from class). The current Dalai Lama, to take one example, summarizes these doctrines in Tibetan Buddhism as follows:

> Negative actions always bring about suffering, and positive actions always bring happiness. If you do good you will have happiness; and if you do bad, you yourself will suffer. Our karmic actions follow us from lifetime to lifetime, which explains why some people who indulge constantly in negativity are still

successful on the worldly level or why others who are committed to spiritual practice face myriad difficulties.[9]

"Capital" for the future, however, may be accumulated by avoiding negative acts and cultivating positive ones. Positive acts are those that benefit other "sentient beings," or at least cause them no harm. Karma rewards such acts by granting favorable rebirths. These in turn open opportunities for further positive behavior which point toward still higher incarnations, and eventually, as the Dalai Lama explains, to liberation, to release from suffering, even escape from the great wheel of death and rebirth.[10] But this (leaving out the complexities of Hindu caste) is exactly what Weber described. Weber classified it as theodicy because it attempts to construct a rational justification for the existence of evil (suffering), which appears as an indispensable part in that process of self-education and testing by which human beings who choose to do so can grope toward salvation (nirvana). In my earlier discussion of Augustine and the orthodox reading of Job, I suggested that rational explanations of human suffering—including Western accounts of original sin and redemption as well as the Eastern doctrines of reincarnation and karma—could all be contained within the concepts of free will and testing. Such explanations would be logically similar, although in terms of internal consistency some might be more elegantly rationalized than others. Weber admired "Karma doctrine" for this reason. So also does the Dalai Lama, who advised Western readers that reincarnation and karma could "be understood as cause and effect" just as "physicists understand that for every action, there is an equal and opposite reaction."[11] Suppose now we accept all this—concurring with the Dalai Lama that reincarnation and karma postulate laws as regular as those of physics, and with Weber that the resulting theodicy is "the most consistent ... ever produced by history"—should we then also conclude that these teachings successfully resolve the problem of evil?

We hardly can afford to go that far. The doctrines of reincarnation and karma purport to teach how humans (or some of them) may escape the thralldom of evil, yet they do not touch the more fundamental question of why evil holds the human species in thralldom to begin with. Suffering (evil) is said to be caused by "illusion," which obscures the real emptiness of all material phenomena, including the desperate strivings of one's own consciousness. "This false conception of 'I' arises," according to the Dalai Lama, "because of one's lack of knowledge concerning the mode of existence of things. ... That all objects are empty of inherent

existence is obscured and one conceives things to exist inherently; the strong conception of 'I' derives from this. Therefore, the conception that phenomena inherently exist is the afflicting ignorance that is the ultimate root of all afflictions."[12]
Learning with the eye of spirit how to see illusion (we are told), can open a strait
gate that leads to nirvana, the only possible release from suffering. But if next we
inquire why all first-born sentient beings had to be born into this blind fog of illusion—from which it will cost them eternities of pain to extricate themselves (if
they ever do)—the answers become increasingly obscure. Comparisons to rational laws of physics, equal and opposite reactions, necessities of cause and effect, are
now no longer relevant. "How do self-attachment and so forth arise in such great
force?" asks the Dalai Lama, and answers his question only by saying, "Because
of the beginningless conditioning." *Thus* is the human condition, he is telling us,
because *thus* it always has been. So we circle back on familiar turf, to those same
sorts of circumlocutions that mired Augustine long before the 14th Dalai Lama—
and long after the first Buddha.[13]

Failure and Successes of Theodicy

If Housman's judgment of Milton—"Malt does more than Milton can to justify
God's ways to man"—is correct (as I suppose it is) then the same verdict must be
extended to all who labored in the same vineyard.[14] This will include Job's elo-
quent "friends" as well as the ancient architects of karma doctrine; it includes
Augustine, Dante, Leibniz, and a host of others whose poetry and metaphysics,
brilliant and beautiful as some of them certainly are, never broke free from the
metaphysical gaps and muddy speculations that have characterized theodicy
since its beginnings. One cannot conclude, however, that theodicy proved totally
unsuccessful. On the contrary, religion, which has been supremely successful,
could hardly have reached its present universality of acceptance had it not been
for theodicy.

Attacking the problem of evil, theodicies have targeted what was most troublesome for believers in each milieu of religious development. Thus karma
amended the arbitrariness of nature and death by promising impeccably fair treatment to all "sentient beings." In the West, it was the absence of such fairness that
inspired Job's protests, and these in turn pointed toward a conclusion that any
moral relation between the God of Western monotheism and his creatures would

be untenable except on the supposition of life after death (a supposition at which the Eastern architects of reincarnation and karma had already arrived). Augustine, systematizing Christianity a thousand years later, found this supposition established as revealed truth. Thence he could argue that God's plan required suffering in order both to prepare worthy souls for salvation and cull out those unworthy of being saved. Although neither of these doctrinal innovations disposed of the problem of evil, one offered a wedge of hope against evil's most grievous manifestation (death), and the two taken together corrected inconsistencies in earlier doctrine, as well as providing a marvelously effective instrument for enforcing social (and class) morality.[15]

Utilitarian arguments of this type can be constructed for most of the changes introduced into orthodox beliefs by that radical branch of theodicy whose Western prototype would be the Promethean reading of Job. Cumulatively, their effect was to make religion more rewarding to believers by improving its psychological fit, ironing out cognitive dissonances, and integrating it functionally into the social order.[16] At this level, it may be tempting to read progress into theodicy, seeing it as moving toward cosmic understanding in lockstep with science (Leibniz), or toward a terrestrial millennium in step with republican virtue (Milton), or both. Before committing ourselves to such benign interpretations, however, it should be noted that theodicy's discernible movement has often been circular rather than directional. It often consisted, that is, in shuttling back and forth between opposite and equally unattractive alternatives. Something like this, I think, is at work in the back-and-forth between gods with warm, tangible bodies immanent in nature and remote creator gods standing outside nature. Nature in most mythologies (and most religious systems) is both matrix and charnel house. But gods who are themselves part of nature (as I have more than once pointed out in preceding chapters) are unlikely to be reliable defenders of mortal beings against nature, whereas those standing outside nature may seem no less indifferent to mortal aspirations than nature itself. To vacillate between these alternatives perhaps conveys the semblance of escaping both, but contributes little to any final disposition of the problem of evil.[17]

Theodicy's successes, then, have been not final but intermediate. At the intermediate level they are eminently rational. Theodicy, East and West, comprises a process of rationalization. If we follow Weber, we will rate karma as the most rational of all. But Augustine, when he interpreted the fall of Rome as a punishment and test for Christians, marshaled elaborately reasoned accounts of humility deformed by pride, of chaste matrons whose own lust collaborated in the sexual surrenders forcefully imposed on them. So Dante, despite his conviction that poetry conveyed the glory of God more persuasively than scholastic discourse, nonetheless spared no pains of rational explanation to show why this was so, and relied for his underlying logic on Aquinas, the prince of rationalists. And Milton, whose reworking of Genesis rides on a sequence of stunning visual images, described his project as an "argument" that would make God's ways seem just and reasonable.[18] Nor was the rationality of these theodicists unrelated to their real world. Reincarnation and karma project to cosmic scale the working model of a just society. Milton's grandest rhetoric in *Paradise Lost* rubbed elbows with his own actions during the Puritan Revolution and Commonwealth. The modeling of heaven, hell, and purgatory by Dante on his native city of Florence has been famous among critics (and historians) for centuries. Augustine, working from observations of contemporary morals and manners that included his own immersion in them, developed psychological explanations for human behavior that seem scarcely less rational and empirical than those of modern clinical therapists.

The point I am getting at is that a different kind of epistemology informs the defenses and rationalizations of theodicy from that which governed the original discovery of spiritual beings. Ancient though theodicy may be, the discovery of spiritual beings was older. It coincided with the crisis of consciousness, marking the passage from biology to culture. We learn of it through tradition and myth, through scriptures that record divine messages to sacred recipients. We learn of it from the reported journeys of mystics into a world beyond our own. Theodicy, on the other hand, defending the reputations of already discovered spiritual beings, has worked in the materials of cumulative social experience out of which stem also technology and science.[19]

Kant and the (Western) Credibility Crisis

The scientific revolution of our own era had its first breakthroughs in western Europe. I do not believe this was because Western minds were more inclined to rational thought than minds of other regions. In any case, the conspicuous rationality of karma (by contrast, say, to that of original sin) would warn against such an assumption. Science depends on rational thought, but depends especially on the application of thought to empirical observation, and even more especially to observations that link into cause-and-effect spirals with technological development. The West in respect to science and technology lagged behind both China and the Middle East until about 1200—that is, till only two or three hundred years before the beginning of our so-called modern era. Empirical science then gave to Europe a commanding lead in industrial technology over all other regions of the world. This differential can be attributed in part to openings and limitations imposed on cultural innovation by the physical realities of geography and geology. As to the scientific revolution itself, its origins have been explored in a rich historical literature; my purpose in commenting on the regional distribution of rational thought is simply to preclude the sorts of causal assumptions often conveyed by such phrases as "the scientific mind" of the West or the "spirituality" of Eastern belief systems.[20]

Since technology and science pursue the same sorts of instrumental thought that also guide theodicy, it had seemed reasonable (and dutiful) to Western rationalists like Leibniz to complete their theodistic projects by grounding them in rational and scientific validations of religion. The failure of these projects discredited the cause of orthodox theodicy. The initiative then passed to political rebels like Milton, to Promethean romantics like Blake or Shelley and Byron, to skeptics like Hume and Kant. They set the moods that would dominate the Age of Secularism.[21] When Hume wrote his definition of the problem of evil (quoted at the opening of chapter 7), he was not laying the groundwork for some new solution to that problem; on the contrary, he was bringing religion itself under skeptical attack. The secular era—starting from the Enlightenment and stretching into the post–Second World War decades of the twentieth century—reduced religious belief to what was probably its lowest ebb since the original encounter with spiritual beings. Kant recalled that he had been waked from the slumber of more or less orthodox faith by reading Hume. This led to reexamination of the so-called rational proofs (upon which Leibniz, among many others, had grounded his theodicy), and spurred Kant to a critique more thorough-going and systematic even than Hume's.[22]

Yet Kant remained less a skeptic and far more religious than Hume. Indeed, his entire life's work might be described as theodicy. Combining Leibnizean rationalism with a skepticism in part derived from Hume, he hoped to reestablish religion at a height beyond reach of skeptical attack. Deconstruction of the rational proofs was a necessary first step because their vulnerability made reli-

gion itself vulnerable—so long as religion depended on them. Kant in his great
critiques severed religion from the rational proofs, making it depend instead on
moral attributes presumably inexplicable except as the gift of benevolent spiritual beings. The core of religious belief would then be a recognition of "all [moral]
duties as divine commands." Pursuit of duty, however, remains problematical.
"We can already foresee," Kant wrote, "that this duty will require the presuppo-
sition of another idea, namely, that of a higher moral Being through whose universal dispensation the forces of separate individuals, insufficient in themselves,
are united to a common end." As to moral law, "each individual can know of himself, through his own reason, the will of God which lies at the basis of his religion. ... The concept of a divine will, determined according to pure moral laws
alone, allows us to think of only *one* religion which is purely moral, as it did of
only *one* God."

The shift from intellectual to moral grounding led Kant to reexamine the limitations of theodicy. In an essay written near the end of his life (inspired, one
might suppose, by rereading Job), he focused on the ambiguous conclusion of
Job in which God, after his thunderous rebuttal, ends by rewarding and rehabili-
tating him. Kant thought this must for Job have been a chillingly unsatisfactory
outcome, since God not only ignored his questions, but at the end simply crushed
him into acquiescence. Faith capable of surviving "such a vexing resolution of
[the believer's] doubts ..." Kant concluded, could exist only "in the soul of a
man who, in the midst of his strongest doubts, could yet say: 'Till I die I will not
remove mine integrity from me, etc.' For with this disposition he proved that he
did not found his morality on faith, but his faith on morality: ... the kind of faith
that founds not a religion of supplication, but a religion of good life conduct."
Kant is attributing to Job an absolute acceptance of moral obligation, based not
on belief, as in standard religious accounts of moral behavior; on the contrary,
belief now becomes the necessary consequence "of his morality." Gone are those
"infallible proofs" from which Leibniz deduced God's existence; divinity itself
will now be only a probability—a speculation—induced, or inferred, from the evidence of morality.

So how is morality known? It is known in two ways: introspectively, by finding
its laws in one's own consciousness; and objectively, by observing those laws in the
behavior of other human beings. Both ranges of observations might be thought of
as empirical. Taking Job as an ideal type for his theory, Kant can then assert,
"Theodicy, as has been shown here, does not have as much to do with a task in the

interest of science as, rather, with a matter of faith." This sentence, which opens the "Concluding Remark" of Kant's essay, signals a crucial shift of meaning, since theodicies had been deeply concerned with science; but those sorts of theodicies, Kant now warns, can never succeed. Must we give up religion because of theodicy's failure? Instead, having altered the meaning of the term, Kant sends theodicy on a new mission. This will be to validate faith through the evidence of human morality, which alone (as he had concluded earlier) bears unimpeachable witness to the divine presence.[23] The problem of evil (if I may recycle a well-worn phrase) has here been stood on its head. In its original form it could be stated as follows: We know (or wish to know) the existence of God but it is difficult (or impossible) to believe in a God who 1) tolerates evil; or 2) is too weak to cope with evil. In the Kantian reformulation, it goes something like this: We know (or infer) the existence of God from the empirical observation of goodness (morality) in the human heart, since that would be inexplicable unless a benevolent God placed it there. To know (or infer) God, therefore, is to be assured of God's goodness.

Theodicy to Fideism

Kant's essay, while not signaling the end of theodicy, acknowledged the failure of theodicies modeled on empirical science. For Western religions this marked a strategic defeat which opened the gates to barbarians and secularizers. Within the span of a single lifetime defenders of the faith would be reduced to nostalgic, self-pitying lamentions like those of John Henry Newman. "But we do not have 'Right Reason,'" Newman wrote in 1864, "... we have fallen, partial, corrupt reason with its all dissolving skepticism of the intellect. ... What force can be a breakwater against the deluge?"[24] Kant, who had permitted himself not much in the way of nostalgia or self-pity, became after his death an emblem of Christian faith. His influence was powerful both in the transcendental movement that dominated Protestant literary culture in England and North America during the middle years of the nineteenth century, and in that romantic glorification of faith associated with the sermons and lectures of Friedrich Schleiermacher. Although separated by time and geography, these two movements shared certain distinctive features. Both perceived nature's middle ground as significant not for itself, but as a screen of shadows and illusions that permitted fragmentary glimpses into the vast transcendent reality beyond.

If the red slayer thinks he slays,
    Or if the slain thinks he is slain,
They know not well the subtle ways
    I keep —

The lines are from "Brahma," written in 1857 by Ralph Waldo Emerson, one of the first Americans to read Darwin.[25] On the other hand, Schleiermacher in 1799 (four years before Emerson's birth) was teaching that "every finite thing ... is a sign of the Infinite," and discussing nonpersonal immortality in terms suggestive of some familiarity with Brahmanism. He and Emerson would have had no difficulty understanding each other across the generational gap.[25]

Lines of communication for the Anglo-American connection traveled from Germany by way of enthusiasts like the English poet Samuel Taylor Coleridge to the Romantic set in England, then through Thomas Carlyle and transatlantic voyagers such as Emerson across the ocean to Transcendentalists in America. Coleridge, younger by half a century than Kant, was fluent in German and lived and studied in Germany during the 1790s when Kant was at the pinnacle of fame. As portrayed in Rene Wellek's book, *Kant in England*, Coleridge appears "more religious" than Kant, often impatient of Kant's cautious metaphysics; always hungry for "a breakdown of human Intelligence in order to substitute pure Faith."[26] Schleiermacher's connection parallels that of Coleridge. Forty years younger than Kant, he remained openly contemptuous of metaphysics. What connects him to Kant was that both were struggling to ground faith in "empirical" observations of subjective experience. "Everything *experiential* is supra-rational," Schleiermacher had written. "There is an inner experience to which [religious beliefs] may all be traced; they rest upon a given; and apart from this they could not have arisen, by deduction or synthesis, from universally recognized and communicable propositions." [27] No less a child of the Enlightenment than Kant, Schleiermacher had suffered his own crisis of belief followed by some sort of reconversion. This did not mean that he dissented from Kant's famous deconstruction of the rational proofs, but rather that he considered such labors an exercise in redundancy. Religion was not known (or *un*known) by proofs; it could only be *experienced*. To have religious experience was to realize absolute dependency on God. "Our point," Schleiermacher declared, "... is that these proofs can never be a component part of the system of doctrine; for that is only for those who have the inner certainty of God, as we have already described it, and of that they can be directly conscious at every moment."[28]

Theodicy at this extreme may accurately be termed *fideism*, meaning a faith that believes itself validated by the intensity of inner belief.[29] Fideism stands in close proximity to what might be called *neo-empiricism*, a stance claiming for subjective inner experience the same validity that science attributes to objective empirical observation. In the long historical connection, both fideism and neo-empiricism mark a reaching back to that earliest moment of religious belief—the crisis of consciousness—in which evil (not the "problem of evil" but evil itself) was constrained by the discovery (or invention) of spiritual beings. More ruthless than Kant in jettisoning intellectualism, Schleiermacher (like transcendentalists in England and America) pointed to sanctuaries and retreats that would remain open for religious believers through the long winter that followed. The secular winter lasted a hundred and fifty years. After the Second World War these same retreats and sanctuaries would become marshaling grounds for counterattacks against secularism. That would be exactly the time for rediscovering Schleiermacher, whom we will meet again, briefly; but the next chapter is about secularism. Focused on the intellectual cutting edge of secularism, it examines the materialist critique of religion carried in the nineteenth and early twentieth centuries mainly by followers and fellow travelers of Marx and Engels and suggests that failure of that critique helped to open the way for the global resurgence of religious faith that marked the last half of the twentieth century.

11

Marxism and the Failed Critique of Religion

When Karl Marx chose for his doctoral thesis a comparison of two classical materialists, Democritus and Epicurus, he was declaring his independence of Hegelian idealism. And lest there be any doubt as to his views on religion, he included in his 1841 foreword a romantic invocation of Prometheus:

> Philosophy makes no secret of it. Prometheus' admission: "In sooth all gods I
> hate" [Aeschylus, *Prometheus Unbound*] is its own admission, its own motto
> against all gods, heavenly and earthly, who do not acknowledge the conscious-
> ness of man as the supreme deity. ... Prometheus is the noblest of saints and
> martyrs in the calendar of philosophy.

[handwritten margin note: Criticism and not discover is what marks Marxism with + Thus is its weakness]

Three years later, in a critical essay on Hegel, Marx wrote that criticism of religion "is the premise of all criticism," and went on to characterize religion as "the opium of the people." All this was twenty years before the first volume of *Das Kapital* in 1867 and four years before Marx and Friedrich Engels, now partners, issued their famous challenge in the *Communist Manifesto*: "The proletarians have nothing to lose but their chains. ... Workingmen of all countries, unite!" The quotations and titles are well-known; what is important here is their chronology. Criticism of religion preceded both the call for proletarian revolt and the analysis of industrial capitalism. This order of priority conveyed a sense that socialist theory as developed by Marx and Engels began from, and remained deeply grounded in, the rejection of religion. If such were the case, one would expect to find religion clearly defined and its negation located within the "dialectic" of class conflict. That indeed has been a widely held assumption, but almost certainly mistaken.[1] The fact is that religion is not clearly defined in Marxist writings nor its historical origin adequately accounted for. A linkage between disbelief and working-class revolution is hinted at but not spelled out. Religion is linked negatively to ideology—the latter generally understood as "false consciousness" promoted by the ruling class—but whether religion simply forms part of ideology, or necessarily existed prior to it, remains unexplained.[2] This lack of precision at the cutting edge of secular thought, as I will try to show, undermined the prevailing secularism of the "modern era," thus clearing the way for the resurgence of religion that came after the Second World War.

The Break from Hegelian Idealism

Marx and Engels tell us their break from Hegelian idealism—and presumably from religion as well—was inspired by Ludwig Feuerbach's *Essence of Christianity* (1841). Feuerbach had proposed a materialist account of religion, to the effect that humans in primeval times imagined gods in their own image, then projected and worshipped those same gods; as they came to realize the gods were reflections of themselves, they would gradually recognize the divine essence of their humanity. Marx and Engels adopted a similarly "materialist" (but no less ambiguous) formulation. Was this real or metaphorical? Or somewhere in between? The Prometheus of Marx's doctoral thesis appears profoundly Feuerbachian, as does the fuzziness of the boundary drawn there between human and divine. Well versed though he was in Greek mythology—knowing that Prometheus, born of gods and titans, had to be a god—Marx nonetheless assigned him human status: "noblest of saints and martyrs in the calendar of philosophy." Whence came this divine aspiration attributed to the human species? Was it inherent in the cosmos? Had Feuerbach simply substituted a Spinozean pantheism for Christianity's orthodox theism? And did Marx and Engels concur? They soon distanced themselves from Feuerbach, yet they would not hesitate to impose on proletarians the god-like tasks of Prometheus.[3]

Despite these ambivalences of concept and explanation, Marx and Engels remained nonbelievers and foes of institutionalized religion. This heritage from the Left Enlightenment they powerfully transmitted to their followers thus helping to ensure that through the next century and a half Marxist parties would serve as prime targets for religion's multitudinous defenders. At the same time—more than any other nineteenth-century tendency of radical anti-capitalism—Marxism remained open to labor unionism and working-class politics. Marxist activists proved influential leaders in both these enterprises. It may not be irrelevant, therefore, to ask how successful they were in pursuing the party line on religion and whether it proved an asset or hindrance in organizing workers, nor to inquire why Marx and Engels themselves had chosen to make criticism of religion the "premise" for their project in revolutionary political economy. Such questions may seem more pertinent to our own times than to those in which Marx and Engels actually lived. Any investigation of their stance toward religion must begin by noting that their careers fell within the opening century of the Age of Secularism. *Non*belief, for the first time in more than fifteen hundred years was becoming intellectually—even to some extent socially—tolerable.

Orthodox religionists, Protestant or Catholic, still controlled most major institutions such as city and state governments and universities throughout western Europe, yet they faced increasingly articulate resistance from educated opponents among the upper classes. Thus, for example, when John Stuart Mill in England declared that the "whole of the prevalent metaphysics of the present century" constitutes a "tissue of suborned evidence in favor of religion," he was saying approximately what Marx and Engels were saying, and targeting the same German idealist metaphysics they were rebelling against.[4] While for Mill the main enemy was Kant, it was of course Hegel for Marx and Engels. Different though the systems of these philosophers were, it would not be inaccurate to describe both as idealist constructions designed to protect religion. To protect it against what? Against the oncoming Era of Secularism: against the rise of skeptical rationalism; against cumulative disillusionments attached to the memory of religious wars that had raged across Europe for almost two hundred years; against the encroachments of empirical science into orthodox belief. Marx and Engels in all these controversial areas stood on solid ground to the extent that their peers in class status and education were likely to remain tolerant toward criticisms of religion that many of them already shared.[5] Yet obviously no such immunity would attach to radical criticisms of class hierarchy.

From Feuerbach to the Manifesto

The Hegelian dialectic in a broad sense had idealized the cosmos as an ongoing spiritual process. More narrowly, that portion of it that paralleled human history

could be analogized to Christian doctrine. God's decision to create a world populated by creatures (including humans) established the antithesis. Conflict stemmed
from the willed act of human creatures to use their God-given liberty for rebellion
against the creator. Resolution, after many turns of the dialectic, must await the
advent of Christ, begotten out of mortal flesh by divine spirit, and thus providing the
synthesis within which the opposites—mortal and divine, creator and created—will
at last be rejoined. According to the famous legend, Marx had arrived at his class
interpretation of human history by an intellectual *tour de force*, that is, by translating
Hegel's idealist dialectic into a materialist one. Thus, instead of pushing the narrative through a sequence of metaphysical abstractions, the dialectic would now be
made to convey human class struggles in the language of historical realism.

A full-dress presentation of the materialist dialectic occurs in the *Communist
Manifesto* (1848). There are some baffling conceptual problems about this transformation, of which I will mention (at this point) only one. If history comprises a series
of struggles in which exploited (therefore antithetical) classes overpower one another to establish each in turn its own dominance, there would seem no possible escape
from this repetition unless a class formation occurred that somehow had the power
(or lack of power!) to break out of the circle. Recalling the original model—that is,
the Hegelian dialectic that symbolically enacted the Christian story—it is obvious
the crucial role belonged to Christ, who by his sacrificial death terminates the long
chain of contradictions between creator and created. Yet when the idealist dialectic
is turned upside down and all the actors become "real, active men, as they are conditioned by a definite development of their productive forces," what sort of class formation could be expected to play a comparable role? "The idea—fundamental for
Marx from then on," writes the Marxist historian, Eric Hobsbawm, "that the proletariat was a class which could not liberate itself without thereby liberating society as
a whole, first appears as 'a philosophical deduction rather than a product of observation.' … [Thus] 'the proletariat makes its first appearance in Marx's writings as
the social force needed to realize the aims of German philosophy.'" Needed, that is,
to materialize the idealized figure of Prometheus.[6]

Did Hobsbawm say *deduction*? He did. Marx and Engels always insisted on
their socialist theory as *scientific*, rather than Christian or utopian. Science, however (at least as understood in the nineteenth century), rests not on deduction
from alleged universals, but *inductions* from empirical observation. Engels, in
The Condition of the English Working Class In England (1845), had provided an
empirical and shattering portrayal of the beginnings of capitalist manufacturing.

His work undoubtedly contributed to the predictive accuracy of *Capital,* on which the two authors later collaborated, yet hardly offers much evidence for the Promethean (or Christ-like) role assigned to proletarians in *The Communist Manifesto.* "A horde of ragged women and children swarm about here, as filthy as the swine that thrive upon the garbage heaps," Engels wrote, describing a typical industrial slum. "The race that lives in these ruinous cottages ... must really have reached the lowest stage of humanity. ... The neglect to which the great mass of workingmen's children are condemned ... brings the enfeeblement of the whole race. ... Liquor is almost their only source of pleasure. ... As inevitably as a great number of working men fall prey to drink, just so inevitably does it manifest its ruinous influence upon the body and mind of its victims."

How could a "race" so reduced in vital energy and self-esteem find courage to break free from religious superstition and raise the banner of revolt? Engels, no less an enthusiast than Marx, did his best to discover empirical answers to this question. "Faulty education," he speculated, "saves [the new proletarian] from religious prepossessions, he ... knows nothing of the fanaticism that holds the bourgeoisie bound. ..." For Engels, raised in a hardshell Protestant milieu, any estrangement from religion, even if arrived at by default, was a positive factor; and he found hope also in the first flickerings of class consciousness. "The English workingman who can scarcely read and still less write, nevertheless knows very well where his own interest and that of the nation lies." "They begin to perceive that, though feeble as individuals, they form a power united. ... The consciousness of oppression awakens ... the workers attain social and political importance." Entries such as these remain few in number, cautious and tentative in tone, whereas the overwhelming thrust of Engel's book is on despair and degradation—disease, malnutrition, wretchedness of the workers, suffering and death of their women and children.[7] Yet only three years later, when these same proletarians reappear in the *Communist Manifesto*, they have taken a new lease on life. A key passage describing their "condition"—and announcing their historic mission—runs as follows:

Modern industrial labor, modern subjection to capital, the same in England as in France, in America as in Germany, has stripped him [the proletarian] of every trace of national character. Law, morality, religion, are to him so many bourgeois prejudices, behind which lurk in ambush just as many bourgeois interests. ... All previous historical movements were movements of minorities. ... The proletarian movement is the self-conscious, independent movement of the immense majority. ... The proletariat, the lowest stratum of our present society, cannot stir, cannot raise itself up, without the whole superincumbent strata of official society being sprung into the air.

What a contrast! The industrial worker, reborn, transcends not only bourgeois nationalism, but bourgeois law, morality, religion as well, and not by default but as a result of purposeful thought. Deconstructing the mysteries of ideology, the proletarian energizes "the immense majority" of humankind (there is no empirical evidence whatever in Engels' book to support this assertion) whose fate now rests on the integrity of working-class consciousness. Here is a transformation comparable to the last movement of Beethoven's Ninth Symphony, and we need to understand they share some of the same ingredients. Marxist theory's worldwide impact would be inconceivable without the Promethean hero, who becomes a teacher, first of other segments of the working class, then of the human species at large.[8]

Dialectics of the Welfare State

Two mistakes of Marx and Engels in the 1840s were their anticipation of immediate revolution and their belief that proletarians must necessarily reject religion. On both points, Engels had pushed beyond what his observations of English working-class life could sustain, and Marx went along with this. Together, they developed a historical argument building upward from peasant revolts in the seventeenth century, through the great revolutions of the eighteenth and Chartism in the nineteenth, all anchored within real (empirical) history, but then leaping to an imagined future insurrection led by England's proletarians that would engulf the nations of the world. Revolution, Engels wrote in 1845, soon "must break out ... in comparison with which the French Revolution ... will prove to have been child's play." They supported the revolutions of 1848 (Engels in military action in the Rhineland), but viewed these as bourgeois and constitutionalist—merely preliminary to the proletarian insurrection they were predicting. Many years later, blaming himself for their failed prophecy, Engels ascribed it to "youthful ardor." I am concerned here with Marxism itself, not with apportioning credits and demerits between its founders. I suppose Marx to have been no less youthfully ardent than Engels; they were barely two years apart in age; both were gripped by Promethean visions that perhaps led them to *transcend*—or at least go beyond—what the empirical evidence warranted.[9]

Moreover, they were hampered by misperceptions inherent in their class background, especially with respect to religion. Secularism, as I noted earlier, had, by the early nineteenth century, become tolerable in educated middle-class circles. But this was not the case for lower-class cultures. Engels acknowledged that most of what he knew about religion in the mill towns came from reports of Anglican or Unitarian investigative committees. Anglicans were Conservative, Unitarians Liberal, each had their own agendas to push. Both would be suspicious of Methodist chapels and hostile to radical sectaries such as those described by E. P. Thompson, or, for an earlier period, Christopher Hill. The mills were already recruiting Irish immigrants; some doubtless brought their Catholic faith, which to Anglicans as well as Unitarians would seem worse than none at all. I suspect that Engels, with respect to religion, missed a good deal of what was going on around him in Manchester and Birmingham.[10] So, for a variety of reasons, Marx and Engels were mistaken both in their prediction of revolution and their belief that industrial workers would reject religion. The latter especially seemed crucial to them during the 1840s because they believed loss of religion necessary to that total alienation from bourgeois values that they expected would launch the proletarians into revolutionary orbit.

Nonoccurrence of the revolution determined the political landscape within which Marxism and religious faith pursued their complex relationships through the nineteenth and early twentieth centuries. Since the political economy of that landscape has already been thoroughly mapped, I will simply note several of its main features and set them aside for reference. Industrial capitalism burgeoned in western Europe and North America. So also did the industrial working class. Because industrialists required some degree of willing cooperation from their work force, a symbiotic relationship which we now call welfare-state capitalism developed between the two. The keynote of welfare states was industrial growth. The bigger the pie the larger its individual slices. Growth made possible the maintenance—sometimes even improvement—of working-class living standards without requiring changes in the hierarchical structure of society. Thus it mitigated class conflict and provided a buffer against revolution.[11] Welfare states faced outward. Both sets of partners (capital and labor) strove to upgrade the enterprise at the expense of other nations, including similarly structured welfare states. We know by hindsight that world war would be the eventual outcome, but such grim scenarios were not yet readily visible during the nineteenth and early twentieth centuries. Labor radicalism, inside each welfare state, shorn of revolution, produced a cadre of radical workers together with a pseudo-middle class of trade union officials and social democratic politicians who served their constituents as spokesmen and mediators. Continuing across successive life spans, these circumstances generated a class consciousness that was unique to the labor force of industrial capitalism. The more diligently each worker strove to keep self, family (and party comrades) alive, the more invincible became those institutions they hoped eventually to abolish. One might describe this as the "dialectic of the welfare state."[12]

Outwardly functioning as partnerships, welfare states worked inwardly as controlled arenas of class conflict. Although the conflict was basically that of labor against capital, both sets of contestants (labor especially) remained internally divided. A Weberian image of this apparatus would look like a seesaw with the socialist workers on one end and religious workers at the other. The capitalist-controlled government in the middle gives occasional nudges this way or that for fine tuning. We are now deep into the Era of Secularism, which as we know, penetrated working classes less than other levels of society. Details differ from nation to nation and time to time, but the seesaw image remains approximately accurate, I think, for welfare states throughout the Western world. The social relationships it portrays entail several important corollaries. Based in working-class communities more religious than the society at large, Marxist activists often found themselves targeted for teaching disbelief and corrupting Christian morals. Already known as members of a movement that denied religion, they would be hampered in defending themselves. Their logical counter-strategy would involve appeals to class solidarity combined with accusations that the Church—whatever branch happened to be dominant in that particular community—had betrayed its working-class constituency by supporting the capitalist employers. Such indictments, containing enough empirical reality to make them persuasive, nonetheless introduced subtle shifts in the original Marxist stance on religion—shifts, that is, from critiques of religion itself to forms of anticlericalism that often seemed more concerned with purifying the church than criticizing religion.

Prodigal Sheep and Spiritual Shepherds

It is time now to wrap up these speculative abstractions, which I will try to do by means of a single, vividly remembered episode. When I was at sea during the

Second World War I sometimes wrote articles for the Communist magazine *New Masses*, describing conditions in Atlantic and Mediterranean ports I visited. I knew several of the editors and when I was in New York, "on the beach," they would take me to lunch in lieu of payment for the articles. The *New Masses* had its office in the famous old loft building on 12th or 13th Street, east of Broadway, that also housed the Communist Party and *Daily Worker*. Even in those days a guard at the elevator gate checked your business and frisked you for concealed weapons. As we waited, my editor introduced me to the man ahead of us, who turned out to be Louis Budenz, chief editor of the *Daily Worker*. I had not met Budenz and never saw him again, but I see him there yet, a stocky, tired-looking middle-aged man in his not-very-new overcoat (New York can be bitterly cold in February) waiting his turn for the Up elevator.

Born in the 1890s in Indianapolis to a staunchly Catholic, marginally middle-class family, Budenz, after working for the Catholic Young Men's Institute, moved leftward, serving as a state manager in LaFollette's 1924 presidential campaign, and with the onset of the Depression threw himself into the movement for industrial unionism where he became a labor journalist as well as a courageous and often-jailed strike leader. Joining the Communist Party in 1935, Budenz edited a party paper in Chicago, then went on to the top post at the *Daily Worker*. Approximately at the time I met him, he had determined to return to the faith of his childhood. He was laying plans with Bishop Fulton J. Sheen, the celebrated Catholic headhunter and savior of souls, to conduct this transformation in a manner that would prove as damaging as possible to the Communist Party in which, meanwhile, Budenz continued to function as a leading member. "At the *Daily Worker*," he recalled, "I criticized copy, made proposals and revisions on pieces to back the [party] line—and fingered a rosary in my pocket as I did so."[13]

Bishop Sheen was well connected for the public relations of soul-saving, his other most newsworthy conquest being Clare Booth Luce, wife of Henry Luce, who in turn was CEO of *Time-Life* and self-styled inventor of the term, "the American Century." Sheen arranged for Budenz and his till-then common-law wife to be properly united in a "secret" ceremony at St. Patrick's Cathedral (leaked to the press ahead of time). Budenz then issued a statement featured by newspapers and radio stations all over the Western world in which he announced that "by God's grace" he had returned "fully to the faith of my fathers," and ended by declaring that Communism and Catholicism were irreconcilable. "Communism … is in unending conflict with religion and true freedom." The date was October

1945. The United Nations had concluded its founding convention at San Francisco three months earlier. Joining the graduate faculty at Fordham in 1946, Budenz became virtually a full-time consultant to the FBI and various congressional un-American activities committees. According to Harvey Klehr's biographical sketch in *American National Biography*, he testified in at least sixty trials, hearings, and deportation cases and appeared as government witness in the first Communist Party Smith Act trial.[14]

The most decisive of his encounters with Bishop Sheen, Budenz wrote in his autobiography, occurred nine years before he reached his own decision to return to Catholicism. During the first year of the Communist Party's so-called Popular Front period (1937), Budenz, having just taken over the *Daily Worker* editorship, had opened a public debate with Sheen. The debate began with hostile declarations on both sides, but Budenz, pursuing the conciliatory line of the Popular Front, hoped it might move to more harmonious levels. When Sheen suggested they meet for lunch, Budenz accepted, and "in an obscure corner" of a Midtown hotel grill room the two men talked "for an hour in earnest, quiet tones." "He was not disposed to contradict me in our face-to-face discussion," Budenz recalled of their conversation. "What he did, instead, took me totally by surprise."

> Monsignor bent forward and exclaimed: "Let us now talk of the Blessed Virgin!" For those who are beyond the bounds of belief, this incident will have little significance. They will not comprehend what went on in my soul at those words. ... "Very well," I said simply to Monsignor. He saw that I was deeply moved. And so he spoke of the Mother of God.[15]

Whether or not one concurs with Budenz's view of who the good guys and bad guys in this narrative are, there is no doubt the story itself conveys the enormous influence of religion in governing human behavior, even (or especially) under circumstances of intense conflict. How can we explain this power?

Suppose we begin (as Marx did with Hegel) by turning the Budenz episode upside down. We can call it a thought experiment. Not long before he joined the Communist Party, Budenz had been a strike leader at Auto-Lite in Toledo, Ohio. The issue was industrial unionism. Auto-Lite's management brought in the National Guard, which shot several striking workers, killing two. Now we might imagine (and this is not difficult!) that one of the CEOs at Auto-Lite arranged a

clandestine meeting with Budenz and offered him a faculty appointment at
Fordham if he would denounce other union leaders as Communist dupes and tes-
tify against them on charges of incitement to violence. Budenz asks for a day to
think this over. He then consults his spiritual adviser. The adviser, however, is not
Fulton J. Sheen but someone more like Dorothy Day, for example, of the *Catholic
Worker*. "Let us talk now about the Virgin Mary," says the adviser. "Mary, Mother
of God, gave her son to die on the cross for liberation of the world's oppressed
and downtrodden masses. How could you even think of betraying her trust by
selling out the workers who rely on you?"[16]

The Problem of Liberation Theology

Is such a scenario conceivable? It must have been conceivable to Marx and
Engels. They both portrayed early Christianity as driven by the desperation of
enslaved and exploited populations in the Roman empire; Engels represented the
Hussites and Anabaptists as religiously inspired rebels fighting to liberate peas-
ants from feudalism. Why might not religion then inspire working-class rebels
against industrial capitalism? The fact is it has done so—a dramatic (and recent)
example being that of liberation theology in Latin America.[17] While it is true that
most such movements were crushed by their respective ruling classes and dominant clergies, these outcomes could be explained by pointing out that wherever
religion became institutionalized, it generated privileged clerical hierarchies that
merged into the existing ruling class. Marx and Engels usually (but not always)
characterized religion as reactionary because it was prone to being captured by
ruling-class ideologies. Ideology they treated invidiously, as obscurantism intended to conceal class exploitation. They sometimes spoke of religion and ideology
as identical or of the one (religion) as contained within the other. They even suggested that religion had been invented for ideological purposes.[18]

All this made for an empirically based and politically powerful explanatory
system, yet contained two big difficulties. The first was the absence of any satisfactory way of accounting for instances (acknowledged by Marx and Engels
both), when religion actually functioned as a liberating rather than repressive
force. The second difficulty is more complicated, but takes us to the heart of the
matter. Ideological explanations necessarily locate religion's starting point *late* in
human culture since they begin by attaching, or equating, religion to ideology.

Ideology, however—understood as a rationalization, and camouflage, for class and gender exploitation—could hardly have originated before the division of labor. But that left dangling the question of whether religion itself existed prior to class society. If so, it could not be explained as an ideological construct, and its existence would precede, perhaps even run separately from, the dialectic of class struggle that for Marxist theory provides the motive force of social development. "The history of all past society has consisted in the development of class antagonisms," Marx and Engels wrote in the *Communist Manifesto*, "... whatever form they may have taken, one fact is common to all past ages, viz., the exploitation of one part of society by the other." Was religion, then, moving on a track separate from the rest of human history? But that would not be an attractive alternative for nonbelievers, because it came perilously close to concurring with an idealist notion of religion.[19]

Given the gift of hindsight, it is not difficult to specify what they needed at this juncture. They needed a *secular* (materialist) account of the origin of religion separate from the origin of ideology. This would allow religion to function (later on) as the keystone of ruling-class ideology, yet not preclude explaining its liberationist phases by reference to particular historical circumstances (such as colonial regimes, for example, or the importation of slaves, or "guest" workers). At the same time, and perhaps more importantly, it would situate religion in the earliest stages of human development, before division of labor and the advent of class society. Ludwig Feuerbach, whose *Essence of Christianity* had impressed Marx and Engels when they were breaking from Hegelian idealism, seemed at first to be moving in those directions. Religion, Feuerbach declared, is "man's earliest and also indirect form of self-knowledge;" religion reenacts "the childhood condition of humanity." Feuerbach bore down hard on *materialist* formulations: consciousness resides in real material bodies; consciousness learns by sensual experience of real objects; religion is "nothing other than" the projection of human consciousness.[20] Despite these tokens of empiricism, Marx and Engels became increasingly suspicious of Feuerbach's high-flown yet always ambiguous eloquence. What did he mean by passages like the following (of which there are many in his major opus):

> We have reduced the supermundane, supernatural, and superhuman nature of God to the elements of human nature as its fundamental elements. Our process of analysis has brought us again to the position from which we set out. The beginning, middle, and end of religion is MAN.[21]

Was he celebrating a real world of secular humanism, or some sort of panthe-ist paradise? Marx and Engels' own ideological take on religion at least had the merit of being clear in respect to materialism, and they always stayed close to it.[22] Yet they were hard-pressed for a more persuasive explanation of religious origins to set against the idealist epistemologies that dominated German (and most other) philosophy throughout the nineteenth century. The enthusiasm with which they first greeted *Essence of Christianity* had been precisely for that reason; and now—even as they distanced themselves from Feuerbach—they were borrowing uncrit-ically his "definition," which, aside from its incompatibility with their view of ide-ology, was not really a definition at all, but a speculative and romantically inclined narration. To incorporate Feuerbach into their own writings had the effect of inhibiting more far-reaching materialist investigation. I doubt, however, that by this time they were primarily interested in religion as such. What they wanted was to get idealist premises off their backs long enough to work through their materi-alist interpretation of history; and, of course, to push ahead with the critique of industrial capitalism.[23]

Reinhold Niebuhr, in his introduction to a 1964 collection of Marx and Engels on religion, accused them of making a major error by "wrongly" assuming that empirical epistemology must necessarily point to materialist hypotheses.[24] I sus-pect it may have been the other way around: that having already determined on materialist history, they were looking for an appropriately empirical epistemology by which to introduce it. Niebuhr's criticism, however, carries a revealing corollary. In this golden age of science, he is saying, we are obligated to work from empirical epistemologies yet remain free to pursue hypotheses (including causal explana-tions of religion)— idealist *or* materialist—as the *empirical* evidence seems to war-rant. Although I remain unpersuaded by Niebuhr's confidence that any final expla-nation must necessarily be idealist, he was right, I think, to insist that Marx and Engels failed to bring forward a persuasive, consistently *materialist* alternative.

Is Religion Older than Class?

The anti-religious commitment has deep roots. Nineteenth-century Marxists were direct heirs of the Radical Enlightenment. That the radicalism they inherited had been religious before it became political set the historical context for Marx's open-ing line, "The premise of all criticism" is criticism of religion.[25] To deny religion is to assert a materialist interpretation of the human condition. Efforts to construct such an interpretation have always stood at the center of Marxist thought, and for this reason it has been supposed that Marxian interpretations of history must be grounded on some materialist hypothesis for the origin of religion. Yet when one rereads Marx and Engels with an eye to what they actually said, that appears not to be the case. The attempt to reconstruct history in materialist terms becomes a terrifying enterprise. Even such bold travelers as Marx and Engels sometimes backed off. So at the very beginning, having broken from Hegelian idealism, they felt obligated to install some sort of progressive direction finder for the real history that was left behind; thence the world-lifting Promethean role assigned to "new proletarians." Was this a temporary failure of nerve? Engels, in an 1886 retrospective summary of their relations to Feuerbach suggests (on the contrary) that it expressed an outlook long shared by himself and Marx:

> All successive historical systems are only transitory stages in the endless course of development of human society from the lower to the higher. Each stage is necessary, and therefore justified for the time and conditions to which it owes its origin.

Engels, at this writing, left open the question of whether a similar progressive direction could be ascribed to nature at large. In later years he began composing a major work titled *The Dialectic of Nature*. He was searching, I think, for cosmic machinery that would cause the nonteleological unfolding of natural sequences always to be upward-bound. He left this project unfinished.[26]

To assert a "necessary" progress from "lower to higher" amounts to an idealist and unsubstantiated intrusion into what had been projected as a materialist interpretation. So far as internal logic is concerned, that would suffice to discredit it. If to this we now add the conceptual problems referred to earlier—lack of clear definition, uncertainty on when (and how) religion entered culture, fuzziness as to its relationship to ideology, and, finally, their own contradictory opinions of its revolutionary potential—we will be led to conclude that Marxism (as so far developed in the Marxist movement) did not logically *require* the rejection of religious belief.[27] To have spelled this out would have strengthened the Marxist cause. Although it could hardly have altered the basic balance of power—since capitalism's entire apparatus backed by revealed and institutional forms of religion stood on the opposite side—it would have eased the way for anticlerical believers to support radical politics, and might have raised the tolerance level within Marxist parties for philosophers like Ernst Bloch (and some of the Frankfurt School scholars) who were trying to reconcile materialist history with spiritual or pantheist notions of the cosmos.[28] Certainly it would have encouraged research into historical circumstances under which religions actually had worked as liberating forces. And most important, it would have pushed serious *theorizing* of means by which believers and nonbelievers (without mutual deception) might collaborate for commonly held (even if limited) objectives.

Beyond these problems of internal consistency lie the implacable demands of credibility in the real world. Religion (as illustrated, for example, by the Budenz episode) exercises emotional controls over human behavior that seem to transcend materialist explication. This poses a choice of alternatives: to seek transcendental answers as Niebuhr was doing, or, as Marx and Engels attempted, to construct an effective secular explanation. Their lack of success in this latter endeavor was due (so I have been suggesting) to overreliance on Feuerbach; or perhaps it would be more accurate to say that reliance on Feuerbach was due to certain assumptions they shared with Feuerbach and never quite left behind even after they left Feuerbach behind. Feuerbach had populated heaven and earth with candy saints and sugar plum angels.[29] Marx and Engels, operating on a scale far grander but no less anthropomorphic, believed that out there somewhere in the cosmos Beethoven's chorus from the Ninth would still be singing the "Ode to Joy."[30] I am of course misspeaking myself in saying they *believed*. I don't know what they believed, yet when they ascribed world-lifting powers to English factory laborers or self-contained progressive direction to human history, it seems they must have been holding to something like this.

Karl Barth wrote in criticism of Feuerbach that he did not know death.[31] The same criticism, I think, could be extended to Marx and Engels, or more generally to Marxist thought as it pertained to religion. Barth believed death had to be part of religion. A nonbeliever would add that death must be part of any *secular* explanation of religion. Secular explanation of religion would be like a *non-ideological* explanation of ideology—that is, one that derived the self-serving constructs of any particular class from real, historical circumstances of that class. And so—to complete this analogy—an effective secular account of religion would be one that grounded religious belief itself in real historical circumstances of the human condition. Potential components of such an explanation, however, were only beginning to come in reach by the last half of the nineteenth century. Marx and Engels deeply admired Darwin.[32] They made use of Darwinian concepts in their own system to explain the relationship of consciousness to labor—although neither they nor any of their colleagues, so far as I know, attempted to apply similar lines of thought to religion. Having pursued religion's ideological connection back as far as it would go, they made no real effort to push beyond that. To have done so would have forced them to explore the relationship of individual consciousness to the knowledge of death. This, in turn, might have brought them closer to a *secular* grasp of religion. Like Feuerbach, however, they remained more at ease with "species consciousness" than individual consciousness.[33] "The being of the species," Marx wrote in one of his earliest essays [1844],"confirms itself in species-consciousness and exists for *itself* in its generality as a thinking being." He then added the following observation:

> *Death* seems to be a harsh victory of the species over the *definite* individual, and to contradict their unity. But the particular individual is only a *particular species-being*, and as such mortal.[34]

Words marked for emphasis in this quotation were so marked in translation from the original, yet one notes that the inconspicuous little word *only* (not emphasized) is packing a lion's share of the baggage. If particular individuals—*only*—are mortal, will that somehow permit the species at large to escape mortality? Or is it reasonable to describe a species—even the human species—as a "thinking being?" All this of course was in 1844, but the ambiguities were never totally resolved.

In later years, Marx and Engels moved away from the problem of religion.[35] Marx was in failing health. Aging and hard-pressed financially, they both remained engrossed in their world-shaking analysis of industrial capitalism—how could one demand more than that? As to their followers, striving over the decades to win working class support for socialist politics, they were more likely to be evading religious conflicts than promoting secular (therefore controversial) theories about the origin of religion. In any case, the bottom line is that Marxism's failure to come up with an effective hypothesis for the origin of religion left a strategic gap in the secular (materialist) interpretation of human history. Thus for those revivals of religious belief that followed the Second World War, the gates of the Secular City were left standing open.

12

High Tide at Dover Beach

From Tylor's definition of religion in the 1840s till the Second World War one hundred years later, the "social science stance" served as a kind of intellectual free trade zone for the Age of Secularism. In 1942 Talcott Parsons, a professor of sociology at Harvard and perhaps already the most widely known of American social scientists, initiated an academic counteroffensive against the social science stance. The occasion was the "Conference on Methods in Philosophy and the Sciences" at the New School for Social Research in New York City. Parsons' paper, titled "Theoretical Development of the Sociology of Religion," is remarkable in that it adumbrates at a very early date themes of the so-called postmodern era that would not enter common currency till the 1970s. So what is postmodernism? I am tempted to suggest, not quite facetiously, that the Age of Secularism closed down when the postmodern era began. Those of my colleagues who write on such subjects have not yet fixed a firm entry date for postmodernism nor determined precisely what defines this new age. Nonetheless, many historians and most theologians would agree that one of its hallmarks has been an increasing enthusiasm for "belief in spiritual beings," that is, for public manifestations of religion. The social science stance toward religion, as I pointed out in an earlier chapter, first came into existence as a neutral sanctuary within which scholars of both transcendental and secular persuasion could collaborate (or at least coexist) while pursuing "scientific" studies of religion. Why, then, in 1942 would the dean of American social sciences feel impelled to mount an attack against the social science stance?[1]

The Quantum Analogy

Although it had certainly functioned as a neutral zone, the social science stance had also been—*always*—a center of controversy. This becomes strikingly evident from an examination of Parsons' paper. He opened his presentation by declaring that developments he was about to outline represented "a notable advance in the adequacy of our theoretical equipment to deal with a critically important range of scientific problems." He went on to explain how the work of four "important theorists" during the past century had contributed to liberating "sociology of religion" from the "'rationalistic' variation of positivism" within which early pioneers in that field (especially "Tylor and ... Spencer") had been imprisoned. As a result, "the sociology of religion for the first time" now found itself in a situation where it was possible "to combine empirical study and theoretical analysis on a large scale in conformity with the best current standards of social science and psychology."[2]

Parsons' four theorists—Pareto, Malinowski, Durkheim, and Weber—had demonstrated (according to Parsons) the existence of sequences of thought and behavior, relating especially to ultimate matters such as life, death, moral obligation, and social authority, which marched to a different drum than that of ordinary human activities governed by empirical observation and rational calculation. There is nothing thus far in Parsons' essay to suggest some intrinsic reason why nonrational behaviors (which doubtless constitute a substantial part of all human activity) might not be recorded empirically and analyzed rationally by scientifically minded observers. Parsons, however, characterized these types of behaviors as incapable "for analytic purposes" of "being assimilated to the patterns of science." In his conclusion he dealt with them as follows:

> All of these distinctions by virtue of which the cognitive patterns of religion
> are treated separately from those of science have positive significance for
> empirical understanding of religious phenomena. Like any such scientific
> categories, they are to the scientist sanctioned by the fact that they can be
> shown to work. Failure to make these distinctions does not in the present
> state of knowledge and in terms of the relevant frame of reference help us
> to understand certain crucially important facts of human life. What the
> philosophical significance of this situation may be is not as such the task
> of the social scientist to determine. Only one safe prediction on this level
> can be made. Any new philosophical synthesis will need positively to take

account of these distinctions rather than to attempt to reinstate for the scientific level the older positivistic conception of the homogeneity of all human thought and its problems. If these distinctions are to be transcended it cannot well be in the form of "reducing" religious ideas to those of science—both in the sense of Western intellectual history—or vice versa. The proved scientific utility of the distinctions is sufficient basis on which to eliminate this as a serious possibility.[3]

By my reading of this not altogether limpid passage, Parsons is saying: 1) In the scientific study of religion we must admit non-empirical data that would not be acceptable in other branches of science. 2) "These distinctions" are justifiable because they "work" —that is, they fit into and complement already reputably established hypotheses about human behavior and social structure. 3) In the sentence referring to "philosophical significance," Parsons implicitly invokes an analogy to quantum theory in nuclear physics, which, like the "distinctions" he is proposing for "sociology of religion," seems rationally inexplicable but nonetheless "works." 4) Philosophy remains beyond the mandate of us practical social scientists, but we know that "any new philosophical synthesis" will need to expand the philosophy of science so as to accord scientific status in studies of religion to non-empirical data. 5) Religious experience, and the evidences of such experience, are *sui generis*; they cannot be "reduced" to a common denominator (homogeneity) that would be shared with empirical experience and secular hypothesis. Yet they are equal (or more than equal?) in validity.[4]

Cleansing the Temple of Positivism

Parsons' paper was retrospective in that it began by commenting on four eminent scholar-philosophers whose major works had been published in the late nineteenth and early twentieth centuries. Thus it connected more directly to the intellectual scene preceding the Second World War than to what would be developing afterward; yet clearly, its intent was projective. Secularism remained dominant in academic circles during the 1940s and continued so for another twenty years, as the success of Harvey Cox's *Secular City* in 1965 makes evident.[5] Yet religion's postwar revivals were already crackling through the canebrakes of popular culture and mass politics; and it was this sacred fire at lower altitudes, I think, that finally ignited an academic revolt against secularism. There now came a rapid shift. Anthropologists, sociologists, specialists in the comparative study and history of religions began to question their adherence to the social science stance and to seek rationalizations for repudiating that "older positivistic conception" that Parsons had denounced already in 1942. Prominent among the revisionists was Peter L. Berger, a sociologist of knowledge, quoted extensively in chapter 4, whose writings on religion take us to the crux of this intellectual shift. A lifelong Lutheran, Berger had struggled to find some satisfactory balance of his professional career with religious faith. "So, let me state where I have arrived," he wrote:

> The gods are projections of the human mind. The gods are symbols of the human condition. Consequently, religion can be successfully analyzed as a human symbol system—historically, sociologically, psychologically, and linguistically. Consequently, any theology that denies this (be it orthodox, neo-orthodox or what have you) is a dead-end street. One gets nowhere, in theology or any other pursuit, if one's starting point is a denial of demonstrable, empirical reality.[6]

Thus far Berger is describing the view from *inside* the social science stance—that having been substantially his own viewpoint earlier, when (with Thomas Luckman) he was working on his *chef d'oeuvre, The Social Construction of Reality.* "But this," Berger now tells us, "is not the whole story." The "whole story" points to *"another reality,* and one of ultimate significance for man, which transcends the reality within which our everyday life unfolds." Since other realities cannot be known by observation and secular hypothesis—that is, by methods of science—Berger now proposes a different set of signals in which elements of subjective experience, such as the terror of death, or craving for order, or the savoring of aesthetic perception, will serve as keys to the other realm. We need not pursue Berger's epistemology in detail, except to note that its project of "empiricizing" subjective experience in order to validate beliefs arrived at "inductively," derives conceptually at least from initiatives of Kant and Schleiermacher a century and a half earlier.[7]

I turn next to two outstanding scholars of religion, both writing as Berger did, during the 1960s. I must begin with some illuminating remarks made by E. E.

Evans-Pritchard, Oxford professor of social anthropology, while presenting a lecture series on theories of primitive religion: "The persons whose writings have been most influential" (his reference here was to Tylor, Frazer, Marett, Malinowsky, Durkheim, Levy-Bruhl, and Freud), "have been at the time they wrote agnostics or atheists. ... We should, I think, realize what was the intention of many of these scholars if we are to understand their theoretical contributions. They sought, and found, in primitive religions a weapon which could, they thought, be used with deadly effect against Christianity. If primitive religion could be explained away as an intellectual aberration, as a mirage induced by emotional stress, or by its social function, it was implied that higher religions could be discredited and disposed of in the same way." Near the end of his final lecture, Evans-Pritchard returned to the same theme. When a student of religion, he said, begins from an assumption that "souls and spirits and gods of religion have no reality ... then some biological, psychological, or sociological theory of how everywhere and at all times men have been stupid enough to believe in them seems to be called for. He who accepts the reality of spiritual being does not feel the same need for such explanations."[8]

In Pursuit of the Numinous

Evans-Pritchard's suspicion of ulterior motives among pioneers of religious theory was shared by an equally distinguished scholar on the opposite side of the Atlantic, Mircea Eliade, at the University of Chicago. "The beginnings of [the study of] comparative religions," Eliade wrote, "took place ... at the very height of materialistic and positivistic propaganda. Auguste Comte published his *Catechisme Positiviste* in 1852. ...[In 1859] appeared Darwin's *Origin of Species* ... [in 1862] Herbert Spencer's *First Principles*." Eliade then pointed to the linkage between mid-nineteenth-century evolutionary thought and Tylor's progressive theory of religion:

> Tylor identified the first stage of religion with what he called animism: the belief that Nature is animated, that is, has a soul. From animism evolved polytheism, and polytheism finally gave way to monotheism.[9]

One may sense a note of disapproval, similar to that expressed by Evans-Pritchard, in the phrase, "materialistic and positivistic propaganda." Nor was

Eliade sympathetic to evolutionary concepts of religion. Religion was not to be comprehended as a subdivision of natural history. Rather, it was "an experience, *sui generis,* incited by man's encounter with the sacred." Coming in a shock of emotion like physical sensation, the sacred would take hold with a shudder, a *frisson,* an instant of terror or exhilaration. What precisely constituted that experience, Eliade did not explain, but referred to "the famous book, *Das Heilige*" by Rudolf Otto, whom he introduced as a "philosopher of religion," a mediator "between Eastern and Western types of mysticism."[10] In *Das Heilige* (1917), the German theologian Rudolf Otto strives to convey what he took to be the essence of all religion: an awareness of absolute otherness, of power beyond rational or moral comprehension yet somehow engrossing these faculties; beyond words; ineffable. To that which cannot be uttered in words, Otto applied the adjective *numinous*—"a special term to stand for 'the holy' ... perfectly *sui generis*, and irreducible to any other."[11] The core of religious experience, then, was a mystic encounter with the numinous, which Otto (and Eliade) insisted must be essentially the same in all places and all times. By locating the origin of religion in this trans-historic encounter, Eliade rescued religion itself from history and from the indignities of progressive evolution. Was he rescuing it also from the rigors of scientific method?

The three authors just quoted share several attributes in common. Approximate contemporaries, they reached the top of their careers during the 1960s and 1970s, and all were internationally reputed scholars in the fields of sociology of religion and comparative religions. All three (judging from their own statements) were religious believers. Only one (Berger) credited science with significant achievement in the study of religion; the other two held current social science methodology inappropriate to religious studies; and all three agreed that ongoing work on religion must free iself from the limitations of the social science stance.[12] Eliade especially was vehement and bitter on this point. "The historian of religions," he wrote in the closing pages of *The Quest*, "who does not accept the empiricism or the relativism of some fashionable sociological and historicistic schools feels rather frustrated. He knows that he is condemned to work exclusively with historical documents, but at the same time feels that these documents tell him something more than the simple fact that they reflect historical situations. He feels somehow that they reflect important truths about man and man's relation to the sacred."[13] Evans-Pritchard, with his gift for pejorative prose, was able to give this same message one of its most lucid expositions:

As far as study of religion as a factor in social life is concerned, it may make little difference whether the anthropologist is a theist or an atheist, since in either
case he can only take into account what he can observe. But if either attempts
to go further than this, each must pursue a different path. The nonbeliever
seeks for some theory—biological, psychological, or sociological— which will
explain the illusion; the believer seeks rather to understand the manner in
which a people conceives of a reality and their relations to it. For both, religion is a part of social life, but for the believer it has also another dimension.[14]

He then repeated with explicit approval a warning attributed to the Catholic
theologian Wilhelm Schmidt: "'If religion is essentially of the inner life, it follows
that it can be truly grasped only from within. But beyond a doubt, this can be
better done by one in whose inward consciousness an experience of religion
plays a part. There is but too much danger that the other will talk of religion as
a blind man might of colors, or one totally devoid of ear, of a beautiful musical
composition.'"[15]

Schleiermacher Rediscovered

The gist of these expressions by leading sociologists and historians of religion
from Talcott Parsons to Evans-Pritchard and Mircea Eliade is that religion is a
separate domain within which standard modes of scientific inquiry are certain to
prove dysfunctional. The scholars quoted were not only prominent in religious
studies but figures of high reputation in the academic establishments of Great
Britain and the United States. They largely concur that studies of religion must
grant subjective experience the same validity that attaches in other branches of
science to empirical observation; in effect, they are "empiricizing" subjective perception in order to establish a "scientific" base for conclusions inductively arrived
at. A right moment for rediscovering Schleiermacher would happen along by the
mid-1960s. Richard Niebuhr, Sterling Professor of Theology and Christian
Ethics at Yale's Divinity School, writing the introduction for a new edition of *The
Christian Faith*, described Schleiermacher as "the Kant of Protestantism, whose
critiques of theological issues define the basic problems of the nineteenth and
twentieth centuries."[16] Wayne Proudfoot, an upcoming sociologist of religion at
Columbia University, shared Niebuhr's estimate of Schleiermacher's historical

importance but not the enthusiasm for his theology. In *Religious Experience* (which won the 1986 American Academy of Religion Award) Proudfoot, after tracing Schleiermacher's powerful influence on "religious thought and the study of religion during the past two centuries," went on to a critical examination of what that influence actually entailed. Schleiermacher, according to Proudfoot, attributed to "intrinsically religious" (subjective) experiences the absolute power of physical sensation. The effect would be to make religion seemingly "autonomous" and thus foreclose any "possibility of conflict ... [with] new knowledge that might emerge" through scientific research. "Strictures against reductionism are invoked to preclude critical inquiry from outside the religious life. The result," Proudfoot concluded, "is a powerful protective strategy" for defending belief against intrusions of secular criticism.[17] In contrast to Niebuhr's celebrationism, Proudfoot was portraying Schleiermachian theology as obscurantist and defensive. His choice of this project for a major scholarly study pointed of course to its contemporary relevance, and he probably was not surprised when his book encountered opposition.[18] That a critique written a century and a half after Schleiermacher's death could still stir up academic controversy was due to the fact that downgrading Schleiermacher amounted to rejecting the movement Parsons had launched fifty years earlier for opening social science research to "neo-empiricist"—that is, subjective—experience.

Over the long run, that movement has proved increasingly popular. The rise of "creation science" and "intelligent design"—their embrace by the media and partial acceptance in the academy—stand in recent confirmation of its progress. Thus at Berkeley in 1998 a symposium on "'science and the spiritual quest,'" funded by the affluent and increasingly prestigious J. M. Templeton Foundation, attracted academics of various persuasions and commanded headline coverage in the press. "Faith and Reason, Together Again," the *Wall Street Journal* announced; "Science and Religion" are "Bridging the Great Divide," said the *New York Times*; and on *Newsweek's* front cover, "Science Finds God." *Newsweek* even challenged its readers by presenting Talcott Parsons' reflections on quantum mechanics:

> Take the difficult Christian concept of Jesus as both fully divine and fully human. It turns out that this duality has a parallel in quantum physics. ... The orthodox interpretation of this strange phenomenon is that light is, simultaneously, wave and particle. ... So, too, with Jesus, suggests physicist F. Russell Stannard of England's Open University.[19]

Of this Berkeley symposium, the late Stephen Jay Gould wrote that it was enveloped in "a deluge of media hype" as if some "new and persuasive argument," some "exciting and transforming discovery," had been been presented. "In fact, absolutely nothing of intellectual novelty had been added, as the same bad arguments surfaced into a glare of publicity because the J. M. Templeton Foundation, established by its fabulously wealthy eponym to advance the syncretist program (that is, harmonizing science and religion) garnered a splash of media attention by spending 1.4 million bucks to hold a conference."[20] The Templeton Foundation continues to make news in academic circles. My daily newspaper (March 22, 2005) reported that Templeton offers "the world's most lucrative academic prize" of $1.5 million, awarded recently to several world-class scientists including Freeman Dyson of the Institute for Advanced Study in Princeton, and Charles Townes, a Nobel Prize winner in physics at Berkeley. Both might accurately be described as "syncretists," although neither (so far as I know) specifically endorses creation science or intelligent design. Yet their willingness to sup at the Templeton table adds to the prestige of such doctrines and speeds their flow from academia out into the grassroots of local politics. Fifty-six percent of Americans, according to a poll conducted in 2005, thought "creationism should be taught in schools"; 64 percent favored displaying religious messages "such as the Ten Commandments" in public buildings. From my e-mail (May 6, 2005) I learn that a "retired science and elementary school teacher," Kathy Martin, elected one year ago to the Kansas State Board of Education, now presides over committee hearings expected to bring "Creationism" and "Intelligent Design" into high school science classes. In addition to Kansas, eight states are said to be working up similar initiatives. Straws in the wind? "Over the last two decades," the *Los Angeles Times* reports in a front page article (February 2006), "this type of 'Creation Evangelicism' has become a booming industry." Evolution is a fine theory, Kansas School Board member Martin explained, "but it is flawed ... We can't ignore that our nation is based on Christianity—not science."[21]

A Saving Resource?

This chapter is the last in Part Three, "The Will to Believe." Beginning with Hume's famous definition of the problem of evil, Part Three traced the unfolding of that problem from Job and Augustine to our own time. Part Three is the longest in my book for the reason that religion's entire history, biological and cultural, is bracketed within the reciprocal relation between religion and the problem of evil. Religion is a belief system. Belief systems depend on *belief*: that is, they work (or may work) when they command credibility. But the problem of evil destroys credibility. First appearing as the mirror image (consequently the *reversed* image) of belief in spiritual beings, it returns in the guise of credibility gaps that mock and discredit religious authority. Consequently—given the amazing grace with which religious authority bonds into and legitimizes economic and political power—the problem of evil becomes subversive of established social order itself. What I need to stress here is that religion's one failure in what might otherwise seem a triumphal march through cultural evolution, was its inability to resolve the problem of evil. Attempts to abolish the problem (theodicies) have been common to most religious traditions. In the West, drawing on scientific achievements of the sixteenth and seventeenth centuries, theodicy assumed a scientific mode that seemed on the brink of successfully unifying science with religion. These expectations collapsed during the Enlightenment. What followed was the long decline—the Age of Secularism—which by midway into the nineteenth century had brought religion down to perhaps its lowest ebb in history. "The sea of faith was once, too, at the full," Matthew Arnold wrote despairingly in "Dover Beach:"

But now I only hear
Its melancholy, long, withdrawing roar,
Retreating ... down the vast edges drear
And naked shingles of the world.[22]

During the early years of the secular era—targeting science as their main enemy—believers had sought to defend religion by means of somber, romantic prophecies *against* science. When these proved unrewarding in a world increasingly dominated by science and technology, they moved to the more pragmatic strategy of claiming for their own beliefs the *vraisemblance* of empirical observation. Here they found powerful support in messages left by Kant and Schleiermacher, counseling against scholastic rationalisms and insisting instead on the cutting edge of direct religious experience. Faith that vouches for its own faith—*fideism*—is doubtless as old as religion. It must have been the earliest form of religion, and would be the natural recourse for believers struggling to survive under the assaults of secularism. Thus fideism served as a fortress like that of Luther's great hymn, "with salvation's walls surrounded," inside which true believers could dare to smile at all their foes. At best this would have been a meager smile, and smiling, as we know, is the signature of defensive postures. After the Second World War, however, as the spiritual climate grew warmer, defensive smiles blossomed into more aggressive body-language. In this chapter I have summarized a series of interventions by religiously inclined scholars spanning the last half of the twentieth century, from Talcott Parsons midway in the Second World War to the lush Templeton Awards of the 1990s, all aimed purposefully at reconstructing the will to believe. These interventions paralleled and reinforced the resurgence of religion that followed the war. Willed belief in the objectivity of *subjective* experience is the essence of postmodern fideism. Although more venturesome and doubtless more affluent than its ancient predecessors, fideism even in our postmodern era remains essentially defensive. Despite the booming revivals that have punctuated recent history, there exists no possibility of restoring the religious realism that once inspired Augustine, Dante, Leibniz. What we have instead is a kind of stand-off, or tactical disengagement, from the unresolved problem of evil.

Yet, one must not underestimate fideism's power in our current world. It was the rise of this movement that terminated the two-hundred-year-long Age of Secularism, and intellectuals of fideist persuasion who devised the conceptual framework for religion's renaissance after the Second World War. These events bear witness to what appears a central reality of our time: that the will to believe in belief can checkmate the problem of evil. Thus from the nadir of its long credibility crisis, religion emerged, not exactly unscathed, but universal and still dominant. Shall we conclude, then, that belief in spiritual beings has served the human species as a saving resource? The answer emphatically is yes. It would be difficult to imagine that humanity could have arrived at its present level of culture, or even survived physically, apart from the power of religion. Divisive and sectarian as that power has been, and ruthless in pursuit of human enemies, its role for the species at large remained adaptive; that is, it worked consistently as a factor for survival and dominance. Its success in resolving earlier crises confirms this answer; so, also in our own time, do the rollback of secularism and the burgeoning domain of postmodern fideism. One may reasonably expect, then—especially since believers make up the vast majority of our species—that religion will prove no less a resource for survival in the dangerous years ahead than it was throughout the cultural evolution that constitutes our history.

PART FOUR:

Knowing and Believing

13

The Great Lizard Analogy

Return of flood tide at Dover Beach brings us to our own times. Our own times are defined by Hiroshima and Nagasaki, by the race for weapons of mass destruction, by the accelerating pace of ecological burnout. My introductory chapter set these disasters (together with the resurgence of religion) at center stage. It then identified four types of institutions which might be considered essential for mobilizing knowledge, power, and moral authority sufficient to resolve the impending crises. These were: 1) science and technology; 2) governments of nation-states; 3) the industrial apparatus; and 4) religion with its institutional attachments. As potential resources, the first three seemed dubious because while one lacks power to implement its knowledge, the next two, amply supplied though they are with power, remain too deeply enmeshed in industrial growth to be capable of imposing restraints. If state authority, then, and the industrial apparatus, and our scientific and technological establishment, all prove derelict in coping with the oncoming crises, might not religion—either directly or as an inspirational catalyst for the other three—step forward as a saving resource? Efforts to construct a response to that question led to the historical essay that is the main part of this book.

A Backward Glance

What was needed first was a definition broad enough to cover the multiplicity of religious forms and precise enough to distinguish them from other cultural phenomena. Following Tylor, and picking what seemed a common denominator, I defined religion as belief in anthropomorphically benevolent spiritual beings in (or over) nature. Religion by this definition appears virtually universal in our contemporary world. So far as I know, anthropology has never confirmed the existence of any previous society totally lacking religious belief. Thus religion stands among the most ancient and universal of cultural continuities. Like the capacity to invent and learn language, it may have preceded human culture. The logic of natural selection applied to cultural evolution implies that constructs of such universality and duration would be adaptively interlocked with survival and success of the species—unless (or until) some environmental change might alter the impact of the behaviors they promoted.[1]

Working from this hypothesis, I outlined a sequence of critical transitions beginning with the crisis of consciousness, into which religion had entered as *the* saving resource by filling the gap between life and death. What most clearly distinguishes the human from other species, and gives it controlling power over them, is its immersion in culture. Culture—begotten by language out of consciousness— might have found no fertile womb had spiritual beings not intervened to protect consciousness from the paralyzing terror of death.[2] The crisis of consciousness projected religious belief as an agent of cultural evolution. Part Two, following this lead, examines the origins of social morality and the subsequent drift from egalitarian moral codes to codes that accepted (and legitimized) gender and class exploitation. Religion played a crucial part in these transitions, both of which contributed decisively to survival and dominance of human culture.[3] Yet culture that survives by exploitation gives hostages to the problem of evil. The problem of evil has confronted religious believers since before the Book of Job. Part Three, "The Will to Believe," shows that all attempted resolutions failed but that religion was able to bypass, or neutralize, the problem of evil by constructing a postmodern style of fideism, which asserted the empirical validity of subjective experience. Thus religious belief survived the Age of Secularism, from which it emerged—"not exactly unscathed, but universal and still dominant."[4]

Midway into the twentieth century came a decisive change of the human condition. Global environment altered from what had once seemed unbounded resource to depletion and overuse. Behaviors governed by the industrial apparatus, by nation-states, by technological and scientific enterprises, became increasingly destructive in the changing environment. Because political and cultural institutions are deeply intermeshed, the other long continuities of culture (including religion) collaborated in preserving these environmentally dysfunctional behaviors. Yet religion was in certain respects differently positioned from the others. Maintaining a skeptical distance from science, it had always asserted its own priority over social morality and governmental power. These differences reflect, and in a sense reenact, the original entry of spiritual beings thought powerful enough to defend consciousness against death. In that earliest crisis, religion spoke for humanity at large; and to that interlude before the fall— before, that is, any of Job's ancestors posed the problem of evil—its universalizing tendencies have always referred back. Most of our species, doubtless a vast majority, recognizing its benefits and universality, will conclude that common sense recommends continuing reliance on religion.

Great Lizards, Great Brains

Sixty million years before our hominid ancestors came marching in, during the Cretaceous period as the paleontologists tell us, diverse species of meat-eating and vegetarian lizards achieved special perfections that enabled them to dominate the earth. Times changed, however, due to an eccentric asteroid, or other causes speculative or unknown.[5] The same perfections that had engrossed the great lizards rendered them inflexible to environmental change and so they perished, leaving their earthly arena to oncoming contenders. Among these were mammals, among mammals hominoids, among hominoids the hominids, and finally that species which today dominates the earth thanks to engrossment of an organ we call the brain. An ominous analogy? Perhaps. How close are the sides of the analogy?

Taking the great lizard sequence first, somewhere during eons of pre-Cretaceous time genetic selections occurred that favored stomach volume as a competitive asset for certain lizardlike ancestors. The rest then follows as the day the night: large stomachs require large jaws for harvesting vegetation, powerful legs and backs for moving stomachs around, heavy armor to protect stomachs from predators. The predators in turn—all at first kissing cousins to their prey— develop weapons adapted to penetrating heavy armor. And when environmental change sets in, prey and predator alike fall victim to their own genetically rigid dysfunctionality.[6] The human sequence, beginning with similar events, developed differently. Late in the sixty-million-year time span that separates the Cretaceous period from the Pleistocene, a hominid prototype became host to a

mutation that favored enlargement of the brain. This deviation flourished for reasons we can only guess at, which at first could not have had much directional
bearing on subsequent evolution of the brain as chief organ of mental activity.
Thus the defining attribute of human specificity, culture, began literally in
absence of mind. It was the early adumbrations of culture such as memory, signs,
symbols—all made possible by an engrossing brain—that summoned mind into
being.[7] Mind is often described as functioning of the brain. Mind and culture
made up a reciprocal process. Together they proved adaptive by opening access
to higher levels of power and self-awareness, thus enhancing survival potential
against competitors. Consciousness (inspired perhaps by close encounters with
spiritual beings?) then worked to separate humans from the remainder of earth's
organic community. The result was a fix on nature as distanced and objectified,
which in turn suggested projects for purposefully directed alterations; and these,
triumphantly successful at short range, established in the long run circumstances
that would prove necessary and sufficient for the nuclear and ecological disasters
of the twentieth and twenty-first centuries.[8]

So far in this analogy, the point of comparison, or contrast, has been hered-
itary size and armature of the great lizards on the one hand, and enlargement
of human brains on the other. The sequences are similar in that both remain
inside the realm of evolutionary biology. Huge bodies, heavy armament, may
readily be seen as encumbering under adverse circumstances. Enlarged brains
(and skulls) may also have entailed physical disadvantages, but these seem not
to have been decisive, especially since difficulties encountered by the human
species arose not from that organ's size, but from the way it functioned, or—
and is this not identical?—from the way human beings learned to use it. Here
the analogy begins to separate. While one sequence resides totally in the kingdom of hard sciences (space physics, evolutionary biology), the other, as an
outcome primarily of culture, enters the domain of social science and humanities. Since the first realm is supposed to be deterministic, and the second is
said to be governed in part at least by choice and free will, this difference suggests a possibility of divergent outcomes.[9] "Conceding for the sake of argument," Charles Beard wrote in his 1932 introduction (appropriately) to J. B.
Bury's *The Idea of Progress*,

> that the past has been chaos, without order or design, we are still haunted by
> the shadowing thought that by immense efforts of the will and intelligence,

employing natural science as the supreme instrumentality of power, mankind may rise above necessity into the kingdom of freedom, subduing material things to humane and rational purposes.[10]

Differing outcomes might be possible to the extent that culture permits flexibilities of response that genetic heredity precludes. Is culture more flexible than biology? The answer hinges on three crucial questions about human culture. The first involves the amount of choice actually inherent in cultural constructions. The second involves rigidity and determinism in those constructs. The third question centers on the degree to which genetic heredity penetrates (and determines?) culture.

Flexibility and Choice in Cultural Constructions

Traditional wisdom has made diversity and change hallmarks of culture. Sometimes this has been celebrated, more often deplored. To people born during the first half of the twentieth century, culture's transformative power appeared self-evident. Our parents grew up in the railroad era; we immersed our own lives in automobile culture and air travel; our children will—or perhaps they may—live during an age of space exploration. Borrowing from recollections only one or two generations removed, we remember the devastations of two world wars, yet recall the bountiful recoveries that followed. Our own parents courted, made love, and raised children (I was born in 1919) more or less under the aegis of moral standards said to be timeless. Doubting the modern utility of those standards, we tried cautious experiments, and our children shocked us by carrying the experiments further than we had dared. Thus culture proved capable of remodeling not only the physical environment but our own norms of moral behavior.[11]

It was not always this way. If residents of the twentieth century, mesmerized by innovation, tended to celebrate flexibility and change as culturally progressive, earlier generations often viewed them as prodigal or even sinful. Governed by powerful dualisms inherent in most religions (East and West), they relegated change to the material side of their dual cosmologies. Eternity belonged on the spiritual side, but change was a property of matter—and death. Like the birth and death of plants and animals, or like seasons, change had to be cyclical. Yet cycli-

cal change goes nowhere. Thus by the curious paradox of dualism, the only sort
of change that could become meaningful was negation of change—that is, a movement of change itself into the eternal kingdom: salvation, paradise, nirvana; dualism speaking in many tongues. Since journeys to eternity must start on this side
of the boundary, there remained room after all in human culture for institutions of
merit and substance, for continuities that must be taken seriously because they
preserved useful knowledge and sacred traditions, as well as furnishing points of
embarkation for the outward journey.[12]

Ancients and moderns, then, despite differences in attribution of values,
have concurred in assigning to culture deep continuities that serve as matrices
of flexibility and significant choice. Taking this concurrence for a somewhat
grudging acknowledgment of reality, and following the implicit lines of thought,
we can identify cultural continuities first as aggregates of customary knowledge
such as religion, agriculture, metallurgy, astronomy, theology, and subsequently as institutions that incorporate those skills and sciences: tribes, city-states,
temples, observatories, universities. These are the long continuities of culture.
The existence of our species would be impossible without them. Collectively
constructed from the beginning of human history, they have proved both
durable and extraordinarily flexible. Changing with turns of history, they survived, flourished, perished; they were fought for, destroyed, and resurrected in
altered forms with new names.[13] To the extent that choice may be imaginable in
a cosmos whose determinations we do not understand, cultural institutions
provided the human species with a rich menu of choices.[14] If so, it might seem
reasonable to reject any analogy between cultural and biological history on the
ground that the distance between them is too great to allow comparison. But
that would be to misconstrue the point of the analogy. What actually is under
comparison is not separate realms of development but specific responses to
adverse environmental conditions. On one side, the great lizards perished for
failing to modify dysfunctional behavior predetermined by their genetically
inherited body structures. On the opposite side, thus far our species hangs at
the brink of self-destruction because human beings seem incapable of modify-
ing dysfunctional behavior that was programmed (presumably) within human
culture. The definitive question is not whether culture offers flexibility and
choice (we have already concluded that it does) but whether it contains institutions that generate rigidly determined behavior patterns comparable (functionally) to those generated through biological evolution.

Rigidity and Determinism in Cultural Constructions

How were the long continuities of culture constructed? Since general acceptance of Darwinism at the end of the nineteenth century, scholars have tended to
narrate cultural history in evolutionary terms. Even religion is often said to have
"evolved" from naive or simple ideas such as animism or ancestor worship to
more complex ones such as pantheism or monotheism. But the mechanisms
ascribed to cultural history have differed from those attributed to biological history. Ideas, especially in accounts of religious or scientific origins, appear to be
self-animating as if the inner logic of each idea invoked an ensuing stage in the
sequence. Ideas might thus be seen as floating out of the past through a benevolent dialectic in which every antithesis painlessly dissolves into a new and
improved synthesis. With respect to more mundane cultural baggage like tool-
making, or weaponry or agricultural technology, the history of human culture
has favored trial-and-error, spontaneous discovery, teaching-and-learning, cultural diffusion, over the bloody tooth-and-claw mechanisms that usually govern
accounts of biological evolution.[15] One would expect cultural history to emphasize cultural processes of change, but emphasis here verges on exclusion, and
what is being excluded is the recollection that culture also is part of biological
history. Through 99 percent of its time span so far, our species survived in an
environment of scarcity. As the species struggled to prevail over other species,
individuals and groups inside its own perimeters were struggling to dominate
or exploit, or extinguish, one another. The reciprocal process of mind and culture—presumably unique to human beings—came into existence as biological
armament. We need think only of the advantage in survival power, or social preeminence, that an individual confident of supernatural empathy and support
would possess over another, less imaginative, whose mental images served
merely to reproduce the tedium of hunting-gathering and dark nights of blood-
thirsty predators.[16]

A similar differential applies collectively. Weapons of culture, culturally transmitted, served not only to overcome beasts in the forest and monsters of the deep,
but to expropriate hunting-gathering grounds from previous users and drive off
followers of alien deities. If a band, happening on the trick of fire or fabricating
some new rudiment of language, used its gift to overpower neighboring bands,
those events would be likely to reappear later as myths of cultural diffusion,
although the original sequence rested as much on conquest and biological extinc-

tion as on cultural sharing. Cultural evolution reproduces mechanisms of selection, adaptation, and survival similar to those of biological evolution. If biological
evolution is causally determined, cultural evolution to some extent must also be
so determined. Although the two evolutionary sets function in different media by
vastly different timescales, the mechanisms themselves involve rigidity and resistance to change. Rigidity in one set results from the glacial slowness of genetic
adaptation. In the other, it results from the fact that culturally learned behaviors
that achieved survival and dominance for the species as a whole (or for groups
within the species) will remain deeply entrenched, institutionalized into the long
continuities of culture—deepest of all in those that reproduce language, social
hierarchy, the content of individual and collective consciousness. We are not
speaking (yet) of genetic transmission. Measured by genetic or geological time,
such continuities may seem ephemeral as dream tissue; in the scale of human history, which for them is the only relevant measure, their rate of change will be slow
enough to approximate rigidity. And this especially holds for the modern era, in
which relay of information becomes virtually instantaneous.[17]

The discussion of cultural rigidity has centered thus far around continuities
that for cultural reasons become rigid and resistant to change, and, therefore,
potentially dysfunctional to survival in the nuclear/ecological crises. We can turn
next to the third, and last, of the questions posed earlier in this chapter: the
degree to which genetic heredity determines culture.

Genetic Heredity in Culture

When I was several decades younger than I now am, I would have responded to
this problem by asserting an absolute separation between evolution and culture.
Basing my position on a belief that human history's time span was too brief to
allow for significant input from biological evolution, I would have cited Franz
Boas, from whom I had learned (correctly, I believe) that the most "primitive" cultures accessible to anthropological study stand substantially on a par with the most
"modern" in their ability to construct languages capable of precisely expressing
the intricacies of temporal, spatial, causal, and moral relationships.[18] From the
foregoing I would have concluded that history—given the arrival of our species at
a certain common biological starting point—is controlled entirely by culture.
Quoting Marx as well as Boas, I would have declared (and did) that the human

species has no *nature*, only history.[19] My position today is different. I place Boas's "primitive" closer in evolutionary time to our own era than to the biological origins of the mind-culture process. I now think the entire span of human history is long enough to have incorporated inputs of genetic evolution into developments previously understood as exclusively cultural. Sharp separations of culture from biology become logically unacceptable—rather the two appear as merging into and reinforcing (or inhibiting) each other. These alterations imply a new starting hypothesis to the effect that long continuities of culture, initiated through biological selection, became generalized at an early stage across what was then still a small and geographically contiguous gene pool. Incest avoidance, universal in human cultures, provides a more-or-less self-evident model of this passage from genetically hard-wired behavior (instinct) to long cultural continuity. If religion—as I have argued throughout this book—is among the most ancient of cultural constructions, it may have originated in comparable transitions. Like language, it could then be described as "a hybrid of culture and biology."[20]

Why the shift of position? It reflects, of course, new developments in genetics, evolutionary psychology, and cognitive science. Like the vast majority of my contemporaries, with no special training in these fields but deeply concerned at the implications of recent research, I have no choice but to rely on interpretations by specialists whose work I have reason to respect. This at best is vicarious judgment, yet we are not left altogether at the mercy of specialists. From scientists, as well as from historians and philosophers of science, we learn that validation of new knowledge requires not only credentials of discovery, but a capacity on the part of the new to illuminate older knowledge by offering less cumbersome, more persuasive resolutions of troublesome difficulties. Raised in the penumbra of behaviorist psychology, I was aware that the language problem (especially how language is acquired in early childhood) had remained unresolved despite the best efforts of behaviorist research.[21] Nonetheless I was astonished by Noam Chomsky's assault on behaviorism:

> Language learning is not really something that the child does, it is something
> that happens to the child ... much as the child's body grows and matures in
> a predetermined way when provided with appropriate nutrition.[22]

Predetermined by what? How could cultural learning be predetermined except by culture itself? Was Chomsky leading a retrogression to some sort of

Neoplatonism? I hardly thought E. O.Wilson, whose book *Sociobiology* had triggered the ferocious "culture wars" of the 1980s, could be classified as a Neoplatonist, yet he was taking Chomsky's side when he described the mind as "innately structured" by a "'deep grammar'" without which language acquisition would be impossible. The behaviorist explanation was obviously bankrupt. Mathematical simulation alone, Wilson insisted, would demonstrate that not enough time exists in childhood "to learn English sentences by rote."[23]

I had always admired Chomsky. As a culturalist during the "culture wars" I felt under some obligation to disparage Wilson, yet his concurrence with Chomsky sank in, as did the fact that others whose work I also had reason to respect were taking similar positions. Culture includes all that can be passed from one generation to the next by learning. If learning proves inadequate to explain how mind sorts out sensory signals or how it acquires language, the remaining alternatives are Neoplatonic dualism or evolutionary psychology. "Plato," Darwin wrote in one of his early notebooks, "says ... that 'our necessary ideas' arise from the preexistence of the soul [and] are not derivable from experience." "For preexistence," Darwin then added, "read monkeys." Reduced to these stark terms, it becomes understandable why the issue has been bitterly contested. My option was (and *is*) for evolutionary psychology. In deference, however, to uncertainties of a rapidly expanding field, and aware of my own minimal comprehension of how discoveries are made in that field, I will keep my own conclusions as low profile as possible. It seems likely that genetic heredity helped fix the early directions of cultural continuities. This supposition sharpens the argument for cultural rigidity without being essential to the argument, since factors within culture itself might suffice to explain rigidity in cultural constructions. Nor, on the other hand, is it reasonable to insist that genetic heredity (if it be allowed entry at all into the cultural realm) must be reckoned as a determining factor. In that case there would be no difference between biological and cultural evolution, whereas such a difference is readily visible.[24]

An analogy between the great lizard crisis in the Cretaceous period and our own nuclear-biological and ecological crises must be less than perfect because human history creates openings of flexibility and choice that separate cultural development qualitatively from biological evolution. Were this not the case there would be no hope for survival of our species (except in the dual realm of spirit) and no point to writing a book such as this one. Hope rests on the potential that flexibility and choice seem to have kept open even in the long continuities of culture. But one remembers that such continuities were constructed by mechanisms parallel to those of natural selection. Relative to human history's timescale, they remain massively resistant to change. Nor can we omit the possibility (or likelihood, or certainty?) that continuities of very long duration had their beginnings under biological jurisdiction. However that may be, the more rigidly predetermined such continuities are, the tighter the fit of the great lizard analogy. The tighter the fit, the narrower the aperture for survival. Will religion, one of the oldest of those cultural continuities, suffice to guide us through?

Knowing and Believing

Suppose now we run this analogy through a thought experiment. Our starting point will be to imagine that the world's industrialized nations, despite all their scientific and technical baggage, have faltered in coping with the nuclear/biological/ecological crises. Religion courageously steps forward to take the lead. Religion, as we know, is disunited at the denominational level. So the opening gambit will be a call for reconciliation of doctrinal differences in the interest of global, or even cosmic, spiritual consensus. Ecumenicalism, to which all denominations necessarily accord tokens of deference, expresses just this sort of aspiration. Ecumenical leaders, then, agree to place species survival at the head of an agenda said to be divinely sanctioned for the reason that divinity is believed to favor human creatures over all others and to be equally accessible to all members of the human family. Building on its world scope and moral authority, religion launches crusades for global environment. It will press on individual believers the duty of preserving the environment God (or the gods) created for them. It discovers ecological transgressions to be sinful in the same degree that murder and theft (or even sacrilege) are sinful. Thus ecumenical faith inspires and commands commitment by national governments—by scientific/technological establishments—by corporate industry. Industrial nations, yielding to this pressure, begin to downsize their living standards even as pre-industrial societies abandon schemes for rapid industrialization. Around the world, under guidance of churches collectively devoted to benevolent, anthropomorphic deities, the human family rejoices in reducing its progeny to whatever rate, scientifically determined, the global environment can best sustain. Simply to read the foregoing is to know not much of it is likely be acted out.[25]

Yet why not? The argument appears impeccably reasonable, and the project-ed behavior no more difficult to imagine than that of American, English, French, Russian, German, and Japanese populations during the Second World War. In other words, one need only attribute to religion a moral authority comparable to that of national patriotism in the 1940s to render credible the scenario I have just sketched. But this optimistic prospectus would be conceivable only if the ecu-menical inclusiveness at religion's first origin somehow transcended the exclu-sive, domineering behaviors favored by natural selection throughout most of human history. Such behaviors, of course, prevailed because they furnished believers with coercive power over others who believed not at all, or believed and behaved differently. While it might be possible to conceptualize a common denominator of all religious belief, religion itself in its earthly incarnations offers a maze of conflicting doctrine, much of which claims the status of revelation. Understood as revealed truth, religious teachings become lethally particularistic even though their content may be universal love. But that has not normally been their content. Since the original crisis of consciousness (and especially since the intrusion, soon thereafter, of evil empires), most religions some of the time and some religions all the time have taught the expendability and unfitness for salva-tion of vast majorities of the human species.[26] Adaptively though such teachings may have worked in earlier times, in our era they become invitations to nuclear-biological disaster, not means of avoiding it.

It may be helpful here to call up testimony of a contemporary witness—one highly esteemed in the media as an expert on spiritual matters—Bill Moyers, whom I quoted in chapter 2. Starry-eyed over the booming religious revival, Moyers was announcing ecstatically, "Religion is breaking out everywhere." "For many people" this means "turning—or returning—to the Bible as a guide through chaos." The upbeat mood of 1996, however, yielded to darker forebodings. "One of the biggest changes in politics in my lifetime," Moyers writes in 2005, "is that the delusional is no longer marginal. It has come in from the fringe, to sit in the seat of power in the Oval Office and Congress." Millions of Christians, Moyers reports—proffering the information this time not as cause for thanksgiving, but for alarm—"believe the Bible is literally true, word for word."

> For them the invasion of Iraq was a warm-up act, predicted in the Book of Revelation. ... A war with Islam ... is not something to be feared but wel-comed—an essential conflagration on the road to redemption. ... Why care

about the earth, when the droughts, floods, famine, and pestilence brought by ecological collapse are signs of the apocalypse foretold in the Bible? Why care about global climate change when you and yours will be rescued in the Rapture? ... I look up at the pictures ... of my grandchildren ... I see the future looking back at me from those photographs and I say, 'Father, forgive us for we know not what we do.' And then the shiver runs down my spine. ... We do know what we are doing. We are stealing their future. Betraying their trust. Despoiling their world.[27]

To bear witness against the revelationist-fundamentalist side of our religious spectrum for Moyers is courageous and important, yet carries no really new information. We know already how such belief systems work to motivate and *sanctify* acts of mass terror like destruction of the World Trade Towers and the Oklahoma Federal Building; or, equally well, crusades of religious cleansing as they are envisioned by many supporters of President Bush's war in Iraq.[28] What Moyers finds terrifying in 2005 is not some scourge of new aberrations, but behavior normal and commonplace for true believers in many religions, through many historical periods.

Precisely the opposite is what would be required if religion were seriously to confront the nuclear and ecological crises. To work at this level, it would be obliged to recapture its first origin. It would need to reenact the revolt of consciousness against death that became generic to the human species. Such a reaching back, however, comes up against a deeper cleavage. Religion, to resolve the crisis of consciousness, had asserted the *real* existence of benevolent spiritual beings in nature. Lacking any proof by reason or empirical evidence—aside from superficial analogies suggested by seasonal rotation or the rites of spring—religion's only ground for belief was the will to believe. Belief in a friendly presence in nature enhanced the survival ratio of believers. For this reason religion proved adaptive in cultural evolution. It needed no other validation. Knowledge of death, by contrast, entered consciousness as a reasoned induction from empirical experience. Its validation was the capacity of mind to organize sensory signals according to time, space, and causality. Acquired through biological evolution, this is the capacity by which human culture constructed the web of approximations and predictions we call *knowledge*, or sometimes *science*. Religion, however, by favoring belief over empirical experience, commanded the fast track, and returned to this same priority throughout its long struggle against the problem of evil.[29]

Moyers's creedal connections are doubtless more solidly based in ecumenical and spiritual circles than among hard-liners, which (in part) explains his
frank expression of alarm. Yet the nub of the problem remains on Moyers's side
of the spectrum. It resides in the vast territory that stretches from moderate,
humane, ecumenicalist beliefs (like those of Moyers himself) out into thinner
atmospheres of New Age spirituality. Here especially one finds empathy with
environmental anxieties and some concurrence in the logic of ecumenicalism.
It is among such believers, consequently, that the cleavage between knowing
and believing can best be estimated. An immense literature aimed directly at
New Age/spiritual constituencies has been generated by religious entrepreneurs of the past quarter-century. The two excerpts that follow are taken from a
work in the top echelon of this literature, *God and the Evolving Universe*, published in 2002. The credentials of its authors are world-class. One was
cofounder of the famous Esalen Institute at Big Sur. The second was author of
The Celestine Prophecy (1993), "which spent more than three years on the *New
York Times* bestseller list and two years as the best-selling American book in the
world." The third is a "counselor to the terminally ill," and co-producer "of a
feature-length documentary" about Tibetan Buddhism. We are dealing with
representative figures at a high level. Not only are they spiritual believers, but
knowledgeable in science. Their text pays homage to scientific great names and
embellishes science itself with mystic correspondences. At the core of this
book, say the authors,

> ... is our belief that the universe has a telos, a fundamental tendency to man-
> ifest its divinity. Though evolution suffers many close calls ... it has given rise
> for billions of years to greater and greater capacities among the Earth's living
> things. To say that evolution appears to meander is not to say that it has no
> direction. Indeed, many attributes of living things exhibit clear lines of
> progress *across* evolutionary domains.

That was near the end of chapter1. In the closing pages of the last chapter we
read:

> Humans, in short, have since the Stone Age sensed the body's capacity to live
> in ever-closer alignment with the Transcendent, thus acquiring new freedom
> from the elements, new capacities for earthly activities and a joyous, life-giv-

ing radiance. ... It is impossible to say how long it might take for such transformations to unfold, but the prospect ... could inspire new creativity, deter-
mination, and excitement among those of us drawn to the evolutionary
adventure.[30]

God and the Evolving Universe may not win big applause from fundamentalists and revelationists, who do not read the same books as spiritualists and New
Agers. The opposite poles of our religious spectrum are like separate nationali-
ties. They remain hostile and mutually exclusive. Their populations are driven by
different emotions, turned on by different jokes, enthralled with different visions.
Maybe they even believe in different gods. Despite these differences they hold
certain basic convictions in common. Both take the final goal of human purpose
to be individual "salvation"—rather than, say, preservation of our species, or of
biological life on earth. Both share the definitive trait of all religions, that is, they
give priority to *believing* over *knowing*. Believing will continue, as it always has,
to ease the terror of consciousness facing death. During previous crises, this was
the essence of its species-saving power. In the crises of the twenty-first century,
however, belief works to dissolve the reality that knowledge labors to hold in
focus. The knowledge of *that* reality imposes terrifying tasks. But religion,
because it sets faith before knowledge, can offer dispensations that to many will
seem persuasive and conscientiously acceptable. Religion at this level becomes
ideological armor for a politics of denial. What market value, today, has biological
life on earth a thousand years from now? Or one hundred?

The alternatives are bleak but simple. If religion's message is true— if there is
indeed a benevolent deity (or deities) presiding over the cosmos, and if we knew
this as a matter of knowledge rather than faith, then we could dismiss the terrifying crises of the twenty-first century as irrelevant. Human souls would be gathered into the eternal kingdom regardless of what you or I might do, or fail to do,
and planet Earth left to disintegrate like a spent rocket in the abyss. Or, should
some nostalgic environmentalist value attach to Earth as first seat of paradise and
birthplace of humankind, its preservation for a historical monument would present no great difficulty for the Master Builder. On the other hand, if religious truth
is a matter of *faith*—that is, if religion remains in doubt with at least a chance of
proving false—then these crises must be seen as absolutely relevant to every
human being alive, or possibly born in the future.

14

Jerusalem

"What can I do?" Gilgamesh asks. "Where can I go?"

A thief has stolen my flesh.
Death lives in the house where my bed is
And wherever I set my feet, there death is.[1]

Belief in spiritual beings, which saved us more than once in the past, will not work this time. What can we do? We consent, I think—as Gilgamesh finally consented—to live out our lives in the angle of illumination that consciousness and culture hold open. In the opening chapter I reviewed in some detail the kinds of initiatives we ought to be pursuing, as well as the political, economic, and cultural inhibitions that hinder us from doing so. There is no need to run these through again. They have been stated often and eloquently by many writers. We know what the initiatives are, yet dismiss them as unrealistic. In reality, we dismiss them not because they are unrealistic, but too realistic. We find them unthinkable. Most of us would think it unthinkable to readjust our political economy to goals of negative growth. Or to suggest, for example, that by deconstructing the advertising industry we might liberate our collective mind-set from its cosmological glorification of waste. Thoughts like these are actually quite easy to think and we will all be thinking them sooner or later; probably too late, since meanwhile the entabulated wisdom of our long cultural continuities keeps setting them out of reach, as if beyond the pale of practical policy.

Ill fared it then with Roderick Dhu
As on the ground his targe he threw,
Whose brazen studs and tough bull hide
Had death so often turned aside.

Walter Scott (whether he so intended or not) was describing a ritual endemic to evolution, both cultural and biological. His readers could join in mourning the downfall of the picturesque Scottish chieftain while tempering their regret by recognizing that he deserved his fate because he stood as adversary to Fitzjames, who represented a more up-to-date (therefore higher) stage.[2]

Something comparable might be said of the great lizards. I suppose we could even contemplate the human condition under a similar rubric of progress. Our own situation, however, appears radically different for the reason that we are in the middle of it. What the oncoming ecological disasters and proliferating weapons of mass destruction announce—for us—is not advancement to some higher stage but the decimation of human culture—or its oblivion. Given our stewardship over planet Earth so far, we doubtless deserve that ending no less than Roderick Dhu or the great lizards, yet we cannot suppose our grandchildren and great grandchildren deserve it (unless we wish to reinstate original sin). In any case, the issue is not one of just desserts, but preservation of a mutated blossom which (to human eyes) appears beautiful and valuable, and grows on our planet more by accident (so far as we can tell), than by necessity.[3]

Religion's historical paradox is that whereas our species could hardly have survived without it—let alone constructed the culture that makes us human—religion itself, which became a central element of culture through those same evolutionary sequences, works in the twenty-first century (as did the dinosaurs' heavy armor in an earlier epoch) to the detriment of the species. My own stance since childhood has been that of nonbeliever. Nonetheless, I had counted on finding in religion an attachment to humanity at large, a sense of shared obligation for life on earth. I had thought the fact that a majority of human beings are believers—leaving aside the validity of what was believed—ought in itself to make religion a natural channel for collective efforts to save the human species. I was mistaken. I had not understood how much of religion's power is used up in making war against evil empires. Throughout this book, I have defined religion as belief in spiritual beings. What evoked that belief, however, was terror of death, which consciousness—a product of biological evolution—had made irrevocable. The problem of evil, then, preceded the origin of religion.

The fact is that all religions are essentially Manichean. Bill Moyers, whom I quoted at the end of the last chapter, is illuminating also in this context. His naive enthusiasm in 1996 stands in striking contrast to the grim polemics of 2005. For Moyers, the intervening decade must have been grievously painful. Like most journalists (in America at least), Moyers has tended to be celebrationist about religion and cautiously selective in his criticisms. What this conveys is that not religion itself was ever at fault, but only particular varieties (Islamic fundamentalism, Christian fundamentalism, Protestantism that takes the Bible as "literally true," true believers who believe what they read in *Left Behind* novels and wait rapturously for the "The Rapture.") *Real* religion presumably remains untainted by any of these. There can be no question of the hostility Moyers is expressing against the Bush administration and its religious allies; nor of his anger at the ecological and military vandalism that he sees as selling out the life chances of his children and grandchildren. Have we "lost our capacity for outrage," he demands, "our ability to sustain indignation at injustice?"[4] If other religious folk share Moyers's opinions (and I expect some do), then divisions are likely to develop inside the "moral majority," which might bring down the Republican regime, and (perhaps) lead to changes in American policy. Meanwhile, how ought *dis*believers conduct themselves? Will critiques and polemics against religion (such as this book) serve simply to impede the efforts of influential and respected moderates like Moyers? Would nonbelievers be better advised to get back into their closets and wait it out? The question is crucial, and the correct question on which to end this book. The difficulty with leaving the battle to moderates like Moyers is that in religious controversy they remain intellectually disarmed because they believe essentially the same things hard-liners believe. If to be religious is to believe that belief trumps knowledge and that spiritual intuitions are more penetrating than scientific information, on what ground can middle-road religionists like Moyers stand in opposing extremists like Bush and Pat Robertson? They will be obliged to invoke scientific styles of argument at the same time they are discounting science itself.

I noted in earlier chapters that religious belief (on a world scale) tends to be most solidly anchored in industrial working classes and among agricultural laborers and displaced rural populations of the third world. Precisely these groups will suffer most heavily under capitalism's "free market" world empire. They will be trapped between exploitation that provokes desperate outbreaks and endless poverty that seeks solace in faith. At this juncture, something akin to liberation theology must make a comeback if it is to claim any share in the future.[5] To stand against its own reactionary clergies, however, a liberating movement needs powers of demonstration that come only from outside religion. Liberationists inside will need to be in communication with the enemy outside. Might there be signals exchanged, then, simply at the level of species solidarity? Believers, after all, are no less vulnerable than nonbelievers to *worldly loves* (yet note how negative a connotation religion attaches to this luminous phrase!), and both partake, inevitably, in affections that view the world as we often look at children, or young people in love, hoping things might go well for them. Such overlaps of shared experience contain our best hopes—at short range—for resolving the crises of the twenty-first century this side of global disaster.

In the long run—if there is a long run—religion now stands as a negative factor with respect to species survival. Every puncture in the heavy armor of religion therefore increases the chance for survival and minimizes the lacerations civilization will be obliged to endure in that process. Yes, human culture may survive, or may be obliterated, or simply bombed back into the Stone Age—as one of our former culture heroes graciously put it. Those who stand against religion in the twenty-first century—a double-decimal minority—may well be putting their lives on the line. In the ancient language of religious radicalism, they will need the moral fortitude to bear witness against the beast, together with grace and clarity of mind sufficient to express their commitment, yet with no promise of afterlife to lure them on. Must such critics make enemies of all the rest? The persuasive power of nonbelief lies in its transparency, its openness to the real world. Belief, on the other hand, draws power from rejecting reality. How will the daily interchanges of citizens and fellow mortals play out as between these contradictory agendas? My bone-level intuition tells me sometimes there never will be such interchanges; rather it will be, as James Baldwin once wrote, "The Fire Next Time." But apocalyptic rhetoric—conscience-raising and ego-enhancing though it sometimes may seem—works dysfunctionally in this case because it terminates dialogue, whereas survival hangs on the possibility of continuing communication between believers and nonbelievers. Hoping to maximize this possibility, I take my model from a poem by William Blake, which by its barrage of unanswered questions enjoins response. "And did those feet in ancient times ...? And was the holy Lamb of God ...?" Blake's poem (a century and a half after it was written)

entered the popular culture of the 1960s as a hymn denouncing destruction of the
natural environment:

And was Jerusalem builded here
Amid these dark satanic mills?[6]

The young rebels of the 1960s perhaps had not dug very deep into Blake's
metaphors. I will not do so either (here, at least) since I am scouting for common
ground, and I must find myself ultimately in disagreement with Blake on matters
of deepest consequence. As to the dark satanic mills, however, set in their context
of early-nineteenth-century England, we can instantly agree and thus make room
for both in the party of ecological survival.[7] And since I am willing to adjust his
"Jerusalem" to my own metaphoric meanings, why should not he be willing to
tolerate my doing so? For me—secularist and nonbeliever—*Jerusalem* refers
metaphorically to the human community *after* it has groped through those identifications that move from family to tribe, to nation; *after* it has arrived at some
self-sustaining balance with natural habitat; *after* it discovers that survival
requires not only an egalitarian politics inside the species but physical and moral
bonding to earth's multitudinous fellow travelers who share our dwelling place.[8]
So Jerusalem, in my metaphor, means not Augustine's city but the city of earth in
all its evolutionary fragility: thus a declaration of allegiance, for better and worse,
fortune or disaster, till death do us part. Blake, a high believer, probably would not
be willing to tolerate so earthbound a Jerusalem as the one I have sketched. At this
point our paths would separate; we would stand to each other as adversaries. Yet
might we not also continue as fellow travelers?

The poem on Jerusalem—which frames the question about satanic mills—
takes the form, like much of Blake's writing, of a dialogue in metaphor. "Bring
me my arrows of desire," he commands, as if to his chariot driver, "Bring me
my spear,

I will not cease from mental fight
Nor shall my sword sleep in my hand.[9]

Blake was surely a warrior, though hardly one who put much trust in swords
and spears.[10] In the three lines quoted there is only one phrase that is *not*
metaphorical, and for that reason demands to be taken at face value. The phrase

is "mental fight." By it I assume he understood something like standing up publicly in moral and intellectual affirmation. This approximately is what radical sur-
vivors of the Great English Revolution—Levelers, Diggers, Quakers, Seekers,
Muggletonians—intended by "bearing witness against the Beast," and would not
have been far removed from the social milieu in which Blake grew up.[11] It com-
bines principled and total commitment with an ongoing openness to persuasion.

Persuasion? As members of an earthbound species, what we share is our heritage of consciousness and culture. Yet culture itself—our *shared* culture of unlimited industrial growth, war, environmental destruction—renders human existence
tenuous. The great lizard analogy serves warning: the tighter the analogy, the narrower the chance for survival. Yet there remains a crucial difference between biological and cultural evolution: culture *evolved* through its reciprocal relationship
with consciousness. Crises that threaten human culture (unlike those that
destroyed the dinosaurs) are themselves artifacts of culture and thus might prove
more malleable. Defusing them would require that consciousness, *consciously*, take
command of the ship. To take command means rejecting every illusion that our
species enjoys a privileged track. Spiritual beings—our cultural *doppelgangers*—
were not waiting here to welcome us. They came later at our bidding. Nature, into
which science opens limited vistas, doubtless *was* here, yet nature (so far as we can
tell) pays no more heed to human purposes than to those of galaxies and black
holes—or to the entrepreneurial aspirations of dinosaurs and great lizards. Earth's
time is limited. We know it will be long. We think some of it still remains open for
inventing and deploying culture. Ours may be the only such outpost the cosmos
contains—or there may be multitudes, however unlikely our chance of encountering any other.[12] Either way, we go it alone. In either case we see how unique and
fragile consciousness actually is. It would be a pity, dreaming of magic transformations, to collaborate in destroying the ground of human consciousness.

Notes

1. The Human Condition

1. For two overviews of the ecological crises from different perspectives: John Bellamy Foster, *Ecology Against Capitalism* (New York: Monthly Review Press, 2002): 9–25, 69–78; and "Organizing Ecological Revolution," *Monthly Review* (October 2005): 1–10; and Michael B. McElroy, "Religion and Ecology: Can the Climate Change?" *Daedalus: Journal of the American Academy of Arts and Sciences* (Fall 2001): 1–58.

2. Alexander Saxton, "Race, Class and Nation-Building," *Contention* (Spring 1996), 203–24.

3. John Bellamy Foster, *Marx's Ecology: Materialism and Nature* (New York: Monthly Review Press, 2000).

4. On third world industrialization and ecological disaster, see for example, Robert Skidelsky, "The Chinese Shadow I, II," *New York Review of Books*, November 17, 2005, 30–32; and December 1, 2005, 32–40.

5. Robert Heilbroner, "The Human Prospect," *New York Review of Books*, January 24, 1974, 21–23; *An Inquiry into the Human Prospect* (New York: W. W. Norton, 1974).

6. Stephen Jay Gould, *An Urchin in the Storm* (New York: W. W. Norton, 1987), 111–12, as quoted in Foster, *Marx's Ecology*, 203.

2. Homo Religiosus

1. Several examples across the spectrum concur on these points. Scott Atran, *In Gods We Trust: The Evolutionary Landscape of Religion* (New York: Oxford University Press, 2002), 56–57. Marvin Harris, *Our Kind: The Evolution of Human Life and Culture* (New York: Harper Perennial, 1989), 399, agrees with Tylor as to religion's origin in animism and universality. Anthony F. C. Wallace, *Religion: An Anthropological View* (New York: Random House, 1966), viii. Mircea Eliade, *The Quest: History and Meaning in Religion* (Chicago: University of Chicago Press, 1969), 2. Harlow Shapley, ed., *Science Ponders Religion* (New York: Appleton Century Crofts, 1960), vi: "Religion, when defined as the belief in spirits and matters spiritual [ie, Tylor's definition], is found by anthropologists to be an inherent part of all cultures, primitive and advanced." Tylor probably arrived at his presumption of universality not from contemporary evidence but from Greek and Roman classics; see Walter Burkert, *Creation of the Sacred: Tracks of Biology in Early Religions* (Cambridge, Mass.: Harvard University Press, 1996), 1, 2.

2. Gregory S. Paul, "The Secular Revolution of the West," *Free Inquiry*, (Summer 2002); 28–34. Philip Clayton, *The Problem of God in Modern Thought* (Grand Rapids, Mich.: Eerdmans, 2000), 263. Most explanations of the secular era stem from two famous sequences in Max Weber: one, describing how intellectualism and rationality cause "the world's processes [to]

become disenchanted, [to] lose their magical significance," *Sociology of Religion* (Boston: Beacon Press, 1963), 124–25; the other, in *The Protestant Ethic and the Spirit of Capitalism*, (New York: Scribner, 1958), 181, suggesting that although early Puritans believed "care for external goods" ought to be worn lightly (like a cloak easily thrown aside), their economic success "decreed that the cloak should become an iron cage." The first sequence points to scientific revolution as a matrix of secularism, a theme developed by James Turner, *Without God, Without Creed: The Origins of Unbelief in America* (Baltimore: Johns Hopkins University Press, 1985), 7–34; and see Bernard Lightman, *The Origins of Agnosticism: Victorian Unbelief and the Limits of Knowledge* (Baltimore: Johns Hopkins University Press, 1987). The second takes us, by way of industrialization, to the city, which of course preceded the industrial revolution by several millennia but was itself revolutionized by industrialism. The city serves often to exemplify the "iron cage." Not always, however; see n. 7, below. For a sociological appraisal of the impact of secularization on religious belief, Peter L. Berger, *A Rumor of Angels: Modern Society and the Rediscovery of the Supernatural* [1969] (New York: Doubleday, 1990), 1–30, 179–82.

3.   John Stuart Mill, *Nature, The Utility of Religion and Theism* (London: Longmans, Green, 1969), 73. The first two essays, written during the 1850s, were published in 1869.

4.   John Henry Newman, *Apologia pro Vita Sua: Being a History of His Religious Opinions* (New York: Longmans, Green, 1947), 123, 221–22, 181; see also 236.

5.   Shapley, *Science Ponders Religion*, passim.

6.   Dan Wakefield, "Speaking in Tongues," *Nation*, January 23, 1995, 98–101.

7.   Harvey Cox, *The Secular City: Secularization and Urbanization in Theological Perspective* (New York: Macmillan, 1965), 1–14; quote, 3.

8.   Ibid., 220.

9.   Ibid., 125–48. Harvey Cox, "'The New Breed' in American Churches: Sources of Social Activism in American Religion," in *Religion in America*, ed. William G. McLoughlin and Robert Bellah(Boston: Houghton Mifflin, 1968), 368–83. Cox, *Turning East: the Promise and Peril of the New Orientalism* (New York: Simon & Schuster, 1977), 65–66, 164, 169, 172.

10. Harvey Cox, *Fire from Heaven: The Rise of Pentecostal Spirituality and the Reshaping of Religion in the Twenty-First Century* (Reading, Mass.: Addison Wesley, 1995), 100–105.

11. William G. McLoughlin, *Revivals, Awakenings, and Reform: an Essay on Religion and Social Change in America, 1607–1977* (Chicago: University of Chicago Press, 1978), 179–216. McLoughlin and Bellah, *Religion*, ix–xxiv.

12. David B. Barnett, George T. Kurian, Todd M. Johnson, *World Christian Encyclopedia:A Comparative Survey of Churches and Religions in the Modern World*, 2 vols. (New York: Oxford University Press, 2001), table 1.1, p. 4, indicates that "pentecostal charismatics" (most of them in the United States) increased from 2.0 to 8.1 percent of world population between 1970 and 1990. Jackson Carroll, Douglas Johnson, Martin Marty, George Gallup, Jr., *Religion in America 1950 to the Present* (San Francisco: Harper & Row, 1979), 8–27; "technologies of the spirit" (p. 25) included transcendental meditation, yoga, mysticism, and Eastern religion. Bill Moyers, "The Upsurgence of Faith," *USA Weekend*, October 11–13, 1996, 4–5.

13. Harvey Cox, *Fire*, 102–5; "The Transcendent Dimension," *Nation*, January 1, 1996, 20–3, as quoted in Wakefield, *Nation*, January23, 1995, 98.

14. Harvey Cox, *Religion in the Secular City: Toward a Postmodern Theology* (New York: Simon & Schuster, 1984), 29–71. Moyers, "Upsurgence of Faith," 4–5; *Time*, October, 28, 1996, 66–77; December 16, 1996, 60–69.

15. Peter Baker, *Washington Post*, in Santa Rosa (Calif.) *Press Democrat*, February 13, 1997.

16. Cox, *Fire*, 185–241; *San Francisco Chronicle*, April 13, 1997, 3. For statistics on the upsurge of religion in the U.S. and worldwide, see Robert W. Fogel, *The Fourth Great Awakening and the Future of Egalitarianism* (Chicago: Univ of Chicago Pr, 2000), 25-8 & notes 11, 12, pp 287-8.

17. Moyers, "Upsurgence of Faith," 5. Robert Wright, *Time*, December 16, 1996, 68–69. Diana L. Eck, *A New Religious America: How a "Chrustian Country" Has Become the World's Most Religiously Diverse Nation* (San Francisco: Harper San Francisco, 2001), 270–93. Jack Maguire, *Essential Buddhism: A Complete Guide to Beliefs and Practices* (New York: PocketBooks/Simon & Schuster, 2001), ix. Barnett et al., *Christian Encyclopedia*, table 1.1, p. 4, shows 1970-2000 growth rates substantially higher for Muslims, slightly higher for Hindus, slightly lower for Buddhists, than that of world population.

18. Clayton, *Problem of God*, 76 n. 34.

19. Cox, *Religion in the Secular City*, esp. 11–26.

20. Israel and the disintegration of Yugoslavia are prime examples, but almost any contemporary conflict will serve.

21. Sidney Ahlstrom in his monumental *Religious History of the American People* (New Haven: Yale University Press, 1972) comments on the late-nineteenth-century convergence of Protestant ecumenicalism with Anglo-Saxonism, overseas missions and imperialism: 8–9, 733–34, 798–99, 802–4, 833, 849–50, 879–80.

22. Moyers, "Upsurgence of Faith," 4. Huston Smith, *The World's Religions* (San Francisco: Harper, 1991), x, xiv, 390–91. For similar assertions of the shared essence of all religions, Ninian Smart, *The Religious Experience of Mankind* (New York: Scribner, 1984); Wilfred Cantwell Smith, *Toward a World Theology: Faith and the Comparative History of Religion* (Philadelphia: Westminster, 1981). Smart, who set up one of the earliest religious studies departments (University of Lancaster, England), also teaches at University of California, Santa Barbara. Cantwell Smith is former director of the Center for Study of World Religions at Harvard.

23. Eliade, *Quest*, 69.

24. Diana L. Eck, *Encountering God: A Spiritual Journey from Bozeman to Banares* (Boston: Beacon Press, 1993), esp. 188–96; quotes, 195–96. Eck, *New Religious America*, 23–5.

25. McLoughlin and Bellah, *Religion*, xvii. Martin Marty, *The Public Church: Mainline, Evangelical, Catholic* (New York: Crossroad, 1981), ix-x, 6–7.

26. Eck, *Encountering God*, 90.

3. Tylor's Definition and the Social Science Stance

1. Eric J. Sharpe, "E. B. Tylor," *Encyclopedia of Religion*, ed. Mircea Eliade (New York: Macmillan, 1987), 15:107. George Stocking, *Victorian Anthropology* (New York: Free Press/Macmillan, 1987), 156–64. Edward Burnett Tylor, *Religion in Primitive Culture*, vol. 2 of *Primitive Cultures* [1871] (New York: Harper, 1958), 8.

2. Eric J. Sharpe, *Comparative Religion: A History* (New York: Scribner, 1975), 53–58, 59, 66. James G. Frazer, *The Golden Bough: A Study in Magic and Religion* [1887] (London: St. Martin's/Macmillan, 1955) 1:222. Andrew Lang, *The Making of Religion* [1898] (New York: AMS Press, 1968), 46–47. George Stocking, ed., *Franz Boas, A Boas Reader: The Shaping of American Anthropology 1883–1911* (Chicago: University of Chicago Press, 1974), 257. Charles Darwin, *The Descent of Man* [1871] (Amherst, NY: Prometheus Pr, 1998), 97-9.

3. Scott Atran, *In Gods We Trust: The Evolutionary Landscape of Religion* (New York: Oxford University Press, 2002), 264, 266. Daniel Dennett, *Breaking the Spell: Religion as a Natural*

Phenomenon (NY: Viking, 2006), 9. More generally, on the recurrence of definitions similar to Tylor's in post–World War II writings: Walter Burkert, *Creation of the Sacred: Tracks of Biology in Early Religion* (Cambridge, Mass.: Harvard University Press, 1996), 3–5. Melford E. Spiro, "Religion: Problems of Definition and Explanation," in *Anthropological Approaches to the Study of Religion,* ed. Michael Banton (London: Tavistock Publications, 1966), 85–126, esp. 93–95. J. Milton Yinger, *The Scientific Study of Religion* (New York: Macmillan, 1970, 4–5, and n. 4. Susannne C. Monahan, William A. Mirola, Michael O. Emerson, eds., *Sociology of Religion* (Upper Saddle River, N.J.: Prentice Hall, 2001), includes quoted or summarized definitions from Clifford Geertz, "Religion as a Cultural System," 16; Peter L. Berger, *The Sacred Canopy* (1967), 24–25; William James, *Varieties of Religious Experience,* 61–62. Steven Katz in *Mysticism and Religious Traditions* (New York: Oxford University Press, 1983), 56. Marvin Harris, *Our Kind: The Evolution of Human Life and Culture* (New York: Harper Perennial, 1989), 397ff. Anthony F. C. Wallace, *Religion: An Anthropological View* (New York: Random House, 1966), 5, 52. Harlow Shapley, ed., *Science Ponders Religion* (New York: Appleton Century Croft, 1960), vi. Bruce Lincoln opens his brief but intense reflection, *Holy Terrors: Thinking about Religion after September 11* (Chicago: University of Chicago Press, 2003), 2–7, by discussing the necessity, and difficulty, of working from an adequate definition of religion.

4. Stocking, *Victorian Anthropology,* 156, describes Tylor as "a survivor of the Enlightenment, a latter–day *philosophe* attacking theology, superstition, and all practices of civilized life for which common sense can find no justification." To which I would add that Tylor's Quaker background doubtless contributed to his preference for an intermediate stance between the dogmatics of affirmation or negation.

5. On the powerful presence of unbelief in the early nineteenth century, Bernard Lightman, *The Origins of Agnosticism: Victorian Unbelief and the Limits of Knowledge* (Baltimore: Johns Hopkins University Press, 1987), 6–31.

6. Adrian Desmond, *Huxley: From Devil's Disciple to Evolution's High Priest* (Reading, Mass.: Perseus, 1994), 373–74. Lightman, *Origins of Agnosticism,* 9–11, 91–115. James Turner, *Without God Without Creed: The Origins of Unbelief in America* (Baltimore: Johns Hopkins University Press, 1985), 7–34, esp. 14. Thomas Huxley, "Agnosticism" in *Science and Christian Tradition* (New York: Appleton, 1914), 238–39.

7. John Bellamy Foster, *Marx's Ecology: Materialism and Nature* (New York: Monthly Review Press, 2000), 2–6, 51–65. Margaret Jacob, *The Cultural Meaning of the Scientific Revolution* (Philadelphia: Temple University Press, 1988), 73–135, and *re* Leibniz, 48; Jacob, *The Radical Enlightenment: Pantheists, Freemasons and Republicans* (London: Allen/ Unwin, 1981), esp. 87–108. Robert K. Merton, *Science, Technology and Society in Seventeenth- Century England* (New York: Fertig, 1978). Christopher Hill, *The Intellectual Origins of the Puritan Revolution* (London: Oxford University Press, 1965); *God's Englishman: Oliver Cromwell and the English Revolution* (New York: Dial, 1970), 20–22, 243, 258–59; *The World Turned Upside Down: Radical Ideas During the English Revolution* (Harmondsworth, Eng.: Penguin, 1984), 113–40, 179–84. Perez Zagorin, *Francis Bacon* (Princeton, N.J.: Princeton University Press. 1998). Charles Taylor, *Sources of the Self: The Making of the Modern Identity* (Cambridge, Mass.: Harvard University Press, 1989), 230: "The Puritan theology of work and ordinary life provided a hospitable environment for the scientific revolution. Indeed much of Bacon's outlook stems from a Puritan background." Taylor speaks of the "Baconian revolution" (p. 231) and its relationship to the "mechanical philosophy," 149, 159–61. Jonathan Israel, *The Radical Enlightenment: Philosophy and the Making of Modernity, 1650–1750* (Oxford: Oxford University Press, 2001), 242–57.

8. Referring to the kingdom of Egypt a thousand years before Alexander, Ogden Goelet writes, "Polytheistic religions, however, have certain strengths, particularly from a political stand- point … the state does not have to enforce a theological conformity on its citizens," *Egyptian*

Book of the Dead (San Francisco: Chronicle Books, 1994), 14. Elaine Pagels, *The Origin of Satan* (New York: Random House, 1995). On converting the Roman empire to an enforcer of [Christian] doctrinal unity, see Hans Kung, *Great Christian Thinkers* (New York: Continuum, 1994), 80–84; Peter Brown, *Power and Persuasion in Late Antiquity: Toward a Christian Empire* (Madison: University of Wisconsin Press, 1992). Timothy Barnes, *Constantine and Eusebius* (Cambridge, Mass.: Harvard University Press, 1981), 191–271.

9. Jacob, *Radical Enlightenment*, 41–42; *Cultural Meaning*, 33–45. Perez Zagorin, *How the Idea of Religious Tolerance Came to the West* (Princeton, N.J.: Princeton University Press, 2003), 300–301.

10. Dante, standing at the apex of medieval culture, permitted himself a certain nostalgia for pagan tolerance expressed in his obvious dismay at the incarceration of virtuous (but pre–Christian) souls in Limbo and, more sharply, in the portrayal of Virgil as a sort of Weberian *ideal type* for high–minded deism. Dante, *Inferno*, trans., John Ciardi (New York: New American Library, 1953), Canto 4, passim. On Enlightenment and toleration, Israel, *Radical Enlightenment*, 265–66; re "providential deism," 63–64, 471–73. O. P. Grell and Roy Porter, eds., *Toleration in Enlightenment Europe* (Cambridge: Cambridge University Press,2000). Zagorin, *Idea of Tolerance*, chaps. 5–8. Richard Popkin, *The History of Skepticism from Savonarola to Bayle* (New York: Oxford University Press, 2003), esp. re Montaigne, 44–63, and Bayle, 283–302.

11. John Locke, *A Letter on Tolerance* (Oxford: Oxford University Press, 1968), 135, as cited in Walter Burkert, *Creation of the Sacred: Tracks of Biology in Early Religions* (Cambridge: Harvard University Press, 1996), 176.

12. Hill, *World Turned Upside Down*, "Mechanic Preachers and the Mechanic Philosophy," 287–305. Jacob, *Cultural Meaning*, 20–75. Jacob, in *The Radical Enlightenment*, 53–61, portrays Leibniz as rationally dedicated to the "mechanic philosophy" which he hoped would enhance human welfare and lead to a more rational social order. For a brief (and brilliant) sketch of the "mechanic philosophy," see Noam Chomsky, *On Nature and Language* (Cambridge: Cambridge University Press, 2002), 49–52. Taylor, *Sources of the Self*, 276, on Leibniz; Zagorin, *Bacon*, 25–51.

13. Hill, *World*, 13–18. Jacob, *Radical Enlightenment*, "The Newtonian Enlightenment and its Critics," 87–108. Israel, *Radical Enlightenment*, 6–22.

14. Bertrand Russell, *Religion and Science* [1935] (New York: Oxford/Galaxy, 1961), 8.

15. See, for example, Alfred Russel Wallace's retrospective comment on the changing shape of the scientific model in "Evolution and Character," *Fortnightly Review* 83 [1908], 1–24, in Jane R. Camerini, *The Alfred Russel Wallace Reader* (Baltimore: Johns Hopkins University Press, 2002), 163–65.

16. Mircea Eliade, *The Quest: History and Meaning in Religion* (Chicago: University of Chicago Press, 1969), 25, 37–53, 68–69. Sharpe, *History*, 25–26, 46–58.

17. Sharpe, *History*, 10–26, 54–55. E. E. Evans-Pritchard, *Theories of Primitive Religion* (Oxford: Clarendon, 1965), 6–13, 106–110. Stocking, *Victorian Anthropologists*, 79–80.

18. Sharpe, "Preanimism," *Encyclopedia of Religion* (2005), 11:7372–74. Kees Bolle, "Animism and Animatism," *Encyclopedia of Religion* (1987), 1:301. Evans-Pritchard, *Theories of Primitive Religion*, 31–32. Sharpe, *History*, 58–65. Paul Radin, "Introduction," Tylor, *Religion*, ix–xi.

19. Eliade, *Quest*, 24. Sharpe, *History*, 58–65, 178–87; "R. R. Marett," in *Encyclopedia of Religion* (2005), 8:5707. "Andrew Lang," in *Encyclopedia of Religion* (2005), 7:5299–5300. Andrew Lang, *The Making of Religion* (New York: AMS Press, 1968), esp. 46–52. R. R. Marett, *The Threshold of Religion* (London: 1929), 145–68. Radin, "Introduction," Tylor, *Religion*, xvi. And see n. 32 below.

20. Sharpe, *History*, 53: "Tylor came of Quaker stock … leaving school at sixteen, he went into the family firm of brass-founders." Annemarie de Waal Malefijt, *Religion and Culture: An*

Introduction to Anthropology of Religion (New York: Macmillan, 1968), 49–51. Stocking, *Victorian Antropology*, 156.

21. Emile Durkheim, *The Elementary Forms of the Religious Life* (New York: Macmillan/Free Press, 1965), 235–72. On outflanking secular explanations by invoking divine intent, see Daniel C. Dennett, *Darwin's Dangerous Idea: Evolution and the Meanings of Life* (New York: Simon & Schuster, 1995), 67.

22. Israel, *Radical Enlightenment*, 456–64.

23. Mark Ridley, ed., *The Darwin Reader* (New York: W. W. Norton, 1987), 41. Foster, *Marx's Ecology*, 81–8.

24. William Paley, *Natural Theology* [1802], ed. Henry Lord Brougham and Sir Charles Bell, 2 vols. (London: Charles Knight, 1836), esp. chaps. 1 and 27. Frederick Ferre, "Introduction," Paley, *Natural Theology: Selections* (Indianapolis: Bobbs-Merrill, 1963), xiii, xxviii. On the argument from design: John Stuart Mill, "Theism" in *Nature, The Utility of Religion and Theism* (London: Longmans, Green, 1969), 167–75. Dennett, *Dangerous Idea*, 70–71. Richard Dawkins, *The Blind Watchmaker* (New York: W. W. Norton, 1987), 21–41.

25. Alfred Russel Wallace, "Geological Climates and the Origin of Species," *Quarterly Review* 126 (1869): 391–4, in *The Alfred Russel Wallace Reader: A Selection of Writings from the Field*, ed. Jane R. Camerini (Baltimore: John Hopkins University Press, 2002), 160–63.

26. The agnostic mode of nonbelief includes a willingness to accord legitimacy to transcendental hypotheses, i.e., to those based more on belief than empirical evidence.

27. Philip Clayton, *God and Contemporary Science* (Edinburgh: Edinburgh University Press, 1997), 173–74. Daniel C. Dennett, *Consciousness Explained* (Boston: Little, Brown, 1991). Francis Crick, *The Amazing Hypothesis: The Scientific Search for the Soul* (New York: Scribner, 1994). Alden M. Hayashi, "Profile: Steven Pinker and the Brain," *Scientific American* 281, no.1 (July 1999): 32. Steven Pinker, *The Language Instinct: How the Mind Creates Language* (New York: Harper Perennial, 1994), 359–62.

28. John Stuart Mill ("Theism," 156–57) pointed out that the argument from design undercuts the other argument most frequently used in support of theism, that from the "general consent of mankind." To the extent that the argument from design is persuasive, it eliminates the need to attribute "general consent" to a universal intuition presumably of divine origin.

29. Walter Burkert in his 1989 Gifford Lectures (as cited above, chap. 1, n. 1) tells us that the effort "to grasp the distinctive features of religion remains at the level of observable behavior; the claims of factual truth or real existence of the gods are not of primary concern in the study of past religions." Steven Weinberg, Nobel Prize physicist and professor at the University of Texas, responding to letters about his famous "Sokal's Hoax" article (*New York Review of Books*, October 3, 1996) wrote that "[they]have me dead to rights in calling my views dualistic. I think that an essential element needed in the birth of modern science was the creation of a gap between the world of physical science and the world of human culture. ... If you want to find astronomy all muddled with cultural or moral values, you would turn to Dante's *Paradiso* rather than Galileo's *Dialogo*." See also Weinberg interview in John Horgan, *The End of Science: Facing the Limits of Knowledge in the Twilight of the Scientific Age* (Reading, Mass.: Addison-Wesley, 1996), 76. Weinberg's position coincides with that of the National Academy of Sciences, representing the 1,800 presumably most eminent scientists in the United States. Polled individually, over 90 percent of NAS members identified themselves as religious nonbelievers. Yet publicly the NAS declared (1998), "Whether God exists or not is a question about which science is neutral," and, in 1981, "Religion and science are separate and mutually exclusive realms of human thought whose presentation in the same context leads to misunderstanding of both scientific theory and religious belief." Edward J. Larson and Larry Witham, "Scientists and Religion in America," *Scientific American* 281, no.3 (September 1999): 89–93.

30. Stephen Jay Gould concurred with Weinberg and the NAS, although he might have resisted being classified as a dualist. In *Rocks of Ages: Science and Religion in the Fullness of Life* (New York: Library of Contemporary Thought/Ballantine, 1999), Gould set forth a "central principle of respectful noninterference. ... NOMA, or Non–Overlapping Magisteria" (p. 5) which clears the way for both "our drive to understand the factual character of nature (the magisterium of science), and our need to define meaning in our lives and a moral basis for our actions (the magisterium of religion)"(p. 175). While the acronym is new and we are offered some *bons mots* to keep it company ("science gets the age of rocks and religion the rock of ages," p. 6), Gould makes no claim to having invented NOMA, insisting rather that it represents "a long-standing consensus among the great majority of both scientific and religious leaders"(p. 64). Gould's NOMA then corresponds approximately to what I have been calling the social science stance toward religion and, thus far at least, I can cite Gould in support of my argument.

31. John Calvin, *The Institutes of the Christian Bible,* as quoted in Christopher Hill, *God's Englishman: Oliver Cromwell and the English Revolution* (New York: Dial, 1970), 219–20: "What avails it, in short, to know a God with whom we have nothing to do?"

32. Scott Atran, *In Gods We Trust: the Evolutionary Landscape of Religion* (New York: Oxford University Press, 2002), 8, 9. Sharpe, *History,* 58–65, 178–87. Lawrence Sullivan, "Supreme Beings," *Encyclopedia of Religion* (New York: Collier/Macmillan, 1987), 14:166–81. Theodore Ludwig, "Monotheism," *Encyclopedia* (1987), 10:68–75. Robert McDermott, "Monism," *Encyclopedia* (2005), 9:6143–50.

4. The Crisis of Consciousness

1. Alexander Alland, *Human Nature: Darwin's View* (New York: Columbia University Press, 1985), 19, attributes "survival of the fittest" to Herbert Spencer. Anthony F. C.Wallace, *Religion: An Anthropological View* (New York: Random House, 1966), argues that rituals aimed at "transformations of state in human beings or nature" (p. 106), which he compares to ritual behaviors of wolves, apes, etc., (p. 220ff.), come first, and if successful in raising group consciousness, will be repeated and rationalized by mythic narratives. Wallace (p. 102) quotes Franz Boas's *Mind of Primitive Man*: "'The ritual itself is the stimulus for the origin of the myth. ... The ritual existed and the tale originated from the desire to account for it.'" Edward O. Wilson, *Sociobiology: The New Synthesis* (Cambridge, Mass.: Harvard University Press, 2000), 559–61. Milton Yinger, *The Scientific Study of Religion* (New York: Macmillan, 1970), 17; Walter Burkert, *Creation of the Sacred: Tracks of Biology in Early Religions* (Cambridge, Mass.: Harvard University Press, 1996), 28–30, 85–101.

2. Although *myth* in everyday speech usually refers to a falsified or inflated account its real meaning, according to Mircea Eliade, *Myth and Reality* (New York: Harper & Row, 1968), 5–6, is that of "a sacred history; it relates an event that took place in primordial Time ... myth tells how, through the deeds of Supernatural Beings, a reality came into existence. ... The actors in myths are Supernatural Beings." Eliade, *The Sacred and the Profane: The Nature of Religion* (New York: Harcourt Brace Jovanovich, 1959), 95. Standard dictionaries confirm this usage, as in *Compact Oxford English Dictionary* (1971): "1. A purely fictional narative usually involving supernatural persons ... or events."

3. Christopher Hill, *The World Turned Upside Down* (London: Penguin, 1975), 292–96. Jonathan Israel, *Radical Enlightenment: Philosophy and the Making of Modernity, 1650–1750* (Oxford: Oxford University Press, 2001), 457. Noam Chomsky, *On Nature and Language* (Cambridge: Cambridge University Press, 2002), 51–52.

4. Burkert, *Creation of the Sacred,* 31, quoting the Roman poet Publius Statius. Paul Radin, *Primitive Religion: Its Nature and Origins* (New York: Dover, 1957), 7–9.

5. Rodney Cotterill, *Enchanted Looms: Conscious Networks in Brains and Computers* (Cambridge: Cambridge University Press, 1998), 335, writes that the key question is "why consciousness confers an evolutionary advantage"; see also 428–49, 434. Burkert, *Creation of the Sacred,* 32. Yinger, *Scientific Study of Religion,* 8. Scott Atran, *In Gods We Trust: the Evolutionary Landscape of Religion* (New York: Oxford University Press, 2002), 269–70. Matt Ridley, *Genome: The Autobiography of a Species in 23 Chapters* (New York: Harper Perennial, 1999), 220–22.

6. David Sloan Wilson, *Darwin's Cathedral: Evolution, Religion and the Nature of Society* (Chicago: University of Chicago Press, 2002), 44–45, lists several possible hypotheses offered by "evolutionary theory" on the origin of religion, one of which is substantially similar to the explanation developed in this chapter. Nicholas Humphrey, "The Uses of Consciousness," in *The Mind Made Flesh: Frontiers of Psychology and Evolution* (New York: Oxford University Press, 2002), 65–85.

7. Edward O. Wilson, *Sociobiology: The New Synthesis* (Cambridge, Mass.: Harvard University Press, 2000), 499–513.

8. John Gardner and John Maier, trans. and ed., *Gilgamesh* (New York: Vintage/Random House, 1985), 245. D. Bruce Dickson, *The Dawn of Belief: Religion in the Upper Paleolithic of Southwestern Europe* (Tucson: University of Arizona Press, 1990), 8–9, describes what I have called the "crisis of consciousness" as follows: "Human beings, in common with all living things, are destined to die. This basic attribute of existence is nonmanipulable; it cannot be altered. Unlike all, or at least most, other creatures, human beings are aware of their inevitable death. It is this human consciousness of the fact of death that renders it horrendous. ... If human beings are to live in the world, they must face the ultimate circumstances of life without giving over to despair and capitulation. At its essence, religion is humankind's primary emotional and intellectual means of struggling with the ultimate circumstances of the human condition. ... the abiding need to cope with the human condition leads to the emergence of religion throughout human history."

9. Peter L. Berger, *A Rumor of Angels: Modern Society and the Rediscovery of the Supernatural* (New York: Anchor Books, [1969] 1990), 31–35, 52–53, 62–54. Berger and Thomas Luckman, *The Social Construction of Reality: A Treatise on the Sociology of Knowledge* (New York: Anchor Books, 1967). On Berger and the social stance, chap. 12, n. 6.

10. Mircea Eliade, *The Quest: History and Meaning in Religion* (Chiago: University of Chicago Press, 1969), 25. Evelyn Underhill, *Mysticism: A Study in the Nature and Development of Man's Spiritual Consciousness* (New York: NAL/Meridien, 1974), 380–412. *Gilgamesh,* 26–29.

11. Eliade, *Myth and Reality* (New York: Harper & Row, 1968), 93–98; *The Sacred and the Profane: The Nature of Religion* (New York: Harcourt Brace Jovanovich, 1959), 122–25. John of the Cross, *The Dark Night of the Soul,* chap. 6; Saint Teresa, "El Castilo Interior," Moradas Sextas, chap. 9, as quoted in Underhill, *Mysticism,* 389–90, 394.

12. John of the Cross, "En Una Noche Escura;" Saint Teresa, *Vida,* chap. 20, par. 24. Madame Guyot, *Vie par elle meme* (Paris, 1791), part 1, chap. 21, in Underhill, *Mysticism,* 371, 384; also 389.

13. Underhill, *Mysticism,* 134, 137–38, 373, 426.

14. *King James,* "Song of Solomon," 2:8–12.

15. Underhill, *Mysticism,* 137–38; J. B. Pratt, *The Religious Consciousness* (New York, 1921), 418, quoted in Underhill, *Mysticism,* 138, n. 3.

16. Underhill, *Mysticism,* "Preface to the First Edition," xiv–xv; 446–47.

17. Radin, *Primitive Religion,* 8–9.

18. Berger, *Rumor of Angels,* 102.

19. "Creation Hymn," Wendy Doniger O'Flaherty, *The Rg Veda: An Anthology* (Harmondsworth, Eng.: Penguin, 1981), 25–26, in *World Religions: Eastern Traditions,* ed. Willard G. Oxtoby (New York: Oxford University Press, 1996), 25. Above, chap. 3, n. 19.

20. See n. 12 above.

21. David P. Barash, *The Hare and the Tortoise: Culture, Biology, and Human Nature* (New York: Viking Penguin, 1986), for example, or Stephen Pinker, *How the Mind Creates Language* (New York: Harper Perennial, 1995), esp. 16–24. Burkert, *Creation,* 18–19: "Religion may well be older than the kind of language we know, insofar as it is bound to ritual ... [which] reflects a preverbal state state of communication, to be learned by imitation. ... It seems to be more primitive and may be more ancient than speech; it clearly has analogies in the behavior of animals."

22. Marvin Harris, *Our Kind: The Evolution of Human Life and Culture* (New York: Harper Perennial, 1989), 463. On "gene–culture coevolution," see below, chap. 13, n. 20.

24. *King James. Deuteronomy,* 3:2–7. Elliot Sober and David Sloan Wilson, *Unto Others: the Evolution and Psychology of Unselfishness* (Cambridge, Mass.: Harv University Press, 1998), 4, 9.

25. Burkert, *Creation of the Sacred,* 13.

5. Morality, Gender and Class

1. Edward O.Wilson, *On Human Nature* (Cambridge, Mass.: Harvard University Press, 1978), 16–17.

2. *Oxford Dictionary of English Etymology,* ed. C. T.Onions (Oxford: Oxford University Press, 1992). King James ver., Exodus 20:12–14.

3. Exodus:20.

4. In a famous letter honoring the 50th anniversary of the Declaration of Independence Jefferson summoned mankind (again) to free itself from "monkish ignorance and superstition" in order to be guided by self-evident truth; cited in Fawn Brodie, *Thomas Jefferson: An Intimate History* (New York: W. W. Norton, 1974), 468.

5. Scott Atran, *In Gods We Trust: The Evolutionary Landscape of Religion* (New York: Oxford University Press, 2002), 39. Frans de Waal, *Good Natured: The Origins of Right and Wrong in Humans and Other Animals* (Cambridge, Mass.: Harvard University Press, 1996), 210, 217–18. Elliott Sober and David Sloan Wilson, *Unto Others: The Evolution and Psychology of Unselfish Behavior* (Cambridge, Mass.: Harvard University Press, 1998). Bert Holldobler and Edward O.Wilson, *Journey to the Ants: A Story of Scientific Exploration* (Cambridge, Mass.: Harvard University Press, 1994), 61–63.

6. Charles Darwin, *Origin of Species* (New York: Collier, 1961), "Instincts," 2:251–84. Instincts before Darwin were generally thought to be "implanted by nature" (Aquinas) or "designed by God" (Descartes), with the exception of Lockean associationists who tried to explain them as learned behavior: David MacFarland, ed, *The Oxford Companion to Animal Behaviour* (Oxford: Oxford University Press, 1981), 309–10. See also A. J. Riopelle, "Instinct," and M. R. Denny, "Instinctive Behavior," in *Encyclopedia of Psychology,* ed. Raymond J. Corsini (New York: John Wiley, 1994), 1:258–60.

7. Wilson, *On Human Nature,* 149–67, and *Consilience: the Unity of Knowledge* (New York; Knopf, 1998), 297–98.

8. Charles Darwin, *Descent of Man* [1871] (Princeton, N.J.: Princeton University Press, 1981), I:71–72, as quoted in de Waal, *Good Natured,* 40; see also 19–20, 24–34. Wilson, *On Human Nature,* 6: "Human emotional responses and the more general ethical practices based on them

have been programmed to a substantial degree by natural selection over thousands of genera-tions." Nicholas Humphrey, *The Mind Made Flesh: Frontiers of Psychology and Evolution* (New York: Oxford University Press, 2002), 59–61.

9. On hunter/gatherer egalitarianism, Robert Boyd & Peter Richerson, *The Origin and Evolution of Cultures* (NY: Oxford, 2005), 266. Christopher Boehm, *Hierarchy in the Forest: the Evolution of Egalitarian Behavior* (Cambridge: Harvard Univ Pr, 1999), "Egalitarian Behavior and Reverse Dominance Hierarchy," *Current Anthropology* (1993) 34: 227-54. Rodney Stark, with whom I would disagree on many other matters, is illuminating with respect to "Gods, Rituals and Morality": *For the Glory of God* (Princeton Univ Pr, 2003), 371-4.

10. Jared Diamond, *Guns, Germs and Steel: The Fates of Human Societies* (New York: W. W. Norton, 1997), 266, 277. Wilson, *Human Nature*, 82–92.

11. She has arrived at a Durkheimian persuasion. "The believer," Durkheim wrote, "is not delud-ing himself when he believes in the existence of a moral force on which he depends ... this force indeed exists—it is society." Quoted in *Durkheim on Religion*, ed. W. S. F. Pickering (London: Routledge & Kegan Paul, 1975), 134.

12. David Sloan Wilson, *Darwin's Cathedral: Evolution, Religion and the Nature of Society* (Chicago: University of Chicago Press, 2002), 20–25; quoted, 22.

13. Wilson, *On Human Nature*, 169–90. Theodora Kroeber, *Ishi in Two Worlds: A Biography of the Last Wild Indian in North America* (Berkeley: University of California Press, 1961) 137, 24–39. De Waal, *Good Natured*, 30. E. H. Winter, "The Enemy Within: Amba Witchcraft ..." as quoted in *The Anthropology of Evil*, ed. David Pocock in David Parkin (London: Basil; Blackwell, 1985), 46: "The inter-village world is an amoral arena where people seek their own goals irrespective of the harm which may be done to others. The world of the village is differ-ent. Within it people should not use one another as means in the pursuit of their own person-al goals. ... The village ... is a moral universe ... the largest one to be found among the Amba." Winter's account suggests that primitive village life would tend to perpetuate the social egali-tarianism and moral introversion of hunter-gatherer bands. For observations of comparable behavior among prehuman primates, Richard Wrangham and Dale Peterson, *Demonic Males: Apes and the Origins of Human Violence* (Boston: Houghton Mifflin/Mariner, 1996), esp. 250.

14. Diamond, *Guns, Germs and Steel*, 281, 273. Norman Cohn, *Cosmos, Chaos, and the World to Come: The Ancient Roots of Apocalyptic Faith* (New Haven: Yale University Press, 1993), 25. Bruce M. Knauft, "Violence and Sociality in Human Evolution," *Current Anthropology* 32, no. 4 (August–October 1991): 391–409, as quoted in Wrangham and Peterson, *Demonic Males*, 73-75.Wilson, *On Human Nature*, 88–92.

15. John Gardner & John Maier, trans. and eds., *Gilgamesh* (New York: Vintage/Random House, 1985), 270.

16. Max Weber, *The Sociology of Religion* [1922] 4th ed., rev. (Boston: Beacon, 1963), 107–8.

17. David Sloan Wilson, *Darwin's Cathedral*, 224: "I interpret this spirit of communitas as the mind of the hunter-gatherer, willing to work for the common good but ever vigilant against expoitation. In small groups the spirit of communitas results in egalitarian societies with an absence of leaders." Diamond, *Guns, Germs and Steel*, also stresses the necessary egalitari-anism of hunter-gatherer bands, as in the chapter title "From Egalitarianism to Kleptocracy: The Evolution of Government and Religion." *Kleptocracy* applies to the beginnings of social hierarchy and class exploitation, which Diamond locates at the advent of chiefdoms, rough-ly 5500 BCE in the Fertile Crescent, 1000 BCE in MesoAmerica, 265–92, esp. 276–80. Edward O.Wilson, *Sociobiology: The New Synthesis* (Harvard University Press/ Belknap, 2000), 561–62, 572–73. Richard Levins and Richard Lewontin, *The Dialectical Biologist* (Cambridge, Mass.: Harvard University Press, 1985), 46.

18. Wilson, *Sociobiology*, 562.

19. Thomas Hobbes, *Leviathan, or the Matter, Forms and Power of a Commonwealth, Ecclesiastical and Civil* (Oxford: Blackwell, 1957), part 1, chap. 13, 82.

20. Karl Marx and Frederick Engels, *The German Ideology*. Part 1 with selections from parts 2 and 3 (New York: International Publishers, 1970), 115–16.

21. Diamond, *Guns, Germs and Steel*, 276. Marvin Harris, *Our Kind: The Evolution of Human Life and Culture* (New York: Harper Perennial, 1989), 397–465.

6. The Evil Empire

1. A Catholic prayer, titled (I think) "The Act of Contrition," which was a regular part of Sunday mass in those days. I cite from memory because the point here is how I remembered it.

2. John Henry Newman, whom we could expect to be well informed on this matter, wrote in 1845: "Scripture has its unexplained omissions. … It is a remarkable circumstance that there is no direct intimation all through Scripture that the Serpent mentioned in the temptation of Eve was the evil spirit, till we come to the vision of the Woman and Child, and their adversary, the Dragon, in the twelfth chapter of the Apocalypse." *An Essay on the Development of Christian Doctrine* [1845] (London: Sheed & Ward, 1960), 85.

3. King James ver. Genesis 1:3; Isaiah, 14:12. Isaac Asimov, *Guide to the Bible* (New York: Wings Books/ Random House, 1981), 538–40. Elaine Pagels, *The Origin of Satan* (New York: Random House, 1995), 35–62. Norman Cohn, *Cosmos, Chaos and the World to Come: The Ancient Roots of Apocalyptic Faith* (New Haven: Yale University Press, 1993), 220. Jack Miles, *Christ: A Crisis in the Life of God* (New York: Knopf, 2001), 28, 302. Jeffrey Burton Russell, *The Prince of Darkness: Radical Evil and the Power of Good in History* (Ithaca, N.Y.: Cornell University Press, 1988), 79. In Russell's *The Devil: Perceptions of Evil from Antiquity to Primitive Christianity* (Ithaca, N.Y.: Cornell University Press, 1977), 229, he explains that although the name Lucifer does not appear in the New Testament, it was already appearing in the Apocalyptic literature.

4. King James ver., Saint Matthew 1:4. Russell, *Prince*, 33.

5. Russell, *Prince*, 33, 43.

6. See above, chap. 3, n. 32.

7. "Creation Hymn," *Rg Veda: An Anthology*, trans. Wendy Doniger O'Flaherty, (Harmondsworth: Penguin, 1981), 25–26, as cited in *World Religions: Eastern Traditions*, ed. Willard G. Oxtoby (New York: Oxford University Press, 1996), 25. Asimov, *Guide*, 17–18. Pagels, *Origin*, 130–41, shows that many Roman pagans, including Stoics and Neoplatonists, believed in a unitary creative force (i.e., monism) older than the gods. On the other hand, Norman Cohn, reviewing Pagels's book in *New York Review of Books* (September 21, 1995), 19–20, attributes to "recent scholarship" the view that until "the sixth century BCE the normal, traditional religion of the Israelites was polytheistic."

8. Russell, *Prince*, 1–27, 28. Wendy Doniger O'Flaherty, whose focus of study is Hindu religion, begins with an assumption similar to Russell's, that the problem of evil arises most acutely in connection with monotheism, in *The Origins of Evil in Hindu Mythology* (Berkeley: University of California Press, 1976), 1–13.

9. Russell, *Prince*, 20, and n.. Russell here follows the transition sketched in more general terms by Max Weber, *The Sociology of Religion* (Boston: Beacon Press, 1963), 144–45. Ninian Smart, *The World's Religions* (Englewood Cliffs, N.J.: Prentice-Hall, 1989), 221–22. Cohn, review of Pagels, n. 7 above: "What has long been suspected is now almost certain: that Satan originated as a Judaized version of the Zoroastrian spirit of evil, Ahriman." And see Cohn, *Cosmos*, 77–104, 194–211, 220–28.

10. Russell, *Prince*, 42.

11. See n. 7, above.

12. Theodore Ludwig, "Monotheism," *Encyclopedia of Religion* (New York: Macmillan, 1987), 10:68–75, suggests the movement is not so much from one point to another as a shift of emphasis between two overlapping levels of belief. Evidence from widely separated regions, according to Ludwig, shows many "primal or archaic" peoples holding concepts of a supreme creator deity. "The streams of the monotheistic vision run dimly through the fertile valleys of archaic agricultural religions with their pluralistic experience of the forces of nature centered on Mother Earth." High gods, Zeus for example, become heads of pantheons and gradually approaching supreme command; as, in India, do Varuna, and later Vishnu and Siva. Weber, *Sociology*, 16–20, offers a similar interpretation. See also Ninian Smart, *The Religious Experience of Mankind* [1969] (New York: Scribner, 1984), 33–34; and Scott Atran, *In Gods We Trust: The Evolutionary Landscape of Religion* (New York: Oxford University Press, 2002), 263–64, 274–76.

13. Cohn, *Cosmos*, 12, 21–22.

14. Cohn, *Cosmos*, "Mesopotamians," 31–56. Russell, *Prince*, 5–6, 13, 16, 79. John Gardner and John Maier, trans. and eds. *Gilgamesh* (New York: Vintage/Random House, 1985), vii, 17, 44 n. 12. Russell, *The Devil: Perceptions of Evil from Antiquity to Christianity* (Ithaca, N.Y.: Cornell University Press, 1977), 99 n. 48.

15. Russell, *Prince*, 17.

16. Ogden Goelet, "Introduction," *Egyptian Book of the Dead*, trans. Raymond Faulkner (San Francisco: Chronicle Books, 1994), 14–15, on the political advantages of polytheism in a realm composed of city states; *re* the Egyptian interlude of monotheism (Akhenaten, 1379-1362 BCE), 15; and Goelet, "Commentary," 144.

17. Smart, *World's Religions*, 221–22. Weber, *Sociology*, 144. David Parkin, ed., Introduction, *The Anthropology of Evil* (London: Basil Blackwell, 1985), 22. Augustine, *Confessions*, trans., Rex Warner (New York: Mentor/Penguin, 1963), 145: "With these [Christian] beliefs firmly and irrevocably rooted in my mind I sought, in a kind of passion, the answer to the question: 'What is the origin of evil?' What agonies I suffered, what groans, my God, came from my heart in its labor! And you were listening, though I did not know it."

18. David B. Barnett, George T. Kurian, Todd M. Johnson, *World Christian Encyclopedia: A Comparative Survey of Churches and Religions in the Modern World*, 2nd ed., 2 vols. (New York: Oxford University Press, 2001), table 1.1, 1:4, Global Diagram 2, 1:7, Glossary, 1:25–30. Gregory S. Paul, "The Secular Revolution of the West," *Free Inquiry* 22, no. 3 (Summer 2002): 28–34; Paul cites *World Christian Encyclopedia* for statistics; also Edward Gaustad and Philip Barlow, *New Historical Atlas of Religion in America* (New York: Oxford University Press, 2001), and International Social Survey Program (ISSP), *Religion I* (1991), *Religion II* (2001), accessible online via Inter–University Consortium for Political and Social Research (ICSPR), http://www.icpsr.umich.edu/index.html.

19. Patrick Orville, *The Upanishads: Translated from the Original Sanskrit* (Oxford: Oxford University Press, 1996), xxxvi–xxxvii; on the concept of a single creator deity in later Upanishads, see xlviii. Cohn, *Cosmos*, "Vedic Indians," 57–76. Jack Maguire, *Essential Buddhism: A Complete Guide to Beliefs and Practices* (New York: Pocket Books/Simon & Schuster, 2001); on head count of Buddhists, ix; on origins and separation from Hinduism, 1–31. A. Bruce Long, "Demons," *Encyclopedia of Religion*, 4: 282–87. Wendy Doniger O'Flaherty, *The Origins of Evil in Hindu Mythology*, 5, 55–59. Mircea Eliade, "Demonologie," *Zalmoxis* 1(1938), 197–203, as cited in O'Flaherty, 5. Weber, *Sociology*, 139.

20. Atran, *In Gods We Trust*, 266-7. George Gallup, Jr., "Afterword: A Coming Religious Revival?" in *Religion in America 1950 to the Present*, ed. Jackson W. Carroll et al. (San Francisco: Harper & Row, 1979), 113–14.

21. Ernst Mayr, *What Evolution Is* (New York: Basic Books, 2002), 133–34, 201, 276.

22. Maria Pia Lara, "Introduction," 1–2, in *Rethinking Evil, Contemporary Perspectives* (Berkeley: University of California Press, 2001).

23. Weber, *Sociology*, 139.

24. The fullest expression of this tendency was Zoroastrianism (see Cohn, *Cosmos*, 96–104). At the beginning stood an undifferentiated monistic force that generated twin deities of good and evil. Since both were creator gods, they made war by creating opposite universes. If equally matched the contest must go on forever; but most Zoroastrianism systems predicted eventual triumph of the good god, Ahura Mazda, and destruction of the evil empire. The realism and internal rationality of such constructs gave them extraordinary survival power. Their weakness (conceptually) was that by withholding from Mazda omnipotence over his own birth, or during his long struggle against the evil twin, they negated his status as monotheistic creator. This was what led Augustine to turn finally against Manicheanism.

25. For a concise statement of this complex relationship, see Ludwig, "Monotheism," 70–2. Henry E. Allison, *Benedict de Spinoza* (Boston: Twayne/Hall, 1975), 60–61, 74–75. Lewis S. Feuer, *Spinoza and the Rise of Liberalism* (Boston: Beacon Press, 1958), 52–57, 229–33.

26. Christopher Hill, *The World Turned Upside Down: Radical Ideas During thr English Revolution* (Harmondsworth: Penguin, 1984), 151–83, 339–43. Margaret Jacob, *The Radical Enlightenment: Pantheists, Freemasons and Republicans* (London: Allen Unwin, 1981), 32–40, 49–53; Jacob, *The Newtonians and the English Revolution, 1689-1720* (Ithaca, N.Y.: Cornell University Press, 1976), 168–69, 201–50; Jacob, *The Cultural Meaning of the Scientific Revolution* (Philadelphia: Temple University Press, 1988), 79–82. Frances A. Yates, *Giordano Bruno and the Hermetic Tradition* (Chicago: University of Chicago Press, 1964). See chap. 8, n. 14, below.

27. Weber, *Sociology*, 18–19, 21–22. On remoteness of creator gods and high gods, Smart, *Religious Experience*, 34.

28. Augustine, *Confessions*, 291: "Also, Lord, in my inner ear I have heard your voice loud and strong telling me that all natures and all substances, which are not what you are but which nevertheless exist, are created by you. Only what does not exist is not from you. Such is the movement of the will away from you, who are, toward something which has less reality; the movement is a fault and a sin and no man's sin can either harm you or disturb the order of your government in any way, great or small." Charles Taylor, *Sources of the Self: The Making of the Modern Identity* (Cambridge, Mass.: Harvard University Press, 1989), 127–30. Kenneth Surin, *Theology and the Problem of Evil* (Oxford: Blackwell, 1986), 12.

29. Luce Irigaray, *Between East and West: From Singularity to Community* (New York: Columbia University Press, 2002), 9–10.

30. There is a vast literature dealing with the presumed superiority of Eastern spiritual experience to that of the West, imprisoned as it is said to have been in modern times within "The Newtonian World Machine." The phrase is from Fritjof Capra, *The Turning Point: Science, Society and the Rising Culture* (New York: Bantam, 1983), 53–74. Harvey Cox, *Turning East: The Promise and Perils of the New Orientalism* (New York: Simon & Schuster, 1977), 91–128. For various examples, Capra, *The Tao of Physics* [1976] (New York: Bantam, 1984); Alan Wallace, *Choosing Reality: A Contemplative View of Physics and the Mind* (Boston: New Science Library/Shambhala, 1989); Gary Zukav, *The Dancing Wu Li Masters: An Overview of the New Physics* (New York: Bantam, 1980); John Horgan, *The End of Science: Facing the Limits of Knowledge in the Twilight of the Scientific Age* (Reading, Mass.: Addison-Wesley, 1996). See below, chap. 7, n. 2.

31. A "Basic Model of Hunting and Gathering Society" has been compiled from various sources by D. Bruce Dickson, *The Dawn of Belief: Religion in the Upper Paleolithic of Southwestern*

Europe (Tucson: University of Arizona Press, 1990). Dickson (160–66) stresses their "class-less or egalitarian" structure and suggests (190–92) that they would show little in the way of religious specialization.

32. Weber, *Sociology*, 108: "In practically every ethical religion found among privileged classes and the priests who serve them, the privileged or disprivileged social position of the individual is regarded as somehow merited from the religious point of view." Jared Diamond, *Guns, Germs and Steel: The Fates of Human Societies* (New York: W. W. Norton, 1997), 265–92.

33. Robert Redfield, *The Primitive World and Its Transformations* (Ithaca, N.Y.: Cornell University Press, 1953), 1–25, quote, 33: "In the idealized typical folk society all members of one's own community are kinsmen; all others are enemies." Frans de Waal, *Good Natured: The Origins of Right and Wrong in Humans and Other Animals* (Cambridge, Mass.: Harvard University Press, 1996), 30. David Pocock, "Unruly Evil," 46, in Parkin, *Anthropology*.

34. Russell, *Prince*, 33, 43. Cohn, *Cosmos*, 82. Paul Carus, *The History of the Devil and the Idea of Evil* (La Salle, Ill: Open Court, 1974), esp. Carus's collection of illustrations.

35. Atran, *In Gods We Trust*, 145, 152–3 and n. 1, 289–90. Edward O. Wilson, *Sociobiology: The New Synthesis* (Cambridge, Mass.: Harvard University Press, 2000), 560–62.

7. The Problem of Evil

1. David Hume, *The Natural History of Religion*, ed. A. Wayne Colver; *Dialogues Concerning Natural Religion*, ed. John Valdimir Price (Oxford: Clarendon, 1976), *Dialogues*, pt. 10, 226–27. Hume's statement of the problem of evil (227, n. 12) paraphrases a quotation attributed to Epicurus in Pierre Bayle, *Dictionary Historical and Critical* (London, 1734–38), "Paulicians," n. E, iv 513n.

2. At one level, this involves the ecumenical argument that while all religions are unique and irreducible, they offer shareable treasures of spiritual wisdom. See above, chap. 2, n. 22. More specifically it invokes criticisms of Western intellectual rigidity and overfixation on empirical rationalism. Cultural rebels of the 1960s had popularized the view that quantum mechanics—the famous "Copenhagen interpretation" and so forth—revealed the crisis of Western scientific culture; and the next step must be to learn disciplines of mind control and spirituality from the great Eastern traditions. Thus Gary Zukav, describing the "Copenhagen interpretation" as "a recognition of the failure of left hemispheric thought ... a *re-cognition* of those psychic aspects which long had been ignored in a rationalistic society," concluded, "The new physics sounds very much like old Eastern mysticism." *The Dancing Wu Li Masters: An Overview of the New Physics* (New York: Bantam, 1980), 40, 72. Harvey Cox, *Turning East: The Promise and Peril of the New Orientalism* (New York: Simon & Schuster, 1977), 91–110. More recently, Roger Walsh (identified as professor of psychiatry, philosophy and anthropology, Department of Psychiatry and Human Behavior, University of California College of Medicine, Irvine), "The Spirit of Evolution," *Noetic Sciences Review* (Summer 1995), in a review of Ken Wilber, *Sex, Ecology, Spirituality: The Spirit of Evolution* (Boston: Shambhala, 1995), writes that although "efforts to revitalize contemplative practices and wisdom" (17) are now widespread in the West, they come "at the end of a millennium in which the possibility of awakening was effectively blocked in the West and to this day mysticism remains widely misunderstood in western culture" (39). See above, chap. 6, n. 30. For a sympathetic and well-informed treatment of these themes, see Alan Wallace, *Choosing Reality: A Contemplative View of Physics and the Mind* (Boston: New Science Library/Shambhala, 1989).

3. John Hick, *Evil and the God of Love* (New York: Harper & Row, 1966), 4.

4. Jeffrey Burton Russell, *Mephistopheles: The Devil in Modern Times* (Ithaca, N.Y.: Cornell University Press, 1986), 11.

5. Ronald Green, "Theodicy," Mircea Eliade, ed., *Encyclopedia of Religion* (New York: Macmillan, 1987), 14:430–41. Alan Watts, *Ways of Zen* (New York: 1957), as quoted in Wendy Doniger O'Flaherty, *The Origin of Evil in Hindu Mythology* (Berkeley: University of California Press, 1976), 4. Mircea Eliade, "Notes de demonologie," *Zalmoxis* 1 (1938): 197–203, as quoted in O'Flaherty, 4.

6. Max Weber, *The Sociology of Religion* (Boston: Beacon Press, 1963), 139. O'Flaherty, *Origin*, 7, 376.

7. David Hume, *The Natural History of Religion*, ed. A. Wayne Colver (Oxford: Clarendon Press, 1976), esp. 25–40. Edward Burnett Tylor, *Religion in Primitive Culture* [1871] (New York: Harper, 1958), 8–9. Near the end of his concluding chapter (537), Tylor writes: "The general study of the ethnography of religion, through all its immensity of range, seems to countenance the theory of evolution in its highest and widest sense." George Stocking, *Victorian Anthropology* (New York: Free Press/Macmillan, 1987), re Spencer, 128–35. Emile Durkheim, *The Elementary Forms of Religious Life* (New York: Collier/Macmillan, 1965). Religion, for Durkheim, is the ascription of sacred status to the transcendental power of society (113).

8. See section "The Dark Night of Consciousness," in chap. 4.

9. Theodore Ludwig, "Monotheism," *Encyclopedia of Religion* (New York: Macmillan, 1987), 10:68–75.

10. Eliade, *Myth and Reality*, 93–98.

11. Prometheus in the original story strove to prevent a self-appointed King of the Gods from usurping total power. Milton enjoyed repeating as a kind of mantra God's summons to his created retainers, "Thrones, Dominations, Princedoms, Virtues, Powers," and assigned exactly the same terminology to Satan when he called his rebel segment of that host into consultation. *Paradise Lost*, Book 5, ll. 600–602, 772). Weber, *Sociology of Religion*, 138. The Nicene Creed (325 CE) as amended at Constantinople (381 CE), see Mary T. Clark, "De Trinitate," in *Cambridge Companion to Augustine*, ed. Eleonore Stumpp and Norman Kretzmann (Cambridge: Cambridge University Press, 2001), 91.

12. Scott Atran, *In Gods We Trust: The Evolutionary Landscape* (New York: Oxford University Press, 2002), 8–11. On monotheistic tendencies in Hinduism and Buddhism, Ludwig, "Monotheism," *Encyclopedia* 10: 69–71. Chap. 6, above, nn. 5, 10. Western-oriented historians of religion tend to see the problem of evil (unresolved) as a kind of badge of honor, testifying to the presumably more acute ethical sensibilities of Western monotheisms. See nn. 3, 4, above.

13. Mircea Eliade, *The Sacred and Profane: The Nature of Religion* (New York: Harcourt Brace Jovanovich, 1959), 68–113. Eliade refers to what I have called pre-secular time as "sacred time." Augustine, *Concerning the City of God Against the Pagans* (London: Penguin, 1984), 434–36. Donald S. Lopez, Jr., ed., *Buddhism in Practice* (Princeton, N.J. : Princeton University Press, 1995), 14. Edward Conze, *Buddhism: Its Essence and Development* (New York: Harper, 1975), 49–50. Philip Clayton, *God and Contemporary Science* (Edinburgh: Edinburgh University Press, 1997), 94, 117.

14. John Stuart Mill argued that monotheists (if well intentioned and rationally consistent) could never believe strictly in omnipotence. "They have always saved [God's] goodness at the expense of his power. ... They have believed that he could do any one thing, but not any combination of things ... And since the exertion of all his power to make [the world] as little imperfect as possible, leaves it no better than it is, they cannot but regard that power, though vastly beyond human estimate, yet as in itself not merely finite, but extremely limited." *Nature, the Utility of Religion and Theism* (London: Longmans, Green, 1969), 39–40, 116–17; and 40n., defending Leibniz against Voltaire. Below, chap. 8, nn. 31, 32..

15. Theodore Greene summed up this aspect of the problem of evil when he wrote that even if we managed to construct from empirical observation infallible proofs for an omnipotent creator

these would be useless to religion since they would convey nothing as to the moral purpose of creation. "Once prove God's existence out of the mouth of non-moral nature and you have a non-moral God of no use to the religious consciousness." Recalling my version of Tylor's definition, I would paraphrase this as follows: Once prove God's existence out of the mouth of non-anthropomorphic nature and you have a non-anthropomorphic God indistinguishable from black holes or big bangs. Greene, "The Historical Context and Religious Significance of Kant's *Religion*," in Immanuel Kant, *Religion Within the Limits of Reason Alone* (New York: Harper & Row, 1960), lix-lx. Traleg Kyabgon Rinpoche, "First, the Bad News," *Buddhadharma: The Practitioner's Quarterly* (Spring, 2006), 56-57. Chogyan Trungpa Rinpoche, "The Lion's Roar," *Collected Works* (Boston: Shambala Publications, 2003), 4: 139-330.

16. Jonathan Israel, *Radical Enlightenment: Philosophy and the Making of Modernity, 1650-1750* (Oxford: Oxford University Press, 2001), esp. 230-57; quote, 233.

17. Isaac Asimov, *Guide to the Bible: The Old and New Testaments* (New York: Wings Books, 1981), 474-87. P. W. Skehan, "Job," *New Catholic Encyclopedia* (Washington, D.C.: Catholic University of America, 1967), 7:999-1001. Robert Gordis, *The Book of God and Man: A Study of Job* (Chicago: University of Chicago Press, 1965). David Daiches, "God Under Attack," in *The Book of Job*, ed. Harold Bloom (New York: Chelsea House, 1988), 37-61. King James ver., Job 1:8-11.

18. Job 1:2-21, 2:3-10.

19. Daiches, "God Under Attack," 39-41.

20. Job 12-32.

21. Job 15:14, 38-41, 42:6.

22. On the hypocrisy of Job's "friends," see Immanuel Kant, "On the Miscarriage of all Philosophical Trials in Theodicy," in *Religion and Rational Theology*, trans. and ed. Allen W. Wood and George Di Giovanni (Cambridge: Cambridge University Press, 1996), 32-3. Job 20:7-17.

23. *City of God*, 17-18.

24. To Job, being tested was simply an unnecessary interruption and the end of the tale found him exactly where he had been at the beginning: a pious man blessed with prosperity in this world. The closing lines (42:16-17) are as follows: "After this lived Job an hundred and forty years, and saw his sons, and his sons' sons, even four generations. So Job died, being old and full of days." Just prior to this conclusion, we are told (42:13-15) that Job had "seven sons and three daughters." In the opening chapter (1: 2), Job already had seven sons and three daughters; the sons were killed by Satan; no mention of the daughters (1:19). It thus remains unclear if the sons and daughters reported as alive and well at the end are the original children restored to life, or a new generation. Skehan (*New Catholic Encyclopedia*, 7:1001) refers to controversy among early Christian fathers as to whether the doctrine of resurrection had been declared (or at least adumbrated) in Job. Skehan concurs with St. John Chrysostom that it was *not*, although a contrary opinion prevailed at the time. "The Vulgate rendering of it, " Skehan writes, "is luminous with St. Jerome's Christian faith on the subject, and it is this rendering which is employed by St. Augustine." And see Thomas Williams, "Biblical Interpretation," *Cambridge Companion to Augustine*, 59-70.

25. *City of God*, Book 1, esp. chaps. 15, 28-29, 36.

26. On the atrociousness of original sin and the justice of Hell, *City of God*, Book 21, chaps. 9-12; on concepts of purgatory and punishment during earthly life for lesser sins, Book 21, chaps. 13-14. Augustine at one time at least believed that human souls "fell" from a prior existence. See James J. O'Donnell, "Augustine: His Time and Lives," 22; and Roland Teske, "Augustine's Theory of the Soul," 120-21, 123 n. 19, in *Cambridge Companion to Augustine*.

27. *City of God*, Book 21, chap. 17. 995.

28. Here I am attempting an abstract from several of the most complex books of *City of God*, including the famous Book 14, in which, as Thomas Merton put it, "the origin of the two cities is sketched in an essay on original sin." Merton, Introduction, *City of God* (New York: Modern Library, 1950), ix–xv.

29. *City of God*, 479–80.

30. *City of God*, 635–36.

31. Eleonore Stumpp, "Augustine on Free Will," *Cambridge Companion to Augustine*, 124–47. According to Stumpp (139), Augustine ultimately declined to answer such questions: "'And if you ask me why ... I confess that it is because I haven't discovered what I should say.'" Her reference is to *De dono perseverantiae*, 8:18.

32. *City of God*, 593.

33. Augustine, *Confessions*, trans. Rex Warner (New York: Penguin, 1963),158; *City of God*, 15; 964–89.

34. O'Donnell, "Augustine," *Cambridge Companion to Augustine*, eds, 8–25.

35. William E. Mann, "Augustine on Evil and Original Sin," *Cambridge Companion to Augustine*, 40–48. Garry Wills, *Saint Augustine* (New York: Penguin, 1999), 131.

36. *Confessions* (1963), 91–109; 145.

37. *City of God*, 490. Inner quote, *Wisdom*, 9:13ff.

38. Max Weber, *Sociology of Religion* (Boston: Beacon Press, 1963), 139.

39. See first section, "Who Begat Satan?" in chap. 6.

8. Promethean Readings

1. Scott Atran, *In Gods We Trust: the Evolutionary Landscape of Religion* (New York: Oxford University Press, 2002), 39. John Gardner and John Maier, trans. and ed. *Gilgamesh* (New York: Vintage/Random. 1985), 31, 245–50, 263–70.

2. *Egyptian Book of the Dead*, trans Raymond O. Faulkner (San Francisco: Chronicle Books, 1994), Ogden Goelet, Introduction, 13–18, and Commentary,137–70. "*The Book of the Dead* promised resurrection to all mankind, as a reward for righteous living, long before Judaism and Christianity embraced that concept."(18) This text, which took shape over many centuries (approximately 2400 to 1550 BCE), was "originally intended solely for the benefit of the king and his family," but was later "adapted for private use ... by anyone who could afford a sarcophagus"(14, 140). One may infer this would not quite have corresponded to "all mankind." Hans Kung, *Great Christian Thinkers* (New York: Continuum, 1994), 74–76. *Confessions of Saint Augustine*, trans. Rex Warner (New York: Penguin, 1963), Books 5–8. Augustine, *City of God*, trans. Henry Bettensen (New York: Penguin, 1984), Book 1, chap. 9. Luther H. Martin, *Hellenistic Religions: An Introduction* (New York: Oxford University Press, 1987).

3. Augustine, *City*, Book 7, chap. 32; Book 17, chaps. 14–18; Book, 19 chap. 22; Book 20, chap. 30. *Catholic Encyclopedia* (Washington, D.C,: Catholic University of America, 1967), "Job," 7:999–1001, reports that Job had no expectation of life after death but that certain lines in Job (esp. 19:25–27) were interpreted by early Christians, including Jerome and Augustine, as evidence for the doctrines of afterlife and resurrection. See David Daiches, "God Under Attack" in *The Book of Job* (New York: Chelsea House, 1988). 37–61. And G. K.Chesterton, "Introduction," *The Book of Job* (New York: Dodge Publishing, 1909).

4. Perhaps the most famous effort to explain doctrinal change without conceding that original revelations might have been inadequate, or not worked quite the way God intended them to work, or, worst of all, been tampered with by human beings for terrestrial purposes, is John Henry Newman's *Essay on the Development of Christian Doctrine* [1845] (London: Sheed and Ward, 1960). Following the scientific mode, Newman described his essay as a "hypothesis," or "theory of Development of Doctrine." (22, 66) The problem facing Newman was how to account for changes in early Christian doctrine during the ensuing eighteen hundred years, while at the same time rejecting Protestant accusations that the changes were in fact corruptions imposed by the Catholic Church and especially the papacy.

5. As in Augustine, *City of God*, Book 11, chap. 18.

6. Milton, *Paradise Lost*, Book I:6–26, in *Milton: Poems and Selected Prose*, ed. Majorie Hope Nicolson (New York: Bantam Books, 1962).

7. Jack Miles, *God: A Biography* (New York: Vintage, 1996), 3–24.

8. Ibid., 11. The sequence referred to is that of the Hebrew Bible, the *Tanakh*, which contains the same books as the Christian but in significantly different order. Also see 19, 411; 8–24, 311, 325–28.

9. Ibid., 311.

10. Aeschylus, *Prometheus Bound*, trans. Rex Warner, in *Prometheus Bound by Aeschylus and Prometheus Unbound by Percy Byssche Shelley* (New York: Heritage Press, 1966).

11. I refer here to Christian orthodoxy, which was of course heresy to Judaic orthodoxy. One could hardly speak of Christian orthodoxy until two or three hundred years after the death of Christ. Augustine was born midway in the fourth century. Although Jewish orthodoxy rejected the Son, it gradually modified the Father to the extent that he could offer Jewish believers a salvation approximately equivalent to that provided for Christians by the Son. Re co-eternity of Father and Son, Augustine, *Confessions*, Book 13, chap. 5 : "See now, there appears to me *in a glass darkly* the Trinity, which is you, my God, since you, Father, *in the Beginning created heaven and earth*—in the beginning of our Wisdom, which is your Wisdom, born of you, equal to you and co-eternal, that is your Son." Augustine, *City of God*, Book 9, chap. 15; Book 21, chap. 15.

12. Elaine Pagels, *The Gnostic Gospels* (New York: Vintage, 1981; and *Adam Eve and the Serpent* (New York: Vintage, 1988); Kung, *Christian Thinkers*, 42–97. R. S.Westman and J. E. McGuire, *Hermeticism and the Scientific Revolution* (Los Angeles: University of California Press, 1977); Frances Yates, *Giordani Bruno and the Hermetic Tradition* (Chicago: University of Chicago Press, 1964). Christopher Hill, *The World Turned Upside Down* (London: Penguin, 1975), chaps. 7–9.

13. Wordsworth, "The French Revolution as It Appeared to Enthusiasts" (1809) and *The Prelude* (1850), Book 9, 108.

14. Christopher Hill, *Milton and the English Revolution* (New York: Viking, 1977), 1–10, 13–116. Barbara K. Lewalski, "How Radical Was Milton?" in *Milton and Heresy*, ed. Stephen B. Dobranski and John R. Rumrich (London: Cambridge University Press, 1998), 49–72. Visit to Galileo, "Milton," *Encyclopedia Americana* (New York: Grolier, 2000), 19:133–39; and see Dava Sobel, *Galileo's Daughter: A Historical Memoir of Science Faith and Love* (New York: Penguin, 2000), 350.

15. Jonathan Israel, *Radical Enlightenment: Philosophy and the making of Modernity, 1650–1750* (Oxford: Oxford University Press 2001), 456–64. Hill, *World*, esp. chapters 7–9; and "Milton and Bunyan: Dialogue with the Radicals," 395–414. John P. Rumrich, "Milton's Arianism and Why It Matters," 75–92; and Lewalksi, 49–72, in *Milton and Heresy*. Milton, *Paradise Lost*, Book 1:23–26. Hereafter, line numbers follow book number in *Paradise Lost* citations.

16. Hill, *World*, comments in his appendix, "Milton and Bunyan," 395-414, that "the view that Satan was the true hero of *Paradise Lost* flourished with the revival of revolutionary romanticism, with Blake and Shelley and Byron." R. J. Z. Werblowsky, *Lucifer and Prometheus: a Study of Milton's Satan* (London: Routledge and Kegan, 1952), 48-9, writes that although Milton made no specific reference to Prometheus in *Paradise Lost*, many critics (especially after the Enlightenment) observed Satan's resemblance to him. But such a resemblance might not have been obvious to Milton in the seventeenth century. As a classical scholar, he was well acquainted with *Prometheus Bound*, the only surviving drama of Aeschylus' Promethean trilogy, and from what was then known about the two missing plays (and about Aeschylus' concept of tragedy) it would have been clear the trilogy had to end by reconciling Promethean rebellion with the divine power of Zeus. Thus its message would have seemed similar to the "orthodox reading" of Job, which probably was not what Milton was looking for in 1660. Warner, Introduction, *Prometheus Bound,*, ix-xix.

17. *Paradise Lost*, 1:254-57. Christopher Hill, *God's Englishman: Oliver Cromwell and the English Revolution* (New York: Dial, 1970), 243.

18. *Paradise Lost*, 1:104; 3:60-67, 90-134, 168-241; 6:699-866; 10:192-211.

19. Denis R. Danielson, *Milton's Good God: A Study in Literary Theodicy* (Cambridge: Cambridge University Press, 1982), 92-130.

20. *Paradise Lost*, 4:388-92.

21. *Paradise Lost*, 4:393-94.

22. *Paradise Lost*, 3:58-64.

23. *Paradise Lost*, 3:93-118.

24. *Paradise Lost*, 3:344-49.

25. *Paradise Lost*, 3:240-50. Rumrich, "Milton's Arianism," 75-92.

26. *Paradise Lost*, 9:908-16.

27. *Paradise Lost*, 9:758-60.

28. *Paradise Lost*, 12:638-49.

29. Danielson, *Milton's Good God*, 24-40, 43-48. Israel, *Radical Enlightenment*, 189-90.

30. *Paradise Lost*, 5:469-74.

31. Milton, *De Doctrina Christiana*, trans. Charles Summer (London: 1825), as cited in *Paradise Lost: An Authoritative Text, Backgounds and Sources*, ed. Scott Elledge (New York: W. W. Norton, 1975), 304, 309. On *De Doctrina Christiana*, see Introduction, *Milton and Heresy*, 1-17. William Empson, *Milton's God* (London: Chatto and Windus, 1965), 16, 203-4.

32. *Paradise Lost*, 5:577-97. Miles, *God: A Biography*, 405ff. In *Paradise Regained*, in *Poems and Selected Prose*, ed., Marjorie H. Nicolson (New York: Bantam, 1962), 467-516, the son shows changes in style of divine power that Milton doubtless regarded as improvements. From the celestial hitman, terrorizing the cosmos with nuclear thunderbolts, the son has changed to a quiet, thoughtful individual, less powerful (physically) than Satan, by whom he is levitated at will from mountaintop to mountaintop, being finally left stranded on the highest minaret of the Jerusalem temple from which he is recued by a band of angels. At the end, instead of rising in triumph to sit at the right hand of the Father, "he unobserved / Home to his mother's house private returned" (516).

33. John Stuart Mill, *Nature, the Utility of Religion and Theism* (London: Longmans, Green, 1969), 38-40, 116. Alfred North Whitehead, *Religion in the Making* [1926] (Cleveland: World Book, 1960), esp. 152-54; Whitehead, *Adventures of Ideas* (New York: Macmillan, 1933), esp. 352-65. Empson, *Milton's God*, 130, re Milton's God: "You may also say that he is an emergent or evolutionary deity, as has been believed at times by many other thinkers, for

example Aeschylus and H. G.Wells." Karen Armstrong, *A History of God: The 4,000-Year Quest of Judaism, Christianity and Islam* (New York: Knopf, 1994). Any author undertaking a "history" or "biography" of God assumes that God changes through time; and this is different from recognizing that people's beliefs change. Armstrong, for example, writes of God's relation to Israel: "He [God] had chosen Israel to be his helpmate. ... In this vision of salvation, God is not gazing down on humanity condescendingly but ... actually dependent upon mankind. Jews have the unique privilege of helping to re-form God and create him anew." Santiago Sia, *God in Process Thought: A Study in Charles Hartshorne's Concept of God*, with a Postscript by Charles Hartshorme (Dordrecht/Boston: Martinus Nijhoff Publishers, 1985). Freeman Dyson in his 1985 Gifford Lectures acknowledged the influence of Hartshorne's theology, which he traced back to the sixteenth-century Italian cleric and heretic, Socinus: Dyson, *Infinite in All Directions* (New York: Harper & Row, 1988), 119–20, 295. On Hartshorne, see also John Horgan, *The End of Science: Facing the Limits of Knowledge in the Twilight of the Scientific Age* (Reading, Mass.: Addison-Wesley, 1996), 263–65. For the "modern" doctrine of panentheism, Philip Clayton, *God and Contemporary Science* (Edinburgh: Edinburgh University Press, 1997), 82–124; and "The Temptations of Immanence: Spinoza's ONE and the Birth of Panentheism" in Clayton, *The Problem of God in Modern Thought* (Grand Rapids, Mich./ Cambridge, UK: Eerdmans, 2000), 387–439.

34. Empson, *Milton's God,* 179, describes the Cambridge Platonists, a group with whom Milton was in close contact, as seeking "to dissolve God into Goodness itself" instead of conceiving him as the divine monarch.

9. Theodicy

1. I admire John Ciardi's translation and find his effort to suggest the effect of the Italian rhyme generally successful. But when he ends the crucial last stanza of *Inferno* by rhyming "stars" with "cars," I have no choice but turn to a prose translation. Mark Musa, trans., *The Inferno* (Bloomington: University of Indiana Press, 1955), 34:131–39. All other quotes from *The Inferno* are from the Ciardi translation (New York: Mentor, 1954).

2. See above, chap. 8, n. 2. Dante, *Paradiso,* trans. John D. Sinclair (New York: Oxford University Press, 1961), n. 29: "There are those who look askance at the 'theological' Beatrice and talk of 'a cold creation,' but that arises from a cold preconception and reconstruction of Dante's vision." And see Rachel Jacoff's introduction, in John Freccero, *Dante: The Poetics of Conversion* (Cambridge, Mass.: Harvard University Press, 1986), ix–xvi.

3. *Inferno,* Canto 1, lines 1–3.

4. *Inferno,* Canto 1.

5. *Purgatorio,* trans. John D. Sinclair (New York: Oxford University Press, 1961), Cantos 27, 30, 31; and *Paradiso,* Cantos 14–16.

6. *Purgatorio,* 16:50–81; Sinclair, *Paradiso,* 217–18.

7. *Purgatorio,* 18:46–75. On Virgil and virtuous pagans, *Inferno,* Canto 4, and Ciardi, Notes, 39–54.

8. *Paradiso,* 1: 100–142; 5: 16–24; 7: 16–51.

9. *Inferno,* 1:61–75; 2:49–137

10. *Inferno,* 26:55–131; Ciardi, *Inferno,* Notes, 225. Freccero, *Dante,* 16–18, 136–51.

11. Freccero, *Dante,* 18 and.277, n. 41; 138–39.

12. *Paradiso,* 33: 55–72, 82–120.

13. Sinclair, *Paradiso* Notes, 490. Sinclair quotes the Danteist C. H. Grandgent: "In the last four cantos, he achieves what no other poet, before or since, has attempted without so much as a

shadow of success: the presentation of a world beyond the perceptions of sense" (490). Joseph Anthony Mazzeo, *Structure and Thought in the Paradiso* (New York: Greenwood, 1968), 42: "*The Paradiso* and indeed the whole of the *Divine Comedy* is a translation into terms of sensible light of a timeless vision of a spiritual or intellectual light; an adaptation for physical eyes of what was seen by the eyes of the soul."

14. Aquinas dominates Cantos 11–14 of *Paradiso*. Sinclair, *Paradiso*, 159, describes Dante as "the learned pupil of Aquinas," and writes (160) that "Aquinas ... more than any other summed up for Dante the Christian doctrine of God." Freccero, *Dante,* and Mazzeo, *Structure and Thought,* without discounting Aquinas, stress a continuity through Augustine from Neoplatonism, both pagan and Christian, to Dante.

15. Philip Clayton, *The Problem of God in Modern Thought* (Grand Rapids, MI: Eerdmans, 2000), 215–16, places Leibniz in a sequence "from at least Plotinus, via Pseudo-Dionysius to early medieval thinkers such as John Erigena, through the Renaissance rediscovery of the Neoplatonic thinkers (and of the Hermetic tradition) to Nicholas of Cusa and Bruno, and on into the early modern period in the work of Descartes, the Cambridge Platonists, and now Leibniz." See also Kai Nielsen, *God, Scepticism and Modernity* (Ottawa: University of Ottawa Press, 1989), 1, on "natural theology"

16. Jonathan Israel, *Radical Enlightenment: Philosophy and the Making of Modernity* (Oxford: Oxford University Press, 2001), 152, 331–41. Susan Neiman's *Evil in the Modern World: An Alternative History of Philosophy* (Princeton, N.J.: Princeton University Press, 2002) contains illuminating discussions of Leibniz, 18–31, and of Bayle, Voltaire, and Hume, 116–69. Richard Popkin, *The History of Scepticism from Savonarola to Bayle* (New York: Oxford University Press, 2003), 283–302. Diogenes Allen, Introduction, in Gottfried Wilhelm Leibniz, *Theodicy*, ed. Diogenes Allen (Indianapolis: Bobbs-Merrill, 1966), xviii n. 8.

17. Clayton, *Problem*, 263: "During the 'classical' period of theistic proofs, starting with Anselm and Thomas Aquinas, but running as late as Leibniz ... readers and writers alike took it as (more or less) a matter of course that God exists. The function of the proofs was merely to lift this obvious truth to the status of a rational, even necessary, inference."

18. *Theodicy*, par. 44, p. 21; Main Essay, pars. 7, 8, p. 35. In other writings Leibniz used all the standard proofs: Clayton, *Problem*, 191–98.

19. *Theodicy*, Main Essay, par. 122, p. 81; par.1, p. 31, par. 273, p. 133; pars 277–78, p. 134, par. 289, p. 137.

20. *Theodicy*, Main Essay, pars. 278, 280–84, pp. 134–36; Prel. Diss., par. 44, pp. 21–22.

21. On Original Sin, *Theodicy*, Main Essay, pars. 76–106, pp. 59–68.

22. *Theodicy*, Main Essay, pars. 31–32, p. 45; par. 20, p. 40.

23. *Theodicy*, Main Essay, par. 19, pp. 38–39.

24. *Theodicy*, Prel. Diss., par. 44, p. 21; Main Essay, pars. 7,8, pps. 34–35. *Re* the calculus, Clayton, *Problem*, 221. See also Neiman, *Evil in the Modern World,* 24–25.

25. Voltaire, *Candide* (1759). Haydn Mason, *Voltaire: A Biography* (Baltimore: Johns Hopkins University Press, 1981), 70–92. Leaving aside Voltaire, philosophers, especially in recent times, have not (according to Clayton, *Problem*, 200–201) viewed *Theodicy* as a great success.

26. Nielsen, *God, Scepticism*, 210–11.

10. Empiricizing the Spiritual

1. Philip Clayton, *Explanation from Physics to Theology: An Essay in Rationality and Religion* (New Haven: Yale University Press, 1989), 127–28. Susan Neiman, *Evil in Modern Thought:*

An Alternative History of Philosophy (Princeton, N.J.: Princeton University Press, 2002), 105. Charles Taylor, *Sources of the Self: The Making of the Modern Identity* (Cambridge, Mass.: Harvard University Press, 1989), 241. John Locke, *A Letter on Tolerance* (Oxford: Oxford University Press, 1968), 135, in Walter Burkert, *Creation of the Sacred: Tracks of Biology in Early Religions* (Cambridge, Mass.: Harvard University Press, 1996), 176.

2. See chap. 7, section titled "Is Any Religion Exempt from the Problem of Evil?"

3. Wendy Doniger O'Flaherty, *The Origin of Evil in Hindu Mythology* (Berkeley: University of California Press, 1976), 376, 2, 8. Patrick Olivelle, *Upanishads: A New Translation* (Oxford: Oxford University Press, 1996), locates karma doctrine in the Brhadaranyaka Upanishad, one of the "two earliest," which he identifies as pre–Buddhist and probably dating from "the seventh to sixth centuries BCE," xxxvi, xlvii–xlviii, 64–67.

4. O'Flaherty, *Origin of Evi,l* 372, 15, 373.

5. Max Weber, *The Religion of India: The Sociology of Hinduism and Buddhism*, (Glencoe: Free Press, 1958), 121. Weber, *The Sociology of Religion* (Boston: Beacon Press, 1963), 145.

6. Weber, *Religion of India*, 118–33.

7. *Ibid.*, 122–3.

8. Marianne Weber, *Max Weber: A Biography* (New York: Wiley, 1975), 90–91. Gordon Craig, in *New York Review of Books* (February 13, 1992), reviewing a recent study of Weber by Lawrence Scaff, writes, "In the last analysis, Weber's choice among the contending orders or value systems of his time was intellectualism, the reliance on scientific knowledge.'"

9. Jack Maguire, *Essential Buddhism: A Complete Guide to Beliefs and Practices* (New York: Pocket Books/ Simon & Schuster, 2001), 3–30. Karen Armstrong, *Buddha* (New York: Penguin, 2001), 21–35. Dalai Lama, *The Way to Freedom* (San Francisco: HarperCollins, 1994), 90.

10. Ibid., 72, 137, 161.

11. Ibid., 170, 68.

12. Armstrong, 106–11. Dalai Lama, *The Buddhism of Tibet and the Key to the Middle Way* (New York: Harper & Row, 1975), 26.

13. Ibid. Later, in a powerfully minimalist plea for universal responsibility, economic egalitarianism, environmental ethics and world disarmament, the Dalai Lama reaffirms his commitment to Tibetan Buddhism (including karma), but yields priority to ecumenicalism and doctrinal pluralism: *Ethics for a New Millennium* (NY: Riverhead Books/ Penguin, 1999), 133-8, 161-231.

14. A. E. Housman, "Epilogue," in Louis Untermeyer, ed., *Modern British Poetry: A Critical Anthology* (New York: Harcourt Brace, 1936), 162–63.

15. Augustine, *Confessions*, trans. Rex Warner (New York: Penguin, 1963), Book 6, chap. 11: "Or is it true that death will cut off and put an end to all care and all feeling? ... But no, this cannot be true. It is not for nothing, it is not meaningless, that all over the world is displayed the high and towering authority of the Christian faith. Such great and wonderful things would never have been done for us by God, if the life of the soul were to end with the death of the body."

16. Clayton, *Explanation*, 135.

17. Prometheus myths and Milton's paradise epics all center on this sequence. Philip Clayton's impressive study, *The Problem of God in Modern Thought* (Grand Rapids, Mich.: Eerdmans, 2000), aims at establishing a compromise by which the distant God may also take up residence as a warm body inside nature. In our modern era, such halfway covenants between theism and pantheism are often called (as they are by Clayton) *panentheism*. Yet since panentheism leaves the creator deity on the high seat, I do not see how it can avoid making that deity vulnerable to the problem of evil.

18. On Weber, see above, nn. 4 and 5. Augustine, *City of God*, trans., Henry Bettenson (New York: Penguin, 1984); for examples, see Book I, chaps. 15, 28. Dante, *Paradiso*, trans. and ed., John Sinclair (New York: Oxford, 1961), 408 and Sinclair's notes, 199, 414, 490. Milton, *Paradise Lost*, 1:6–26.

19. Christopher Hill, *The World Turned Upside Down* (London: Penguin, 1975), 395–404. Eric Auerbach, *Mimesis: The Representation of Reality in Western Literature*, trans. Willard Trask (Princeton, N.J.: Princeton University Presss, 1953), 174–202. Augustine, *Confessions*, on the "innocence" of children, for example, Book 2, chap. 1; or on the sublimation of sexual energy into intellectual or 'spiritual' output, Book 6, chap. 11. Dalai Lama, see nn. 10, 11 above.

20. Jared Diamond's *Guns, Germs and Steel: The Fates of Human Societies* (New York: W. W. Norton, 1997); and J. M. Blaut, *Eight Eurocentric Historians* (New York: Guildford, 2000) are examples of explanations for the world dominance of western Europe and North America that rely on factors such as geography, geology, distribution of plants and animals, rather than invoking alleged psychic differentials such as spirituality or scientific-mindedness. Blaut, a geographer, happens to be aggressively critical of Diamond, a "bioecologist" (p. 15), but for my purposes what will be relevant is their areas of overlap rather than disagreement.

21. "Of the sacred Milton ... let it ever be remembered," Shelley wrote in his "Author's Preface" to *Prometheus Unbound* [1820] that he was "a republican, and a bold enquirer into morals and religion." Two hundred years after the opening of the Long Parliament, Shelley could declare unequivocally that Satan was the hero of *Paradise Lost* (whether Milton so intended or not); and Shelley went on to identify Satan with his own hero (Prometheus), although he thought Prometheus superior in moral and "poetical" attributes. Prometheus, in Western skies, was by this time the rising star of romantic revolution. We will meet him again in the next chapter (twenty-five years later) at the apex of his trajectory. On Milton and the Promethean connection see above, chap. 8, n. 16.

22. Susan Neiman, *Evil in Modern Thought: an Alternative History of Philosophy* (Princeton: Princeton University Press, 2002), 81.

23. Immanuel Kant, *Religion Within the Limits of Reason Alone*, trans. Theodore M. Greene and Hoyt Hudson (New York: Harper & Row, 1960). Greene, Introduction, "The Historical Context and Religious Significance of Kant's *Religion*": on background in rationalism and pietism, xiv, xvi, xxxi; influence of Hume and writings on religion in earlier major works, xxxi–xxxviii; deconstruction of the rational proofs, xli–xlvii. Greene, xliii, writes of Kant, "Throughout the *Critique of Pure Reason* he had firmly in mind a new MORAL proof of a beneficent and just Deity; in limiting the range of 'knowledge' [i.e., by rejecting the metaphysical proofs] he was but clearing the ground for 'faith.'" Greene, lx, concurs with Kant that it is better to depend on the "moral proofs of God's existence" than on scientific, or "natural," proofs, even if such were available. See above, chap. 7, n. 14. Kant, in *Religion*, offers several variations on an argument from moral law as the universal core of religion to the inferred or necessary existence of a benevolent deity; see also 89, 95; for the moral definition of religion, 142. David Hume, *An Inquiry Concerning Human Understanding*, ed. and intro. Charles W. Hendel (New York: Liberal Arts Press, 1955), xv. Neiman, *Evil in Modern Thought*, 66. Kant's reference to Job ("Now I find such an authentic interpretation expressed allegorically in an ancient holy book.") in "On the Miscarriage of all Philosophical Trials in Theodicy," is in *Religion and Rational Theology*, trans. and ed. Allen W. Wood, George Di Giovanni (Cambridge: Cambridge University Press, 1996), 32. See also 24, 30, 33–34. For the date of this essay [1791], Gabrielle Rabel, ed., *Kant* (Oxford: Clarendon, 1963), 233. Clayton, *Problem*, 266–67.

24. John Henry Newman, *Apologia pro Vita Sua: Being a History of His Religious Opinions* (New York: Longmans, Green, 1947), 123, 181, 221–22, 236.

25. Ralph Waldo Emerson, "Brahma," in *Oxford Guide to American Literature* (New York: Oxford University Press, 1965), 255–57.

26. Friedrich Schleiermacher, *On Religion: Speeches to its Cultured Despisers*, trans. John Oman (New York: Harper, 1958), 18-19, 88, 99-101. Rene Wellek, *Immanuel Kant in England, 1793-1838* (Princeton, N.J.: Princeton University Press, 1931), 66-202; quote, 91. John Stuart Mill, certainly in a position to know, concurs that Coleridge was *the* chief interpreter of Kantian thought ("the Germano-Coleridgian doctrine") for early Victorian England. While making clear his own philosophical disagreement, Mill described Coleridge (far more positively than Wellek) as one of "two great seminal minds of England in their age." The other, for Mill, was Bentham. John Stuart Mill, *On Bentham and Coleridge* (New York: HarperTorchbook, 1962), 40, 99, 103, 108, 114.

27. Friedrich Schleiermacher, *The Christian Faith*, vol. 1 (New York: Harper Torchbook, 1963), 66-67.

28. *Christian Faith*, 136-37. In an important study, *Religious Experience* (Berkeley: University of California Press, 1985), the sociologist of religion, Wayne Proudfoot, confirms Schleiermacher's lead in developing concepts of an autonomous, irreducible "religious experience" and shows the central role of that concept in opposing secularism, and in the eventual resurgence of belief after the Second World War. Sharply critical of Schleiermacher, Proudfoot characterizes "religious experience" arguments as logically flawed, and, for their proponents, nicely self-serving. Clayton, *Explanation*, 137, concurs both with Proudfoot's estimate of Schleiermacher's importance and the fallibility of his doctrine.

29. Kai Nielsen, *God, Scepticism and Modernity* (Ottawa: University of Ottawa Press, 1989), 211-12, 226-27.

11. Marxism and the Failed Critique of Religion

1. Karl Marx, "Foreword to Thesis: the Difference between the Natural Philosophy of Democritus and the Natural Philosophy of Epicurus," "Contribution to the Critique of Hegel's *Philosophy of Right*," both in Karl Marx and Friedrich Engels, *On Religion* (New York: Schocken Books, 1964), 13-14, 41-42. Marx and Engels, *The Communist Manifesto: A Modern Edition* (London: Verso, 1998), 77.

2. "False Consciousness," is a term never employed by Marx, nor by Engels till the 1890s. I use it here in its simplest variation to convey the meaning Marx and Engels usually attached to "ideology." Martin Seliger, *The Marxist Concept of Ideology: A Critical Essay* (Cambridge: Cambridge, 1977), 30-31 nn. 20, 21. Raymond Williams, *Keywords: A Vocabulary of Culture and Society* (New York: Oxford University Press, 1976), 126-30.

3. Frederick Engels, *Ludwig Feuerbach and the End of Classical German Philosophy*, in Marx and Engels, *Selected Works in One Volume* (New York: International, 1968), 602-3. Richard Lichtman, "The Marxian Critique of Religion," in *Marxism and Christianity: A Symposium*, ed. Herbert Aptheker (New York: Humanities Press, 1968), 75: "Feuerbach's 'reduction' of religion ... must not be misunderstood. ... The intention is not to lower God or religion to *mere* anthropology, but to raise man to the level of the divine." Jonathan Israel, *Radical Enlightenment: Philosophy and the Making of Modernity, 1650-1750* (Oxford: Oxford University Press, 2001), 159-74.

4. John Stuart Mill, *Nature, the Utility of Religion and Theism* (London: Longmans, Green, 1969), 72.

5. Terrell Carver, *Friedrich Engels: His Life and Thought* (London: Macmillan, 1989), 1-59. Israel, *Radical Enlightenment*, 3-22.

6. Marx and Engels, *The German Ideology*, ed. C. J. Arthur (New York: International, 1970), 47. Eric Hobsbawm, "Introduction," *Communist Manifesto*, 22-23; interior quotations, Leszek

Kolakowski, *Main Currents of Marxism* (Oxford: Oxford University Press,1978), 1:130; and George Lichtheim, *Marxism* (London: 1964), 45.

7. Engels, *The Condition of the Working Class in England* (London: Penguin, 1987), 98, 130, 132-33, 141, 148, 151.

8. *Communist Manifesto*, 48-49.

9. Engels, *Condition*, 64. "Preface to the English Edition" in *Condition*, 38-9. Marx and Engels, *German Ideology*, 66-88. Engels, "Outlines of a Critique of Political Economy," as quoted in Arthur, "Introduction," *German Ideology*, 15.

10. Engels, *Condition*, esp. 157-58. E. P. Thompson, *Witness Against the Beast: William Blake and Moral Law* (New York: Cambridge University Press, 1993). Christopher Hill, *The World Turned Upside Down* (London: Penguin, 1975).

11. E. J. Hobsbawm, *Nations and Nationalism Since 1780: Programme, Myth, Reality* (London: Verso, 1992); for Hobsbawm's list of "illuminating" works, see p. 4. Benedict Anderson, *Imagined Communities: Reflections on the Origin and Spread of Nationalism* (London: Verso, 1991). Ernest Gellner, *Nations and Nationalism* (Ithaca, N.Y.: Cornell University Press, 1983). For older treatments, Carleton J. H. Hayes, *The Historical Evolution of Modern Nationalism* (New York: Macmillan, 1959). Hans Kohn, *The Idea of Nationalism: A Study in its Origins and Background* (New York: Macmillan, 1944).

12. Alexander Saxton, "Race, Class and Nation-Building: the Case of the United States," *Contention* 5 (Spring 1996): 203-4.

13. Louis Francis Budenz, *This is My Story* (New York: Whittlesey/McGraw Hill, 1947), 346.

14. Ibid., 349. Harvey Klehr, "Budenz," *American National Biography* (New York: Oxford, Oxford University Press, 1999), 3:872-73.

15. Budenz, *This is My Story*, 155-64.

16. The quotation is imaginary. Dorothy Day helped to organize the Association of Catholic Trade Unionists but ceased working with them because she disapproved of their focus on electing Catholics to union offices at the expense of working-class interests and trade union democracy. Dorothy Day, *The Long Loneliness* (New York: Harper, 1952), 220-21. Douglas P. Seaton, *The Association of Catholic Trade Unionists and the American Labor Movement from Depression to Cold War* (Lewisburg, Penn.: Bucknell University Press, 1981), 155-56, 158, 208, 218, 231-32 n. 55, 663.

17. That they were mistaken as to the social milieu of early Christianity, now generally located among shopkeepers and urban artisans does not invalidate their attribution of sometimes liberating potentials to religious movements. See Wayne Meeks, *The First Urban Christians: The Social World of the Apostle Paul* (New Haven: Yale University Press, 1983); Peter Brown, *Power and Persuasion in Late Antiquity: Toward a Christian Empire* (Madison: University of Wisconsin Press, 1992), 71-117; Robin L. Fox, *Pagans and Christians* (NY: Knopf, 1987), 265-335, especially 300-1.

18. Marx and Engels tried out various conceptualizations of religion. The major themes, I think, are covered by the following citations. *German Ideology*: religion, together with metaphysics and moral codes, forms part of "ideology" (47); in the very earliest times a "natural religion" expressed human awe at the "alien, all-powerful" force of nature; long after this, the division of labor, esp. that of "material [from] mental labour," brought forward 'the first form of ideologist, *priests*" (51). *Communist Manifesto*: religion is part of bourgeois obscurantism "behind which lurk in ambush" bourgeois class interests (48); the "ideological standpoint" used by the bourgeoisie against "communism" includes religion (58). *Capital* (New York: Modern Library, n.d.), 91-92: "The religious world is but the reflex of the real world. ... The bourgeois reflex [can only] finally vanish when the prac-

tical relations of everyday life offer to man … [none but] intelligible and reasonable relations with regard to his fellow men and nature." In *Marx and Engels on Religion* (147–48)
religion "is nothing but the fantastic reflection in men's minds of those external forces
which control their daily lives"; representing the alien power of nature—and later that of
society—religion confronts each individual as an "alien force." "The Part Played by Labor
in the Transition from Ape to Man" in Engels, *The Origin of the Family, Private Property
and the State* (New York: International, 1972), 258–59: "Tribes developed into nations
and states. Law and politics arose, and with them that fantastic reflection of human things
in the human mind—religion;" religion became the core of "the idealistic world outlook"
which since ancient times "has dominated men's minds."

19. *Communist Manifesto*, 59.

20. Ludwig Feuerbach, *The Essence of Christianity*, trans.George Eliot (New York: Harper
    Torchbook, 1957), 11–13, 62.

21. Ibid., 184; for other Feuerbachisms, among many, that might have irritated Marx and Engels,
    11, 13, 62, 64. And see Marx and Engels, *German Ideology*, 60–64; and Engels, *Feuerbach* in
    Selected Works, One Volume, 603, 611ff.

22. See n. 18 above on the predominance of "ideological"accounts of religion.

23. Their focus on the crucial importance of religion was mainly in the 1840s. John Raines, *Marx
    on Religion* (Philadelphia: Temple University Press, 2002), vii. David McLellan, *Marxism and
    Religion: a Description and Assessment of the Marxist Critique of Religion* (New York: Harper
    & Row, 1987), 31, 56–57.

24. Reinhold Niebuhr, "Introduction," in *Marx and Engels on Religion*, vii–1x

25. The argument of Israel's book (n. 3, above) shows that Radical Enlightenment had to come
    after (religious) Reformation. Milton's *Paradise Lost* points to a similar sequence. Marx and
    Engels (in *German Ideology*) are not saying that German intellectuals were wrong to pay atten-
    tion to religion, but wrong not to move from that to an examination of the civil and political
    establishment.

26. Engels, *Feuerbach*, in *Selected Works*, 598. For various formulations of the concept of progress,
    see Hobsbawm, "Introduction," Marx, *Pre-Capitalist Economic Formations* (New York:
    International, 1965), 12. Marx, "Preface: 'A Contribution to the Critique of Political
    Economy,'" in Raines, *Marx on Religion*, 109–10. Marx and Engels, *Communist Manifesto*,
    50, 59, 62; *German Ideology*, 42–57. J. B. S. Haldane, "Preface," Engels, *Dialectic of Nature*
    (New York: International, 1940), viii: "In 1871 [Engels] came to London and started reading
    scientific books and journals. … He intended to write a great book to show 'that in nature the
    same dialectical laws of movement are carried out in the confusion of its countless changes,
    and also govern the apparent contingency of events in history.'" The term *historical material-
    ism* refers to a materialist (but not necessarily dialectical) interpretation of human history.
    Dialectical materialism designates a materialist interpretation, guided by dialectical
    "method," applicable either to human history or to the entire span of *natural* (cosmic) histo-
    ry. Marx used the first term, never the second; Engels used both more or less interchangeably.
    Williams, *Keywords*, 91–93.

27. To justify such a rejection it would be necessary to show either (a) that religious belief itself
    precluded escape from class exploitation; or (b) that religion inevitably generated clerical hier-
    archies which made escape impossible. Obviously, neither (a) nor (b) could be sustained by
    empirical evidence.

28. Wayne Hudson, *The Marxist Philosophy of Ernst Bloch* (London: Macmillan, 1982). Martin
    Jay, *The Dialectical Imagination: A History of the Franfurt School and the Institute of Social
    Research, 1923–1950* (Berkeley: University of California Press, 1973).

29. Engels, *Feuerbach*, 603. Feuerbach, *Essence*, 11–13.

30. Lewis Lockwood, "Beethoven Beyond Classicism," *New York Review of Books,* July 17, 2003, 27–29, reviewing Maynard Solomon, *Late Beethoven: Music, Thought, Imagination* (Berkeley: University of California Press, 2003), and Esteban Buch, *Beethoven's Ninth: A Political History* (Chicago: University of Chicago Press, 2003).

31. Richard Niebuhr, Foreword, Karl Barth, Introductory Essay, in Feuerbach, *Essence*, vii, x–xxxii.

32. Raines, *Marx on Religion*, 1.

33. Feuerbach, *Essence*, 270: "The necessary turning point of history is therefore the open confession, that the consciousness of God is nothing else than the consciousness of the species."

34. Marx, *Economic and Philosophic Manuscripts of 1844* (New York: International, 1964), 134, 138.

35. See above, n. 23.

12. High Tide at Dover Beach

1. Talcott Parsons, "The Theoretical Development of the Sociology of Religion: A Chapter in the History of Modern Social Science," *Journal of the History of Ideas* 5 (1944):176–90, and 176 n. 1.

2. Parsons quotations, ibid., sequentially: 176, 179, 189, 178, 177, 189.

3. Ibid., 190.

4. Ibid., 190 n. 18.

5. Harvey Cox, *The Secular City: Secularization and Urbanization in Theological Perspective* (New York: Macmillan, 1965).

6. Peter L. Berger and Thomas Luckman, *The Social Construction of Reality: A Treatise in the Sociology of Knowledge* (New York: Anchor Books, 1967). Berger, "A Lutheran View of the Elephant," in Berger, *A Rumor of Angels: Modern Society and the Rediscovery of the Supernatural* (New York: Doubleday/Anchor, 1990), 114.

7. Berger, *Rumor*, 2, 64.

8. E. E. Evans-Pritchard, *Theories of Primitive Religion* (Oxford: Clarendon, 1965), 15, 121.

9. Mircea Eliade, *The Quest: History and Meaning in Religion* (Chicago: University of Chicago Press, 1969), 41.

10. Ibid., 23.

11. Rudolf Otto, *The Idea of the Holy: An Inquiry into the Non-Rational Factor in the Idea of the Divine and Its Relation to the Rational* (London: Oxford University Press 1967), 6, 7, and see 14–15, 19, 30–32, 112–15. Eric J. Sharpe, *Comparative Religion: A History* (New York: Scribner, 1975), 61, points out that Otto's famous descriptive term, "numinous," was used earlier by Lang in *The Making of Religion*, 2nd ed. (1900), 45.

12. Eliade, *Quest*, 52–53; Pritchard, *Theories of Primitive Religion*, 100, 129.

13. Eliade, *Quest*, 53.

14. Pritchard, *Theories of Primitive Religion*, 121.

15. Ibid., 121, citing W. Schmidt, *The Origin and Growth of Religion* (1931), 6.

16. Richard Niebuhr, "Introduction," Friedrich Schleiermacher, *The Christian Faith* (New York: Harper Torchbook, 1963), ix–x.

17. Wayne Proudfoot, *Religious Experience* (Berkeley: University of California Press, 1985), 228, xiii–xiv, xvi. Proudfoot supports Schleiermacher's assertions that "religious experience" must

always be described, or identified, in terms understandable by, and acceptable to, the person having the experience. The experience is subjective and no reduction would be justifiable. But an objective account of the experience requires causal explanation, and reduction then becomes legitimate and necessary (191-92, 196-98). "Failure to distinguish between these two kinds of reduction" tends to become "a protective strategy. The subject's identifying description becomes normative for purposes of explanation, and inquiry is blocked to insure that the subject's own explanation of the experience is not contested"(197).

18. Susanne C. Monahan, William A. Mirola, Michael O. Emerson, eds., *Sociology of Religion* (Upper Saddle River, N.J.: Prentice-Hall, 2001), 56. The editors, who describe Proudfoot's book as a "bombshell," write, "Few sociologists or psychologists refer to Proudfoot's work, and those who do tend to be critical."

19. Stephen Jay Gould, *Rocks of Ages: Science and Religion in the Fullness of Life* (New York: Library of Contemporary Thought/Random House, 1999), 214-18. Larson and Witham, *Scientific American,* September 1999, 89. "Frontlines," *Free Inquirer* (Summer 2002), 26, 27. Dates of the headlines are respectively: *Wall Street Journal,* June 12, 1998; *New York Times,* June 30, 1998; *Newsweek,* July 20, 1998.

20. Gould, *Rocks of Ages,* 214.

21. Margaret Wertheim, "Why Science Can't Show Us God," *Los Angeles Times,* March 22, 2005; ibid., May 6, 2005; ibid., February 11, 2006.. Michael Lerner, "Hostile Takeover: Theocracy in America," *Tikkun,* January-February 2006, 14.

22. Matthew Arnold, "Dover Beach."

13. The Great Lizard Analogy

1. Edward O. Wilson, *Sociobiology: The New Synthesis* (Cambridge, Mass.: Harvard University Press, 2000), 555-62. Alfred Russel Wallace described the normal outcome of natural selection as a continuing adaptation to environmental change. "This must be the case because all alterations in environment are necessarily very gradual. Changes of climate require thousands of years before they attain an amount greater than occurs during the ordinary seasonal or periodic changes to which all animals and plants are already adjusted." Wallace "Evolution and Character," [*Fortnightly Review* 83 (1908): 1-24], in *The Alfred Russel Wallace Reader: A Selection of Writings from the Field,* ed. Jane R. Camerini (Baltimore: Johns Hopkins University Press., 2002), 169. Like his colleague, Charles Darwin and their mentor in geology, Charles Lyell, Wallace assumed uniformity of global evolution. That assumption has more recently been modified by the the recognition that cataclysmic changes have sometimes happened. Against the norm of uniform development, the implications of cataclysmic change, whether by natural or human agency, are obvious.

2. Walter Burkert, *Creation of the Sacred: Tracks of Biology in Early Religions* (Cambridge, Mass.: Harvard University Press, 1996), 12-13, "Because on the whole the history of religions has been a story of success, a good strategy for survival in the long run must have been at work."

3. Ibid., 80-128. Jared Diamond, *Guns, Germs and Steel: The Fates of Human Societies* (New York: W. W. Norton, 1997), 265-92.

4. On Fideisu, "Postmodern style," above, 180.

5. Ernst Mayr, *What Evolution Is* (New York: Basic Books, 2001), 201, 276.

6. Stephen C. Stearns and Rolf Hoekstra, *Evolution: An Introduction* (Oxford: Oxford University Press, 2000), 272-74, 276.

7. David P. Barash, *The Hare and the Tortoise: Culture Biology and Human Nature* (New York: Viking/Penguin, 1986), on the mind-culture spiral, esp. 31–39. On cultural construction and "evolutional landscape," see Scott Atran, *In Gods We Trust: The Evolutionary Landscape of Religion* (New York: Oxford University Press, 2002), 243, 274.

8. Jean Aitchison, *The Seeds of Speech: Language Origin and Evolution* (Cambridge: Cambridge University Press, 2000), 49–104, 161–219. Daniel C. Dennett, *Consciousness Explained* (Boston: Little, Brown, 1991), 189–91. Steven Pinker, *How the Mind Works* (New York: W. W. Norton, 1997), 191–210. Wilson, *Sociobiology*, 547–75.

9. On the cost of big brains, Robert Boyd & Peter Richerson, *The Origin and Evolution of Cultures* (New York: Oxford, 2005), 72-3. Matt Ridley, *Genome: The Autobiography of a Species in 23 Chapters* (New York: Harper/Perennial, 1999), 301-13. Ridley's closing chapter illuminates the absolute obscurity of our notions about free will and determinism.

10. Charles Beard, "Introduction," xl, in J. B. Bury, *The Idea of Progress: An Inquiry into its Growth and Origin* (New York: Dover, 1955).

11. Frequent use of the term "cultural revolution" suggests the transformative power we attribute to culture. "Because social inheritance is Lamarckian, there is more of a theoretical basis for belief in progress in culture … there is that possibility of directional accumulation," Stephen Jay Gould, as quoted in John Horgan, *The End of Science: Facing the Limits of Knowledge in the Twilight of the Scientific Age* (Reading, Mass.: Addison-Wesley, 1996), 123. In the closing pages of *Our Kind: the Evolution of Human Life and Culture* (New York: Harper & Row, 1989), 494–98, the anthropologist Marvin Harris contrasts long continuities and rapid changes of culture and reflects on their implications for the survival of our kind. See also Wilson, *Sociobiology*, 560.

12. Bruce Lincoln, *Holy Terrors: Thinking About Religion After September 11* (Chicago: University of Chicago Press, 2003) 54–55. Mircea Eliade, "Sacred Time and Myths," 68–115, *The Sacred and the Profane: The Nature of Religion* (New York: Harcourt Brace Jovanovich, 1959).

13. Harris, *Our Kind*, 398–420. Burkert, *Creation*, 3, 20, 130, 150, uses the term *"universalia* of anthropology" for what I refer to as long continuities of culture. Wilson, *Sociobiology*, 548–49. Atran, *In Gods We Trust*, 207.

14. Rodney Cotterill, *Enchanted Looms: Conscious Networks in Brains and Computers* (Cambridge: Cambridge University Press, 1998), 377.

15. Thus the idea of divine justice contains in embryo that of individual afterlife. The *Magna Carta* contains in embryo the *Declaration of Independence*, and so forth. So also we debate whether agriculture came to the Americas by way of diffusion or separate discovery (Harris, *Our Kind*, 474–76); and speak of "diffusion" of horse culture across the pampas and the Great Plains, or of mining technology in the North American West.

16. Edward O. Wilson, *On Human Nature* (Cambridge: Harvard University Press, 1978), 114, 116.

17. Diamond, *Guns*, 67–81, 354–75. J. M. Blaut, *Eight Eurocentric Historians* (New York: Guilford Press, 2000), 8–12. Harris, *Our Kind*, 487–91.What Walter Burkert (16) writes of religions applies to long continuities of culture: "[They] are established by learning, they are propagated both through imitation and through explicit verbal teaching. Traditions developed in this way can evidence a kind of cultural fitness for survival without any genetic basis." Elliot Sober and David Sloan Wilson, *Unto Others: The Evolution and Psychology of Unselfish Behavior* (Cambridge, Mass.: Harvard University Press, 1998), 336–37, on behaviors hardwired by biological evolution and the psychological motivations of those behaviors, shaped by cultural evolution. Michael Gazzaniga, "Language and Selection Theory," *Nature's Mind: The Biological Roots of Thinking, Emotions, Sexuality, Language and Intelligence* (New York: Basic Books, 1992), 72–94.

230 NOTES TO PAGES 186–189

18. Steven Pinker, *The Language Instinct: How the Mind Creates Language* (New York: Harper
   Perennial, 1995), 27: "There are Stone Age societies but there is no such thing as a Stone Age
   language. Earlier in this century the anthropological linguist Edward Sapir wrote, 'When it
   comes to linguistic form, Plato walks with the Macedonian swineherd, Confucius with the
   head–hunting savage of Assam.'"

19. Franz Boas, *The Mind of Primitive Man* (New York: Macmillan, 1938), 140–44, 172–73.
   Burkert, *Creation*, 2, chastising cultural specialists for their exclusivist tendencies. Noam
   Chomsky in his famous "Managua Lectures," 161–62 (n. 22, below) applied a similar criticism not only to behaviorists but to the "Marxist tradition" at large and to "the dominant intellectual tradition in American thought," i.e., progressivism.

20. Wilson, *Sociobiology*, 569, estimates a span of two thousand generations since "typical
   Homo sapiens" moved into Europe. Wilson, *Human Nature*, 36–39, on incest avoidance.
   Ridley, *Genome*, 31. Burkert, *Creation*, 8–23, quote, 18. David Barash, *Sociobiology and
   Behavior* (New York/Amsterdam: Elsevier, 1977), 290ff.; Barash, *The Hare and the
   Tortoise: Culture Biology and Human Nature* (New York: Penguin, 1986). When I began
   working on this book fifteen years ago, I first wrote the Introduction and present chapter
   13, "The Great Lizard Analogy." I knew my ideas about religion's relationship to biological
   and cultural evolution were unsystematic and speculative, so I am grateful (and relieved) to
   be able to base my argument now on recent work by anthropologists and evolutionary psychologists on "coevolution." Robert Boyd and Peter Richerson, *Culture and the
   Evolutionary Process* (Chicago: University of Chicago Press, 1985), and by the same
   authors, *The Origin and Evolution of Cultures* (New York: Oxford University Press, 2005),
   especially the summary of propositions that govern their research, 3–5. Scott Atran, *In Gods
   We Trust: The Evolutionary Landscape of Religion*, cited in this and earlier chapters. John
   Bellamy Foster, *Marx's Ecology: Materialism and Nature* (New York Monthly Review Press,
   2000), 203 and 292 n. 53.

21. William James, *Essays in Pragmatism* (New York: Hafner, 1948), 160, 168. Horgan, *End of
   Science*, 70–71. Cotterill, *Looms*, 30–57. Pinker, *The Language Instinct* 154. Francis Crick,
   interview, as quoted in Horgan, *End of Science*, 182–83.

22. Noam Chomsky, *Language and the Problems of Knowledge: the Managua Lectures*
   (Cambridge: MIT Press, 1988), 38; quotes 134, 161–63. Chomsky, *Reflections on Language*
   (New York: Pantheon, 1975), 9–11, in Pinker, *The Language Instinct*, 22–24. Michael S.
   Gazzaniga, *The Mind's Past* (Berkeley: University of California Press, 1998), 59. Alden M.
   Hayashi, "Profile: Pinker and the Brain," *Scientific American* 281, no. 1 (July 1999): 32–4.

23. Wilson, *Human Nature*, 63, 67.

24. Charles Darwin, *Notebooks* (1836–44) quoted in John Bellamy Foster, *"Marx's Ecology:
   Materialism and Nature* (New York: Monthly Review Press, 2000), 29. Francis Crick, *The
   Astonishing Hypothesis: The Scientific Search for the Soul* (New York: Scribner, 1994), xii:
   "Now is the time to think scientifically about consciousness (and its relationship, if any, to the
   hypothetical immortal soul) and, most important of all, the time to start the *experimental*
   study of consciousness in a serious and deliberate way." Carl Sagan (dust jacket): Crick is
   telling us that "consciousness and what has long been called the soul are now accessible to scientific investigation." Nicholas Humphrey, *A History of the Mind* (London: Chatto and
   Windus, 1992), 1–30. Barash, *Hare*, 34–60, focuses on problems raised by the speed of cultural evolution, as does his essay, "Evolution's Odd Couple: Biology and Culture," *Chronicle
   of Higher Education*, sec. 2 (December 12, 2001), B7–B10.

25. Kai Nielsen, *God, Scepticism and Modernity* (Ottawa: University of Ottawa Press, 1989), 232.
   Mary Tucker and John Grim, eds., "Religion and Ecology: Can the Climate Change?"in
   Daedalus, Journal of the American Academy of Arts and Sciences, *Proceedings* 130 (Fall
   2001):4.

26. Diamond, *Guns*, 281. For examples (among many), Pat Robertson, *The End of the Age* (Dallas: World Publising, 1996); Jerry B. Jenkins, *Soon: The Beginning of the End* (2003); Tim LaHaye and Jenkins, *Tribulation Force: The Continuing Drama of those Left Behind* (1996); and a dozen or so novels of the *Left Behind* series (Tyndale House, Wheaton, Ill., 1995–), several of which have run first in the *New York Times* fiction bestseller list; the series as a whole had sales of 55 million by November 2003. Joan Didion, "Mr. Bush and the Divine," *New York Review of Books*, November 6, 2003, 81–86. Bruce Lincoln, *Holy Terrors: Thinking About Religion After September 11* (Chicago: University of Chicago Press, 2003).

27. Bill Moyers, "There Is No Tomorrow," *Free/Inquiry* (June/July 2005), 21–23; Moyers, "Welcome to Doomsday," *New York Review of Books*, March 24, 2005, 8–10.

28. See above, n. 26.

29. The seasonal rotation metaphor (doubtless well-known before words existed to carry it), which simply expresses hope for the renewal of life, plant and animal, could hardly serve as an analog for spiritual beings in nature; even less for hopes of life after death. Atran, *In Gods We Trust*, 66: "Once you can track even the seasons—and anticipate that leaves will fall … you cannot avoid overwhelming inductive evidence favoring your own death. … Emotions compel such inductions and make them salient . … This is 'the Tragedy of Cognition.'"

30. James Redfield, Michael Murphy, Sylvia Timbers, *God and the Evolving Universe* (New York: Penguin/Putnam, 2002), 19, 214–15; and dust jacket.

14. Jerusalem

1. John Gardner and John Maier, trans. and eds., *Gilgamesh* (New York: Vintage/Random House, 1985), 245.

2. Walter Scott, *The Lady of the Lake.*

3. Steven Pinker, *How the Mind Works* (New York: W. W. Norton, 1997), 563: "And it is my last opportunity … to get you to step outside your own mind for a moment and see your thoughts and feelings as magnificent contrivances of the natural world rather than as the only way that things could be."

4. Bill Moyers, "The Upsurgence of Faith," *USA Weekend*, October 11–13, 1996, 4–5; "Welcome to Doomsday," *New York Review of Books*. March 24, 2005, 8–10.

5. For a current example from the first world: Michael Lerner, *The Left Hand of God: Taking Back Our Country from the Religious Right* (San Francisco: Harper San Francisco, 2006).

6. *The Poetry and Prose of William Blake*, ed. David V. Erdman. Commentary, Harold Bloom (Garden City, N.Y.: Doubleday, 1970), 94–95. Bloom maintains (823) that "dark Satanic Mills" refers "primarily" to the rational and mechanistic mind-set that Blake identified with Evil, "rather than the actual mills of British industry." But I expect the two metaphoric levels overlapped in Blake's thought. G. E. Bentley, Jr., *The Stranger from Paradise: A Biography of William Blake* (New Haven: Yale University Press, 2001), 246–47.

7. Ibid. Richard Holmes, "Lord of Unreason," *New York Review of Books*, May 12, 1994, 15–17; Michael Ferber, "The Making of William Blake," *Nation*, November 15, 1993, 594–600; both are reviews of E. P. Thompson's book on Blake, see n. 10.

8. For a formal but succinct statement of this doctrine, Kai Nielsen, *God, Scepticism and Modernity* (Ottawa: University of Ottawa Press, 1989), 227.

9. Blake, *Poetry and Prose*, 94–95.

10. E. P. Thompson, *Witness Against the Beast: William Blake and the Moral Law* (New York: New Press, 1993), xi–xxi.

11. Ibid., esp. chapters 3, 6, 13. Bentley, *Stranger from Paradise,* 7–21. Ferber, "The Making of William Blake," 597. Christopher Hill, *The World Turned Upside Down* (London: Penguin, 1975).

12. Ernst Mayr, *What Evolution Is* (New York: Basic Books, 2001), 263: "Following the origin of life on Earth there were nothing but prokaryotes for the next billion years, and highly intelligent life originated only about 300,000 years ago, in a single one of the more than one billion species that had arisen on Earth. These are indeed long odds. Even if something parallel to the origin of human intelligence should ... have happened somewhere in the infinite universe, the chance that we would be able to communicate with it must be considered as zero. Yes, for all practical purposes, man is alone."

Index